Fashion Patternmaking Techniques

[Vol. 2]

Fashion Patternmaking Techniques
[Vol. 2]

How to Make Shirts,
Undergarments,
Dresses and Suits,
Waistcoats and Jackets
for Women and Men

Antonio Donnanno

Illustrations by
Elisabetta Kuky Drudi

promopress

Fashion Patternmaking Techniques [Vol. 2]
How to Make Shirts, Undergarments, Dresses and Suits,
Waistcoats and Jackets for Women and Men.

Original title:
La tecnica dei modelli
Donna-Uomo vol. 2°

Translation: Carol Lee Rathman

ISBN: 978-84-15967-68-2

Promopress is a brand of:
Promotora de prensa internacional S.A.
C/ Ausiàs March 124
08013 Barcelona, Spain
Tel.: +34 93 245 14 64
Fax: +34 93 265 48 83
Email: info@promopress.es
www.promopresseditions.com
Facebook: Promopress Editions
Twitter: Promopress Editions@PromopressEd

First published in English: 2016

Drawings: Elisabetta Kuky Drudi
Cover design: David Lorente
Cover photo design: Haider Ackerman ss12
Cover image: Gianni Pucci

Printed in China

INTRODUCTION

THE PATTERNMAKER'S IMPORTANT ROLE

To make a good pattern, well-proportioned and harmonious in its style and volumes, and precise in its lines, is the essential basis for creating a fine garment and ensuring its commercial success.

There are very few tailors nowadays who think that drawing the pattern directly on the fabric is an indication of merit and that it carries no risk; even less would an industrial garment making company think of using empirically-made patterns thus putting at risk its production. Today, a good patternmaker who has attended a good school is aware of the responsibilities he or she takes on when setting out to prepare a complete pattern, with clear and precise instructions; extreme care must be taken to give an harmonious line to the entire pattern, giving the best interpretation of the sketch and of the style that the designer wished to impart to the garment.

To achieve the best results, a patternmaker requires a perfect knowledge of the geometric techniques for determining the lines of the basic blocks and for the size grading using the simplest and most suitable procedures, to obtain the best result in the least possible time. In this second book, we look at and analyze the various procedures for the basic transformation of the bodice, using dart control techniques and techniques for the creation of volume, drapery, and fitted patterns. Furthermore, techniques for using knit fabrics with the patterns have been introduced, as have the basic garment blocks and every possible transformation imaginable; maternity clothing; a thorough study of the different styles of sleeves for shirts and blouses and dresses; basic blocks for men's vests and jackets; size grading for bodices and dresses; the basics about pattern layouts.

Thus, this manual completes in a comprehensive and logical way the exploration of the themes of the bodice, trousers, and suits and dresses from a technical point of view, leaving to the readers the task of applying these notions to make other patterns, the fruit of their inspiration and imagination.

SUMMARY

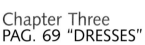

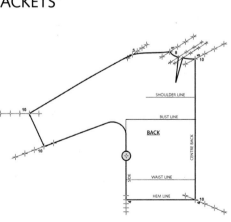

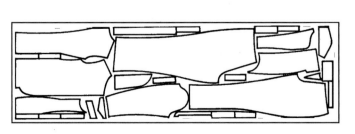

ENGLISH MEASUREMENTS CONVERSION TABLE

CM	INCH	CM	INCH	CM	INCH	CM	INCH	CM	INCH	CM	INCH
1	0.39"	14	5.51"	27	10.63"	40	15.75"	56	22.05"	82	32.28"
1.5	0.59"	14.5	5.71"	27.5	10.83"	40.5	15.94"	57	22.44"	83	32.68"
2	0.79"	15	5.91"	28	11.02"	41	16.14"	58	22.83"	84	33.07"
2.5	0.98"	15.5	6.10"	28.5	11.22"	41.5	16.34"	59	23.23"	85	33.46"
3	1.18"	16	6.30"	29	11.42"	42	16.54"	60	23.62"	86	33.86"
3.5	1.38"	16.5	6.50"	29.5	11.61"	42.5	16.73"	61	24.02"	87	34.25"
4	1.57"	17	6.69"	30	11.81"	43	16.93"	62	24.41"	88	34.65"
4.5	1.77"	17.5	6.89"	30.5	12.01"	43.5	17.13"	63	24.80"	89	35.04"
5	1.97"	18	7.09"	31	12.20"	44	17.32"	64	25.20"	90	35.43"
5.5	2.17"	18.5	7.28"	31.5	12.40"	44.5	17.52"	65	25.59"	91	35.83"
6	2.36"	19	7.48"	32	12.60"	45	17.72"	66	25.98"	92	36.22"
6.5	2.56"	19.5	7.68"	32.5	12.80"	45.5	17.91"	67	26.38"	93	36.61"
7	2.76"	20	7.87"	33	12.99"	46	18.11"	68	26.77"	94	37.01"
7.5	2.95"	20.5	8.07"	33.5	13.19"	46.5	18.31"	69	27.17"	95	37.40"
8	3.15"	21	8.27"	34	13.39"	47	18.50"	70	27.56"	96	37.80"
8.5	3.35"	21.5	8.46"	34.5	13.58"	47.5	18.70"	71	27.95"	97	38.19"
9	3.54"	22	8.66"	35	13.78"	48	18.90"	72	28.35"	98	38.58"
9.5	3.74"	22.5	8.86"	35.5	13.98"	48.5	19.09"	73	28.74"	99	38.98"
10	3.94"	23	9.06"	36	14.17"	49	19.29"	74	29.13"	100	39.37"
10.5	4.13"	23.5	9.25"	36.5	14.37"	49.5	19.49"	75	29.53"	101	39.76"
11	4.33"	24	9.45"	37	14.57"	50	19.69"	76	29.92"	102	40.16"
11.5	4.53"	24.5	9.65"	37.5	14.76"	51	20.08"	77	30.31"	103	40.55"
12	4.72"	25	9.84"	38	14.96"	52	20.47"	78	30.71"	104	40.94"
12.5	4.92"	25.5	10.04"	38.5	15.16"	53	20.87"	79	31.10"	105	41.34"
13	5.12"	26	10.24"	39	15.35"	54	21.26"	80	31.50"	106	41.73"
13.5	5.31"	26.5	10.43"	39.5	15.55"	55	21.65"	81	31.89"	107	42.13"

BODICE BLOCKS AND FANCY SHIRTS

Basic darted bodice block

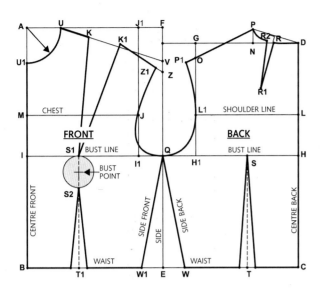

Measurements:

- Semicircumference bust + ease 50 cm/19.69".
- Semicircumference chest + ease 47 cm/18.50".
- Semicircumference waist + ease 36 cm/14.17".
- Semicircumference neck 18.5 cm/7.28".
- Length front waist 43 cm/16.93".
- Length back waist 40 cm/15.75".
- ½ width front chest + ease 20.5 cm/8.07".
- ½ width back shoulders + ease 19 cm/7.48".
- ½ the bust divergence 9.5 cm/3.74".
- Shoulder 13.5 cm/5.31".
- Circumference arm 29 cm/11.42".

Base

On the left side of a sheet of pattern paper, draw a right angle ABC, with:
- A-B Front waist length (e.g.: 43 cm/16.93"). Write CENTRE FRONT.
- B-C Semicircumference waist + ½ ease.
  (e.g.: 92 + 8 = 100 : 2 = 50 cm)
- C-D Back waist length (e.g.: 40 cm/15.75"). Write CENTRE BACK.
- B-E half B-C. Mark the point E.
- A-F like B-E. Mark the point F.
- Draw E-F. Write SIDE.
- D-H half C-D (e.g.: 40 : 2 = 20 cm).
- H-I parallel to B-C. Write BUST LINE (This line is 2-5 cm/0.79"-1.97" above the bust point).
- D-G half shoulders width + ease (e.g.: 36.5 + 1.5 = 38 : 2 = 19 cm).
- H-L ⅓ D-H (e.g.: 20 : 3 = 6.6 cm).
- H-H1 like D-G (Half shoulders width 19 cm/7.48").
- H1-I1 width underarm section* (e.g.: 10.7 cm/4.21").
- Draw G-H1 parallel to D-H.
- Draw I1-J1 parallel to G-H1.
- I-M like H-L.
- Draw L-M parallel to H-I.
- Draw the bust point.

*Note: The underarm section can be obtained using two methods:
1) By personal measurement: Circumference upper arm plus ease divided by 3.14 + 1.5 cm/0.59" (e.g.: 29 : 3.14 = 9.2 + 1.5 = 10.7 cm).
2) By size: ⅕ semi-circumference of the bust without ease + 1.5 cm/0.59" (e.g.: 46 : 5 = 9.2 + 1.5 = 10.7 cm).
- For blocks that do not call for ease (sleeveless garments or ones with low necklines, etc.), the underarm section H1-I1 is made 2 cm/0.79" tighter, for a snugger fit.

Back

- G-O = 2.5 cm/0.98" (this measure decreases if shoulder pads are called for).
- D-N = ½ DG - 1 (e.g.: 19 : 2 = 9.5 - 1 = 8.5 cm).
- N-P = 2.5 cm/0.98".
- Draw D-P. - D-R = ½ DP.
- R-R1 = 9.5 cm/3.74".
- Draw R-R1 perpendicular to D-P.
- R-R2 = 1.5 cm/0.59".
- Draw the neck dart R-R1-R2.
- Make a curved line that follows the shape of the neck and joins D-P.
- P-P1, passing through O, is the shoulder length measurement + 0.5 cm/0.20" (e.g.: 13 + 0.5 = 13.5 cm)**.
- Mark the point Q midway along H-I.
- Draw the Armhole or Armscye P1-L1-Q, shaping it carefully.

Side tapering and back waist darts.
The reduction in the waist measurement in the back is made by tapering at the waist and inserting darts. The amount is obtained by subtracting half the waist circumference from half the bust circumference and dividing the result by 2 (e.g.: 50 - 36 = 14 : 2 = 7 cm). This amount is distributed between the side tapering and the waist darts, so we have:
- E-W = 4 cm/1.57" (or another measurement based on the total waist tapering).
- Draw Q-W = SIDE BACK.
- H-S ½ Bust Divergence (e.g.: 19 : 2 = 9.5 cm).
- C-T like H-S.
- Draw S-T.
- Draw the waist dart with a width of 3 cm/1.18" (or another measurement based on the total waist tapering) and the length T-S down to the bust line.

Front

- A-U = ⅓ of DG on back (e.g.: 19 : 3 = 6.3 cm).
- Draw an arc U-U1 with the centre at A and the measurement A-U.
- I-I1 is like H-H1 + 1 on back (e.g.: 19 + 1 = 20 cm).
- I-S1 = ½ bust divergence (e.g.: 19 : 2 = 9.5 cm).
- F-V = 6 cm/2.36" (less any shoulder pad thickness).
- Join U-V
- U-K = ⅓ of P-P1 on back + 1 cm/0.39"
  (e.g.: 13.5 : 3 = 4.5 + 1 = 5.5 cm).
- K-K1 = the difference between the Bust Circumference and the chest girth + 0.5 cm/0.20" (e.g.: 92 - 86 = 6 + 0.5 = 6.5 cm).
- K1-S1 = K-S1. Join.
- V-Z = ⅓ F-V (e.g.: 6 : 3 = 2 cm).
- K1-Z1 = P-P1 on back minus U-K (e.g.: 13.5 - 5.5 = 8 cm).
- Draw the Armhole or Armscye Z1-J-Q, shaping it carefully.

Side tapering and the front waist dart.
The reduction in the waist measurement is calculated as on the back, subtracting half the waist circumference from half the bust circumference and dividing the result by 2 (e.g.: 50 - 36 = 14 : 2 = 7 cm). This amount is distributed between the side tapering and the waist darts, so we have:
- E-W1, like E-W on the back = 4 cm/1.57".
- Draw Q-W1. SIDE FRONT.
- I-S1 = ½ Bust divergence (e.g. 19 : 2 = 9.5 cm).
- B-T1 = I-S1.
- S1-S2 = 5.8/2.28" cm. DART TIP POSITION.
- Draw S2-T1 using a broken line.
- Draw the waist dart with a width of 3 cm/1.18" (or another measurement based on the total waist tapering) and the length T1-S2, at the edge of the circle.

** For full-bosomed figures do not add 0.5 cm/0.20".

BASIC FITTED SLEEVE BLOCK

Measurements

- Arm circumference 29 cm/11.42" + ease.
- Arm length 58 cm/22.83".

On the left hand side of a sheet of pattern paper,
draw a rectangle A–B–F–E, with:
- A-E like sector bodice +½ sector.
 (e.g.: 10.7 + 5.35 = 16 cm).
- A-B sleeve length measurement (e.g.: 58 cm/22.83").
- A-G = L1-P1 of the basic bodice back minus 1 cm/0.39"
 (In this case: 10 - 1 = 9 cm/3.54").
- Draw G-X parallel to A-E.
- A-N = half A-B (e.g.: 58 : 2 = 29 cm).
- Write ELBOW LINE.
- A-M = ⅔ A-E (e.g.: 16 x 2 = 32 : 3 = 10.6 cm).
- Write CENTRE SHOULDER.
- M-M1 ⅓ A-G (e.g.: 9 : 3 = 3 cm).
- A-I ¼ A-E (e.g.: 16 : 4 = 4 cm).
- G-H 2 cm/0.79".
- Draw H-B1 parallel to A-B (This line is the seam
 line and often it must be moved to the front).
- X-L half G-X + 1 (e.g.: 16 : 2 = 8 + 1 = 9 cm).
- L-L1 half H-L.
- L1-L2 1 cm/0.39".
- G-O 1.5 cm/0.59"
- Draw accordingly the front head E-M1-I-O.
- Draw accordingly the back head E-L-H-O.
- Draw with curve the hem F-B2.

Open sleeve

- Copy the back part of the sleeve E-F-B3-H-L2-L-E,
 and position it on the fold line E-F.
- Copy the part H-B3-B2-O and position it on the
 line B2-O. Or, if the pattern calls for it, on the
 back line H-B3.

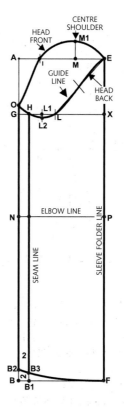

Fig. 1
SLEEVE WITH SEAM MOVED TOWARD THE FRONT

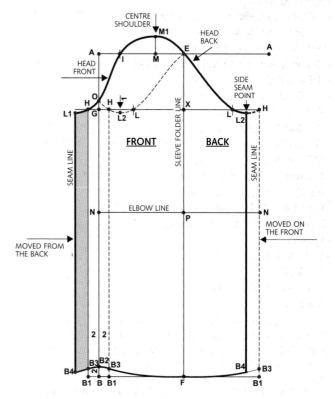

Fig. 2
SLEEVE WITH SEAM ALIGNED WITH SIDE SEAM

Note: The sleeve seam must be kept forward 2–3.5 cm/0.79"-1.38" from the side seam (Fig. 1). To get a sleeve with its seam aligned with the side seam, you have to move the back part H-B3-L3-H, to the front seam line, as shown in Figure 2.

BASIC BODICE BLOCK WITHOUT DARTS

- Draw a right angle A-B-C, with:
- A-B equal to front waist length (e.g.: 43 cm/16.93").
- B-C equal to half the bust circumference plus ease.
  (e.g.: 92 + 8 = 100 : 2 = 50 cm).
- C-D back waist length (e.g.: 40 cm/15.75").
- B-E Half B-C. Mark point E.
- A-F like B-E. Mark point F.
- Draw E-F write SIDE LINE.
- D-H half C-D (e.g.: 40 : 2 = 20 cm).
- Draw H-I. BUST LINE.
- D-G measures ½ Shoulder width + ease + 1 cm/0.39"
  (E.g.: 36.5 + 1.5= 38 : 2 = 19 + 1= 20 cm).
- H-H1 = D-G. Draw H1-G.
- H1-I1 = $\frac{1}{5}$ H-I plus 1.5 cm/0.59" (e.g.: 50 : 5 = 10 + 1.5 = 11.5 cm).
- Draw I1-J1 parallel to H1-G.
- H-L = $\frac{1}{3}$ D-H (e.g. 20 : 3 = 6.7 cm). Draw L-M parallel to H-I.

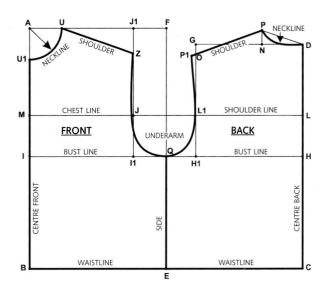

Back
- G-O = 1.5 cm/0.59" (This measure decreases if shoulder pads are called for).
- D-N = ½ DG - 2 cm/0.79" (e.g.: 19 : 2 = 9.5 - 2 = 7.5 cm).
- N-P = 2.5 cm/0.98". Draw D-P.
- Draw P-O-P1 Shoulder length measure + 1 cm/0.39".
  (e.g.: 13.5 + 0.5 = 14 cm).
- Mark the point Q midway along H-I.
- Draw the Armhole or Armscye smoothly connecting P1-L1-Q.

Front
- A-U $\frac{1}{3}$ DG of back (e.g.: 19 : 3 = 6.3 cm).
- Draw the arc U-U1 as a sector of a circle with its centre at A.
- J1-Z = 5 cm/1.97" (This measure decreases if there are shoulder pads).
- Draw U-Z equal in measure to P-P1 on the back.
- Draw the Armhole or Armscye Z-J-Q with ease.

Sleeve
- Draw a rectangle A-B-F-E with:
- A-E = the Bodice section measurement + 1/2 the same section measurement (e.g.: 11.5 + 5.75 = 17.25 cm).
- A-B = Sleeve length (e.g.: 58 cm/22.83").
- A-G = L1-P1 on the bodice + 1 cm/0.39"
  (In this case: 12+1= 13 cm/5.12").
- Draw G-X.
- join G-E with diagonal.
- A-N = half A-B + 2 cm/0.79". Join N-P.
- A-L = half A-E. Draw L-L1.
- L2 = half G-E.
- Move L3 2 cm/0.79" from L1.
- E1 = half E-L2.
- G1 = half G-L2.
- Draw E-L2-G with a curved line as in the figure.
- Draw E-G1-G with a curved line as in the figure.
- Draw B1-L3-F with a curved line.
- Draw B1-L1-F with a curved line.
- Copy the front and back of the sleeve and draw the full sleeve as in the figure.

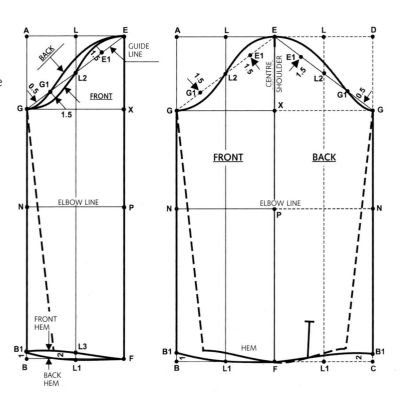

VARIATIONS ON THE BASIC BODICE BLOCK

PRINCESSE SEAM MOTIFS

Princess seams are figure-flattering and are used to absorb bust darts.

They can run from the shoulder, the armhole, or the neckline to curve over the bust point and continue down to the waist dart or the hem at the bottom of the bodice or the dress. When making princess seams, the bust point should be increased slightly to obtain the correct line and fit.

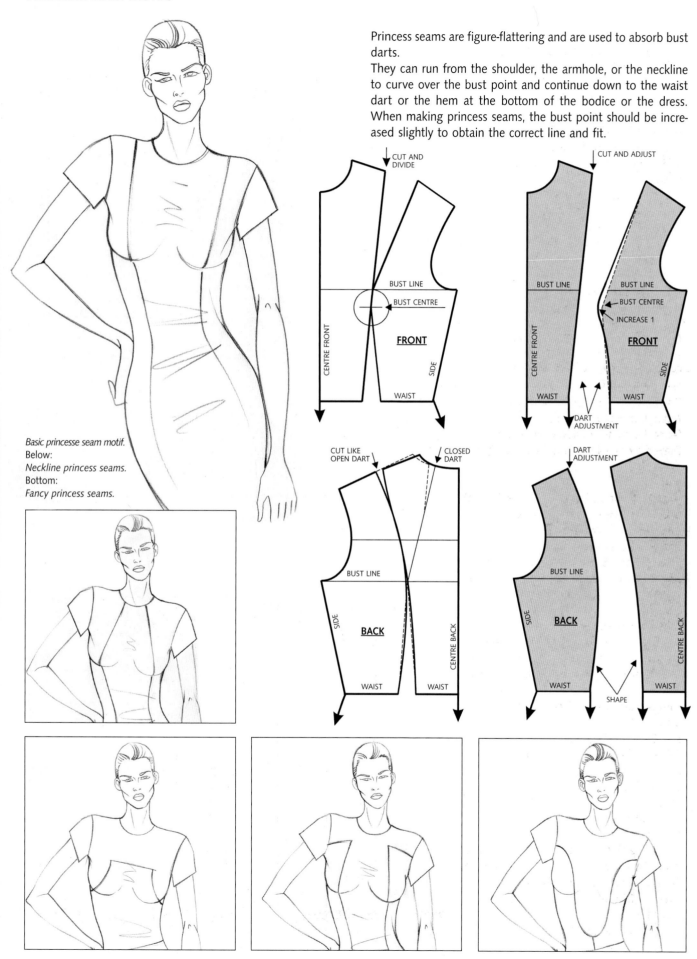

Basic princesse seam motif.
Below:
Neckline princess seams.
Bottom:
Fancy princess seams.

Variations on the basic bodice block

Princess seam motifs

- Draw the basic bodice block with the necessary ease.
- Draw the lines of the motif with the shape and in the position desired, depending on the style.
- If necessary, move the waist darts a few centimetres to the side, for a better line.
- Trace off the front and back parts, after marking the notches. For a full-bosomed figure, close the bust dart on the shoulder, open it on the side and merge it into the cut; if instead the figure is smaller breasted, close the bust dart on the shoulder and move it directly to the edge, absorbing it in the seam.

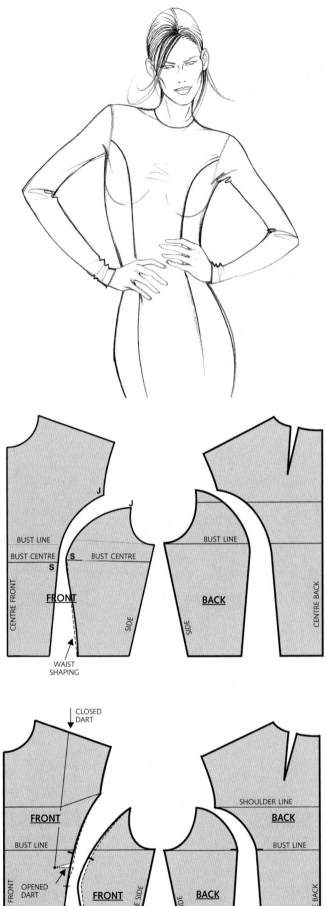

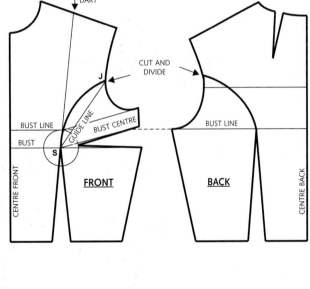

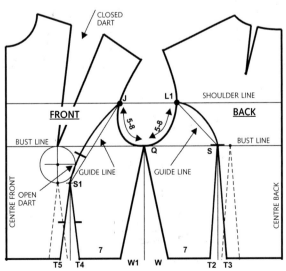

SIDE PANELS OR SIDE YOKES

The side panel, not to be confused with princess seams, is a vertical motif that does not pass through the curved areas, (that is, the bust), but crosses the darts that originate in the waistline and shoulder, suitably shifted and made to merge into the seam.

The waist dart is shifted a few centimetres to the side, to have a more fluid line, while the shoulder dart is moved to the edge, and absorbed loosely in the seam joining the side panel.

- Draw the basic bodice block with the necessary ease.
- Draw the lines of the side panel with the shape and position

desired, based on the sketch.
- If necessary, move the waist darts a few centimetres to the side, for a better line.
- Trace off the front and back parts of the side panel, after marking the notches.
- Close the shoulder bust dart and make it merge in the edge of the side panel, then letting it be absorbed by the seam.
- Join the two parts of the side panel and mark the straight of grain and the notches.

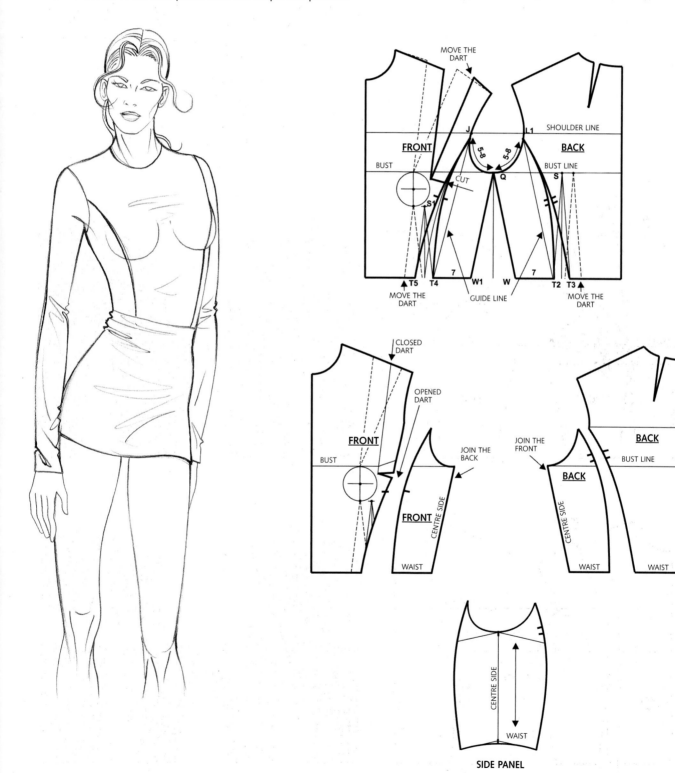

SIDE PANEL

TOP WITH HORIZONAL PLEATS

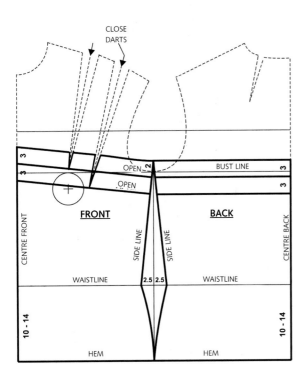

- Draw the basic bodice pattern with darts, with necessary measurements and ease.
- Draw the the bottom line with desired length.
- Trace the neckline with desired measures.
- Draw two horizontal lines front and back for the folds.
- Divide the shoulder dart in two parts and move the tip of one to the first seam and the tip of the other to the second seam.
- Separate the front and the back.
- Slash along the lines drawn and open the darts as shown in figure.
- Divide the lines to insert pleats.

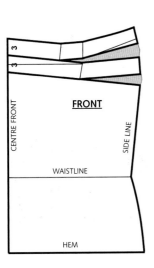

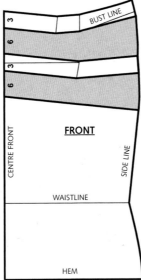

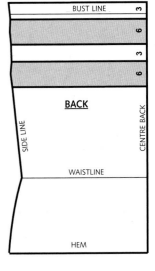

ASYMMETRICAL TOP WITH SLASHES

- Draw the basic bodice block with darts, necessary with ease, with full front and back.
- Draw the shape of desired neckline.
- Move the shoulder dart of the left front to the side.
- Make the desired length and shape.
- Draw the cuts on the front and the back.
- Draw the extension of the shoulder front for the fastening.
- Close the shoulder dart of right front, suppressing it in a cut.
- Copy all the parts of the pattern onto another sheet of tissue paper.

BACK

CLOSE

FRONT   FRONT   BACK   BACK

CENTRE FRONT

BUST LINE   CENTRE BACK   BUST LINE

SIDE   WAIST   WAIST   SIDE   SIDE   WAIST   SIDE   WAIST   SIDE

CLOSE THE DARTS FOR FULL BOSOM

CUT AND OPEN

CLOSE THE DARTS

FRONT   FRONT   BACK   BACK

CENTRE FRONT

BUST LINE

SIDE   WAIST   WAIST   WAIST   SIDE   WAIST   WAIST   CENTRE BACK   WAIST   SIDE

CLOSE THE DARTS FOR FULL BOSOM

BUST LINE

17

BASIC BLOCK FOR BUSTIER

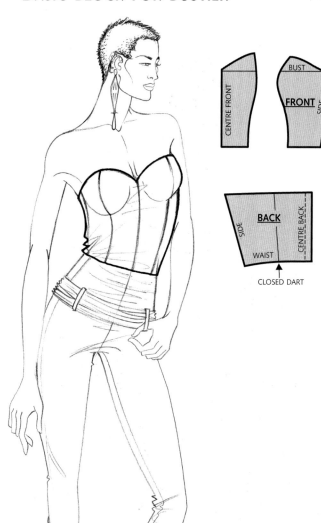

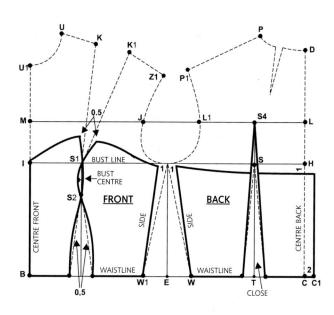

- Draw the basic bodice block with darts, with necessary ease.
- Draw the shape of the desired neckline.
- Widen the front and back bust darts, as shown in figure, it allows for a snugger fit of the bodice.
- Draw the back extension C-C1, for the fastening.

PLEATED BUSTIER

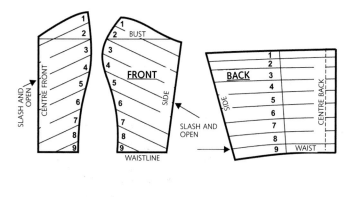

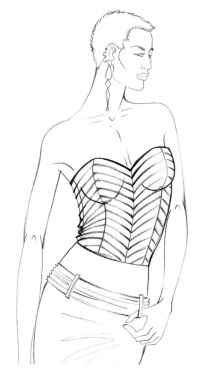

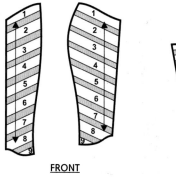

FRONT

BACK

- Make the basic pattern of the fitted top.
- Draw a correct number of parallel lines on the front and back, to make the desired pleating.
- Slash the pattern along the lines drawn and open by 1-2 cm /0.39"-0.79", depending on the type of fabric.
- Paste the strips onto another sheet of paper, keeping them parallel and on the straight of grain.

LOOSE-FITTING CROP TOP WITH CIRCULAR YOKE

- Draw the basic bodice pattern with darts, with necessary measurements and ease.
- Draw the the bottom line with desired height.
- Trace the neckline and the shaped facing with desired measures.
- Draw two vertical lines front and back by the width.
- Separate the shaped facing and close the darts.
- Separate the front and the back.
- Cut the pattern along the lines drawn and open to the bottom as shown in figure or as desired.

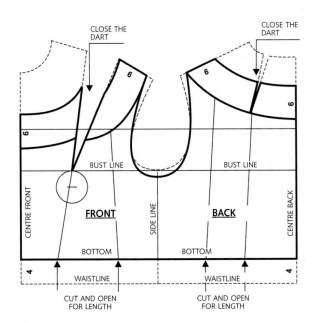

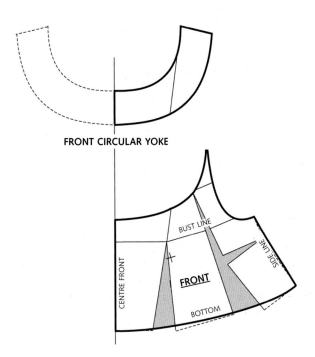

FRONT CIRCULAR YOKE

BACK CIRCULAR YOKE

CROSSED-HEART CROP TOP

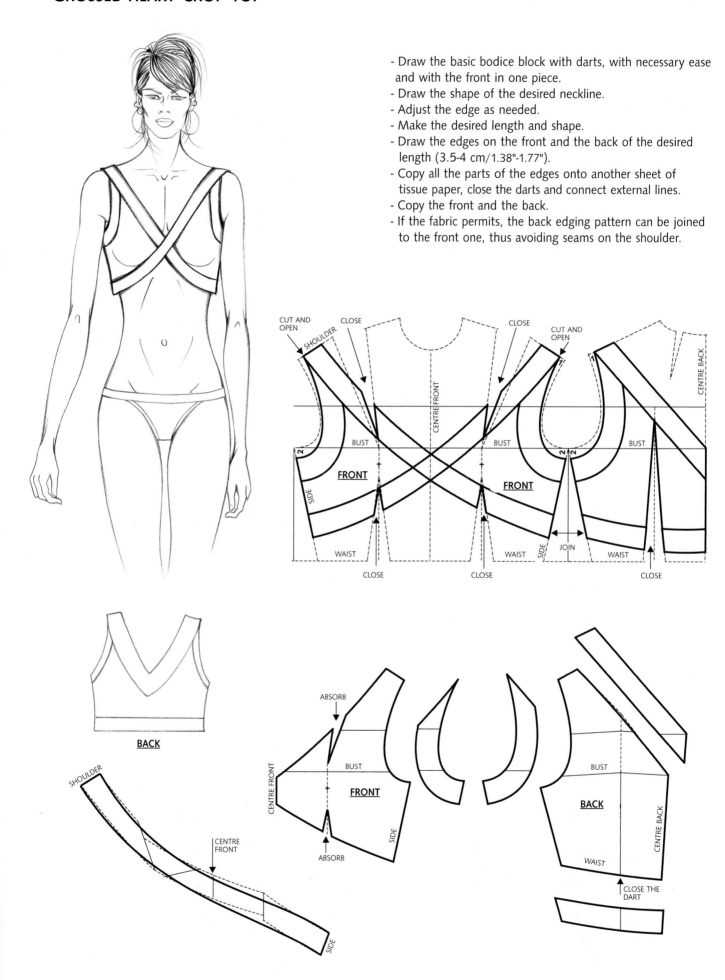

- Draw the basic bodice block with darts, with necessary ease and with the front in one piece.
- Draw the shape of the desired neckline.
- Adjust the edge as needed.
- Make the desired length and shape.
- Draw the edges on the front and the back of the desired length (3.5-4 cm/1.38"-1.77").
- Copy all the parts of the edges onto another sheet of tissue paper, close the darts and connect external lines.
- Copy the front and the back.
- If the fabric permits, the back edging pattern can be joined to the front one, thus avoiding seams on the shoulder.

LOOSE-FITTING ASYMMETRICAL TOP

- Draw the basic bodice pattern with darts, with necessary measurements and ease.
- Draw the front, a mirror image, to make the extension of the centre front.
- Trace the neckline and extend it over the centre front, with the depth and length required.
- Adjust the back neckline, raising it by 1 cm/0.39".
- Shift the waist darts as shown in figure, to make the gathers.
- Divide the bust dart in two equal parts.
- Draw four lines from the tips of the darts to the outer edge of the side, as shown in figure.
- Slash along the lines drawn and open them, closing the darts.
- Reshape the bottom and the neckline.

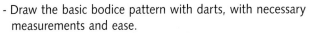

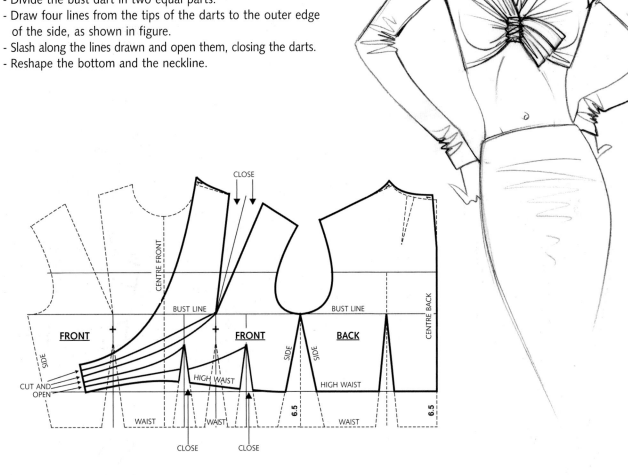

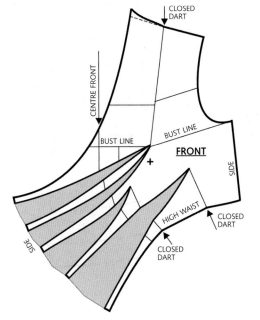

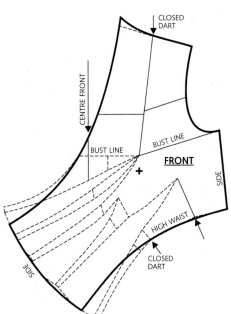

BUSTIER-TYPE TOP

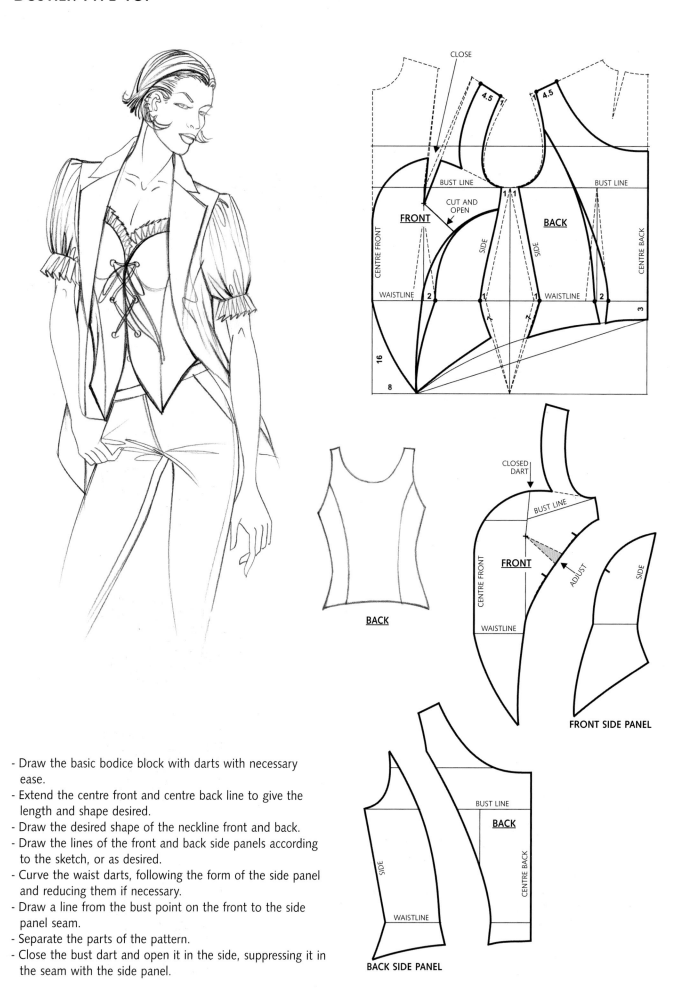

- Draw the basic bodice block with darts with necessary ease.
- Extend the centre front and centre back line to give the length and shape desired.
- Draw the desired shape of the neckline front and back.
- Draw the lines of the front and back side panels according to the sketch, or as desired.
- Curve the waist darts, following the form of the side panel and reducing them if necessary.
- Draw a line from the bust point on the front to the side panel seam.
- Separate the parts of the pattern.
- Close the bust dart and open it in the side, suppressing it in the seam with the side panel.

TOP WITH FANCY SEAMS

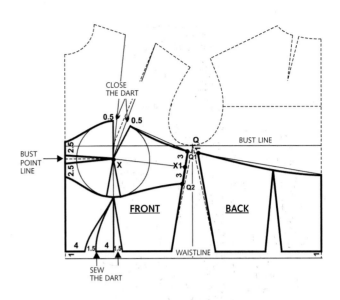

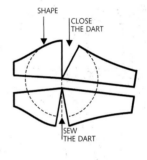

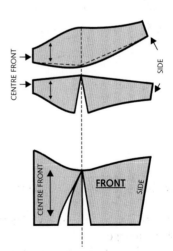

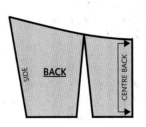

- Draw the basic bodice block with darts, with necessary ease for a top.
- Draw the desired neckline front and back.
- Draw the bust point.
- Extend the bust and waist dart lines to the bust point.
- Draw the line X-X1 ending at the midpoint of Q1-Q2.
- Draw the bust darts in the positions shown in figure and allow greater ease.
- Divide the front waist dart in two parts and give a curved shape to the one closer to the centre front.
- Close the darts above and connect accordingly after separating the two parts.

Tecno crop top

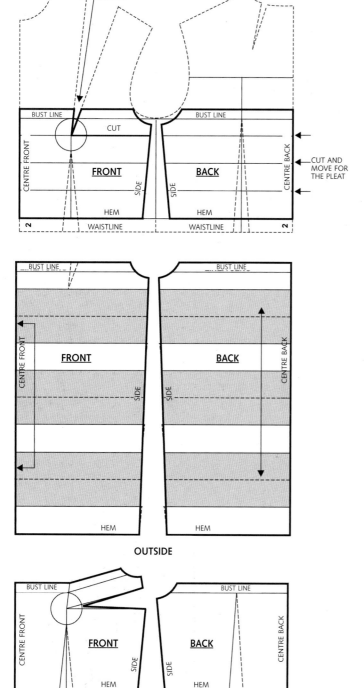

OUTSIDE

LINING

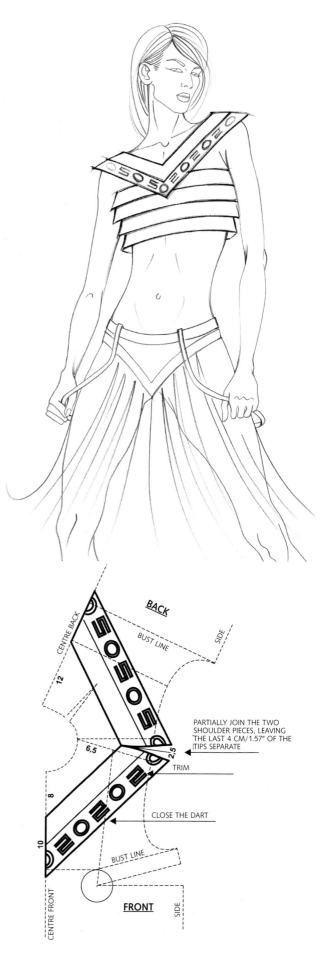

BACK

PARTIALLY JOIN THE TWO SHOULDER PIECES, LEAVING THE LAST 4 CM/1.57" OF THE TIPS SEPARATE

TRIM

CLOSE THE DART

FRONT

- Draw the basic bodice pattern with darts, necessary measurements and ease.
- Draw the line of the bottom at desired length.
- Draw the neckline front and back as shown in figure.
- Copy the front and back for the lining.
- Draw three horizontal and equidistant lines in the front and back to make pleats.
- Separate the front and the back.
- Slash along these lines and paste the parts to another sheet of paper, separating them by double the height of the top fold.
- Move the bust dart to the side.

TOPS WITH GATHERED ACCENTS
DARTS IN THE CENTRE FRONT WITH GATHERS

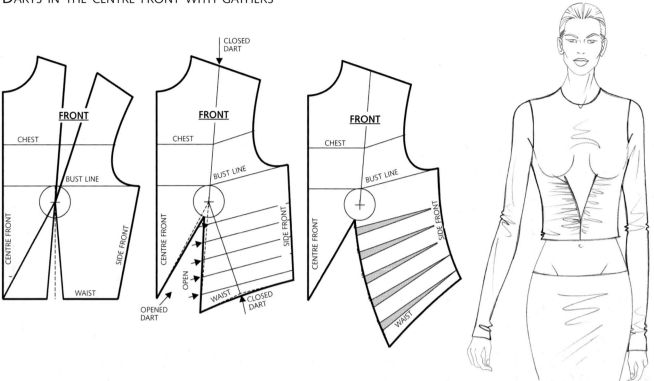

- Draw the basic bodice pattern with necessary darts, measurements and ease.
- Move the bust dart and waist dart to the centre front.
- Draw 5-6 parallel diagonal lines, from the side seam to the front dart.
- Cut along these lines and open by 1-1.5 cm/0.39"-0.59", as shown in the figure, and carefully finish.

CHEST-LEVEL DARTS WITH GATHERS

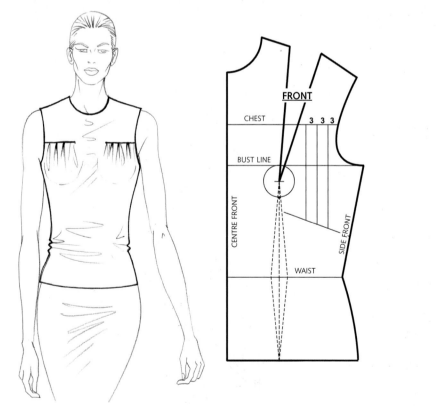

- Draw the basic bodice pattern with darts, with necessary measurements and ease, and eliminate the waist darts.
- Close the part of the bust dart above the line.
- Draw a diagonal line from the side seam to the waist dart.
- Draw three parallel vertical lines, from the chest to the diagonal line drawn.
- Cut along these lines and open by 1.5 cm/0.59", as shown in the figure, and carefully finish.

CROP TOP WITH DIAGONAL GATHERED MOTIF

SIDE DART WITH GATHERS

- Draw the basic bodice pattern with darts,
  with necessary measurements and ease.
- Reduce the depth of the shoulder dart by 50%.
- Close the shoulder and waist darts, redirecting them to the
  armscye.
- Make the two-fold basic front block and draw the diagonal
  line of the motif from the tip of the armscye dart.
- Draw three lines from the tip of the opposite armscye dart to
  the diagonal line.
- Slash along the lines and open, as shown in the figure.

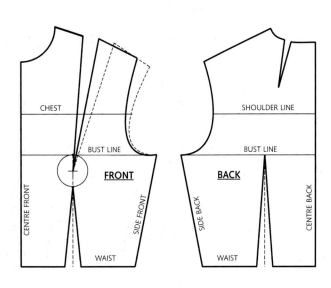

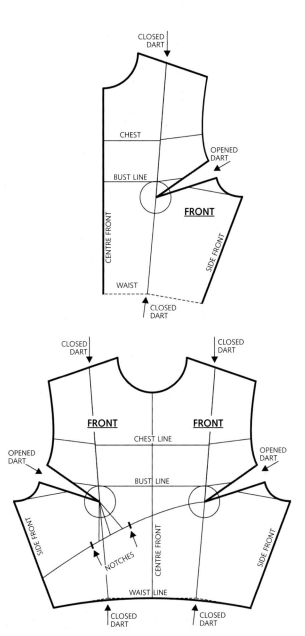

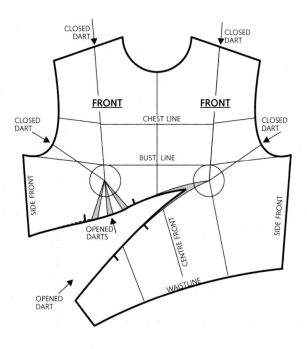

BASIC CROPPED KIMONO TOP WITH GUSSET

WITH BLOCKS AT RIGHT ANGLES

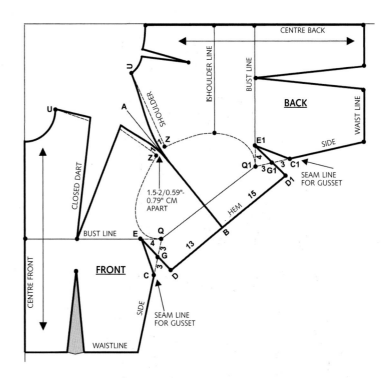

- Position the front and back darted bodice blocks at right angles, about 1.5-2 cm/0.59"-0.79" apart at the second shoulder point Z.
- Connect the points Q-Q1 from the front to the back (bust line).
- Q-E and Q1-E1 4 cm/1.57".
- Q-G and Q1-G1 3 cm/1.18".
- G-C and G1-C1 3 cm/1.18".
- Connect E-G-D and E1-G1-D1, based on desired sleeve length.
- Trace the bottom line D-D1.
- Point B is half D-D1 minus 1 cm/0.39".
- Draw A-B, centred between the Z points.
- Join the shoulders of the back and the front.

MADE USING THE LONG-SLEEVED KIMONO BLOCK WITH GUSSET

This short-sleeved top is made using the long-sleeved kimono block with gusset, described elsewhere, volume 1.
The length is drawn setting the sleeve hem perfectly on the bias, with the desired length and fullness, as shown in the figure.

GUSSET
- Draw a horizontal line B-C, 8 cm/3.15"; and a vertical one A-F bisecting B-C.
- B-A equals the length of E-C in the bodice.
- A-C equals the length of E1-C1 in the bodice.
- DE = 7 cm/2.76".
- BD equals the length of E-D in the bodice.
- C-E equals the length of E1-D1 in the bodice.
- Make a curved line connecting D and E.

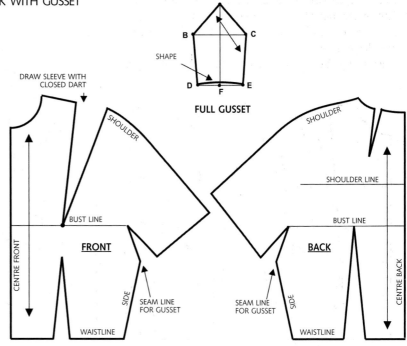

BASIC KIMONO BLOCK

USING THE BODICE BLOCK WITH DARTS

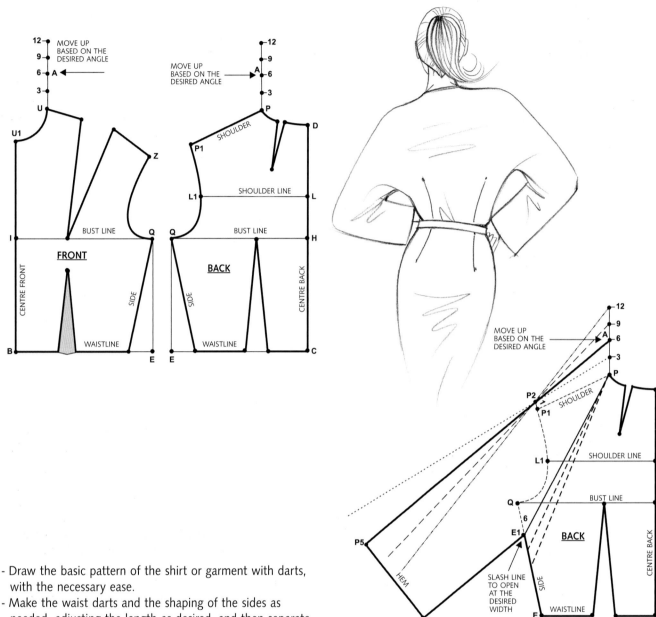

- Draw the basic pattern of the shirt or garment with darts, with the necessary ease.
- Make the waist darts and the shaping of the sides as needed, adjusting the length as desired, and then separate the front and back.

Back
- From the point P draw a vertical line with a height ranging from 3 to 12 cm/from 1.18" to 4.72", depending on the desired angle of the sleeve (e.g. 6 cm/2.36").
- From A, passing through P2, which is 1 cm/0.39" from P1, draw a straight line A-P5.
- P2-P5 is the length of the sleeve from the shoulder point.
- From the point Q, drop 4 to 16 cm/from 1.57" to 6.30" (in this case, 6 cm/2.36"), depending on the sleeve width desired, and draw the point E1.
- Draw the diagonal P-E1.
- Draw E1-E2 parallel to P2-P5.
- Trace the sleeve hem P5-E2 perpendicular to the line P2-P5, making the width of the sleeve at the hem 2 cm/0.79" wider than on the front.
- Slash along the diagonal E1-P, opening it as wide as the style requires (e.g., 8 cm/3.15") and join the separate parts with a curved line.

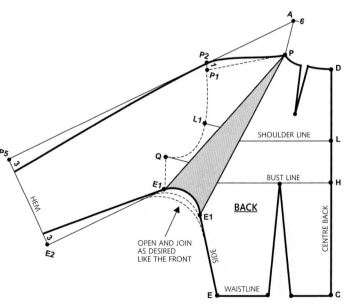

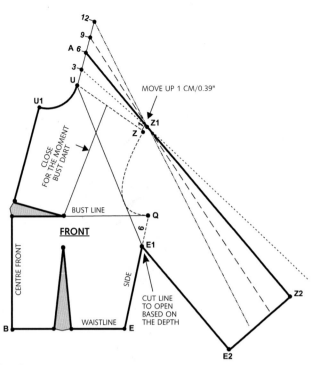

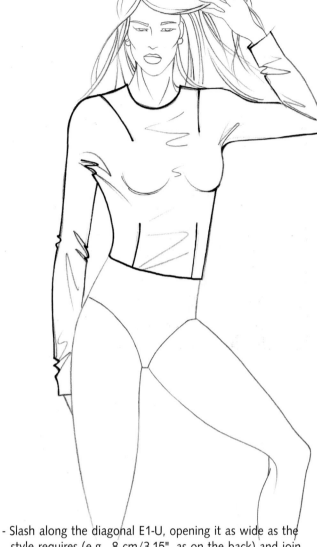

Front

- Draw from the point U a perpendicular line ranging from 3 to 12 cm/from 1.18" to 4.72", based on the desired angle of the sleeve (e.g., 6 cm/2.36" as on the back).
- For the moment, close the shoulder bust dart, opening it at the waist on the centre front, or in another position.
- From A, passing through Z1, which is 1 cm/0.39" from Z, draw a straight line A-Z2.
- Z1-Z2 is the length of the sleeve from the shoulder point, as on the back.
- From the point Q, drop 4 to 16 cm/from 1.57" to 6.30" (in this case, 6 cm/2.36"), depending on the sleeve width desired, and draw the point E1.
- Draw the diagonal U-E1.
- Draw E1-E2 parallel to Z1-Z2.
- Trace the sleeve hem Z2-E2 perpendicular to the line Z1-Z2, making the width of the sleeve at the hem 2 cm/0.79" wider than on the front.

- Slash along the diagonal E1-U, opening it as wide as the style requires (e.g., 8 cm/3.15", as on the back) and join the separate parts with a curved line.
- Reopen the bust dart on the shoulder and restore and connect all the lines. Check the pattern by laying it over the pattern for the back.

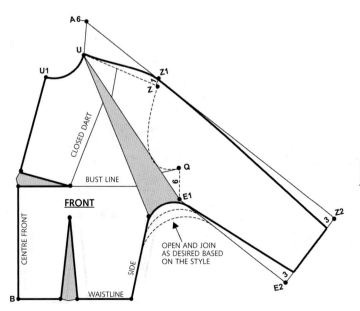

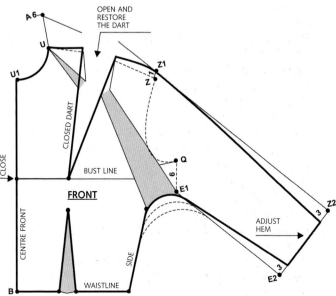

29

BASIC BLOCK FOR KIMONO WITH GUSSET

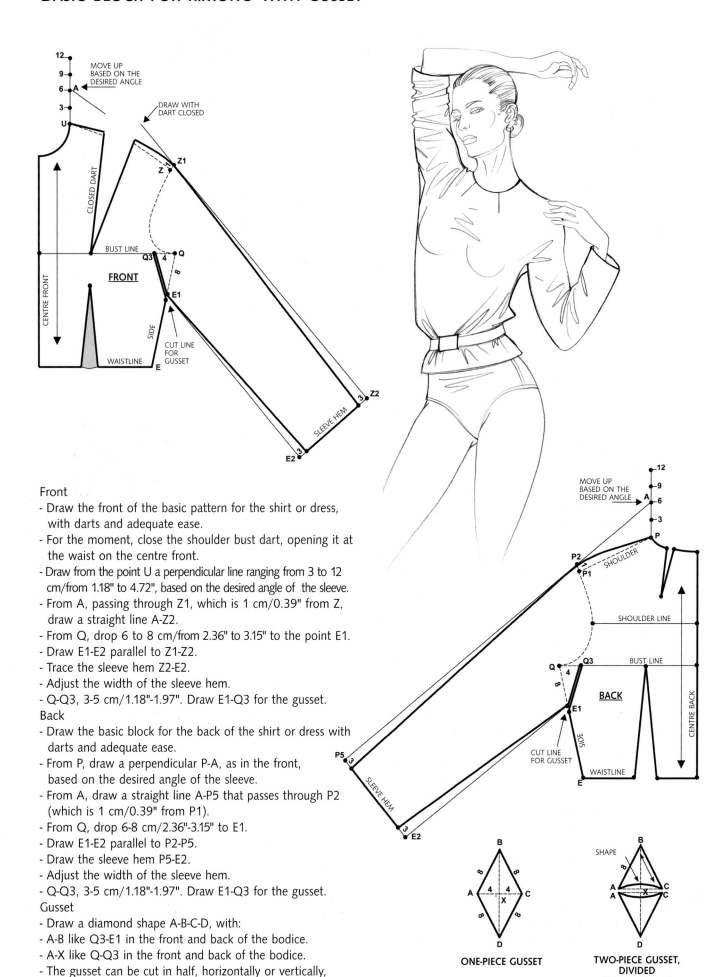

Front

- Draw the front of the basic pattern for the shirt or dress, with darts and adequate ease.
- For the moment, close the shoulder bust dart, opening it at the waist on the centre front.
- Draw from the point U a perpendicular line ranging from 3 to 12 cm/from 1.18" to 4.72", based on the desired angle of the sleeve.
- From A, passing through Z1, which is 1 cm/0.39" from Z, draw a straight line A-Z2.
- From Q, drop 6 to 8 cm/from 2.36" to 3.15" to the point E1.
- Draw E1-E2 parallel to Z1-Z2.
- Trace the sleeve hem Z2-E2.
- Adjust the width of the sleeve hem.
- Q-Q3, 3-5 cm/1.18"-1.97". Draw E1-Q3 for the gusset.

Back

- Draw the basic block for the back of the shirt or dress with darts and adequate ease.
- From P, draw a perpendicular P-A, as in the front, based on the desired angle of the sleeve.
- From A, draw a straight line A-P5 that passes through P2 (which is 1 cm/0.39" from P1).
- From Q, drop 6-8 cm/2.36"-3.15" to E1.
- Draw E1-E2 parallel to P2-P5.
- Draw the sleeve hem P5-E2.
- Adjust the width of the sleeve hem.
- Q-Q3, 3-5 cm/1.18"-1.97". Draw E1-Q3 for the gusset.

Gusset

- Draw a diamond shape A-B-C-D, with:
- A-B like Q3-E1 in the front and back of the bodice.
- A-X like Q-Q3 in the front and back of the bodice.
- The gusset can be cut in half, horizontally or vertically, depending on the pattern.

30

BASIC KIMONO BLOCK

WITHOUT DARTS

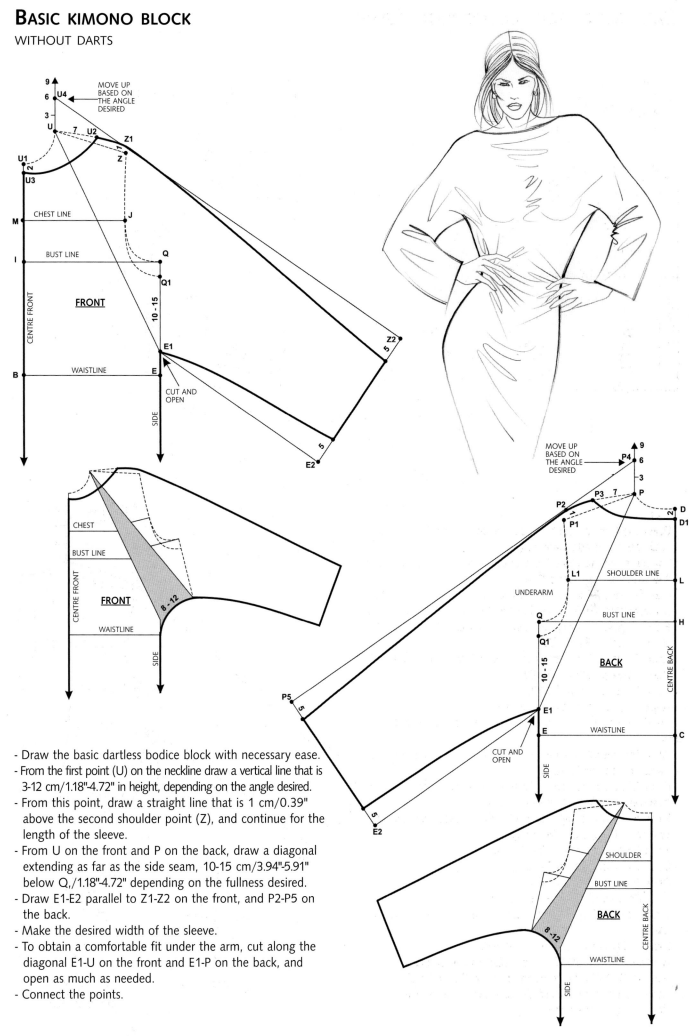

FRONT

MOVE UP BASED ON THE ANGLE DESIRED

CHEST LINE

BUST LINE

CENTRE FRONT

WAISTLINE

SIDE

10 - 15

CUT AND OPEN

CHEST

BUST LINE

CENTRE FRONT

WAISTLINE

SIDE

8 -12

MOVE UP BASED ON THE ANGLE DESIRED

SHOULDER LINE

UNDERARM

BUST LINE

BACK

CENTRE BACK

WAISTLINE

10 - 15

CUT AND OPEN

SIDE

SHOULDER

BUST LINE

BACK

CENTRE BACK

WAISTLINE

8 -12

SIDE

- Draw the basic dartless bodice block with necessary ease.
- From the first point (U) on the neckline draw a vertical line that is 3-12 cm/1.18"-4.72" in height, depending on the angle desired.
- From this point, draw a straight line that is 1 cm/0.39" above the second shoulder point (Z), and continue for the length of the sleeve.
- From U on the front and P on the back, draw a diagonal extending as far as the side seam, 10-15 cm/3.94"-5.91" below Q,/1.18"-4.72" depending on the fullness desired.
- Draw E1-E2 parallel to Z1-Z2 on the front, and P2-P5 on the back.
- Make the desired width of the sleeve.
- To obtain a comfortable fit under the arm, cut along the diagonal E1-U on the front and E1-P on the back, and open as much as needed.
- Connect the points.

ONE-PIECE KIMONO

WITH STITCHED SHOULDERS

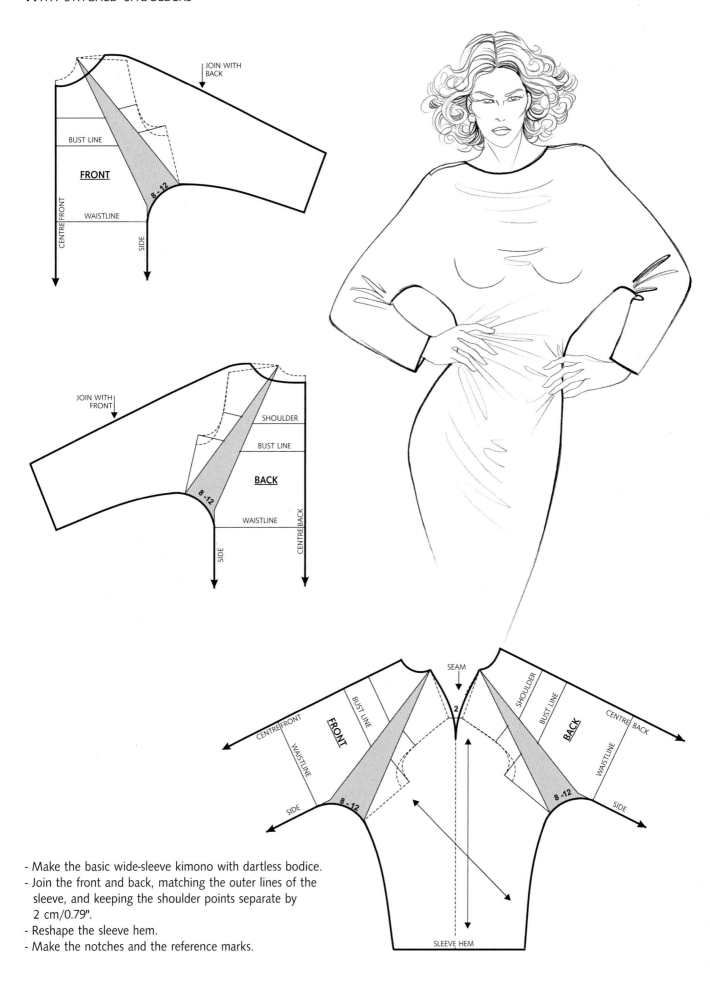

FRONT

JOIN WITH BACK

BUST LINE

CENTRE FRONT

WAISTLINE

SIDE

8 · 12

JOIN WITH FRONT

BACK

SHOULDER

BUST LINE

WAISTLINE

SIDE

CENTRE BACK

8 · 12

SEAM

2

FRONT

CENTRE FRONT

BUST LINE

WAISTLINE

SIDE

8 · 12

SHOULDER

BUST LINE

BACK

CENTRE BACK

WAISTLINE

SIDE

8 · 12

SLEEVE HEM

- Make the basic wide-sleeve kimono with dartless bodice.
- Join the front and back, matching the outer lines of the sleeve, and keeping the shoulder points separate by 2 cm/0.79".
- Reshape the sleeve hem.
- Make the notches and the reference marks.

SEAMLESS KIMONO SLEEVES

WIDE AT CUFF

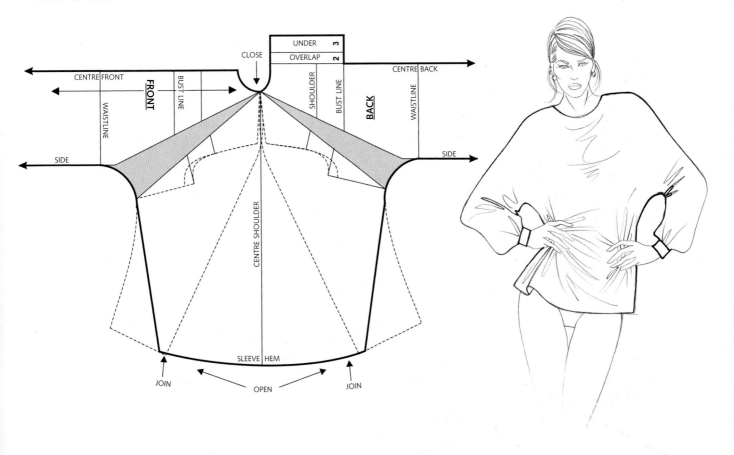

NARROW AT CUFF

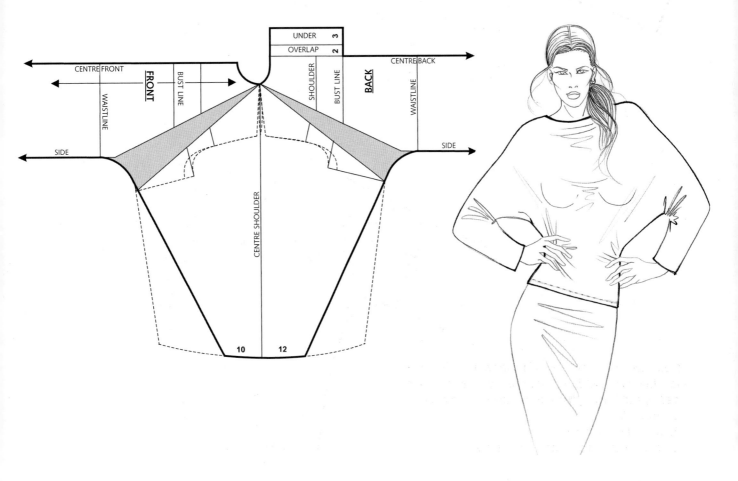

BASIC RAGLAN BLOCK

- Draw the basic shirt or dress block with darts, and keep the front and back separate.

Back

- Draw the vertical P-A as desired, depending on the angle of the sleeve.
- Draw a straight line A-P5, passing through P2 1 cm/0.39" from P1, with P2-P5 equal to the sleeve length taken from the shoulder centre.
- Q-E1 equals 3-8 cm/1.18"-3.15", depending on the depth desired.
- E-E4 equals 6.5 cm/2.56". Draw the vertical line E4-Q2.
- P-P3 equals 3-4 cm/1.18"-1.57". Draw the guideline P3-E1.
- From E1 to P3 equals 12 cm/4.72", for the intersection of the curve: Q3
- Draw E1-Q3-P3.

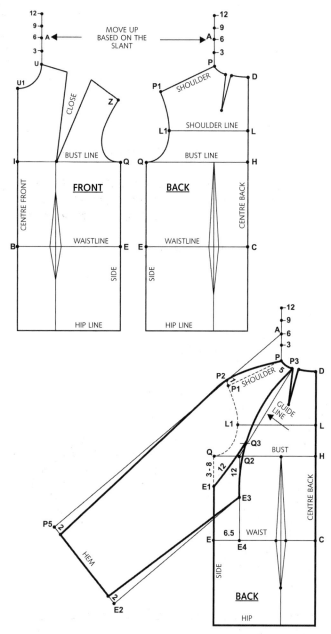

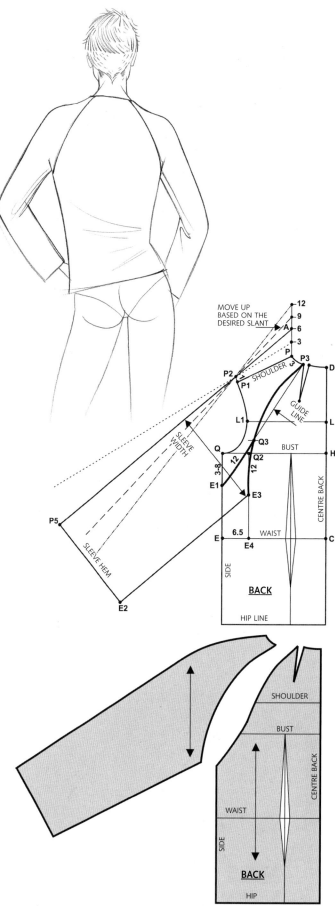

- Draw Q3-E3 like Q3-E1.
- Draw E3-E2 parallel to P2-P5.
- Adjust the sleeve hem depending on the style.

- Adjust the inner and outer lines of the sleeve and the bodice.
- Carefully trace off the sleeve and the bodice.

BASIC RAGLAN BLOCK - FRONT

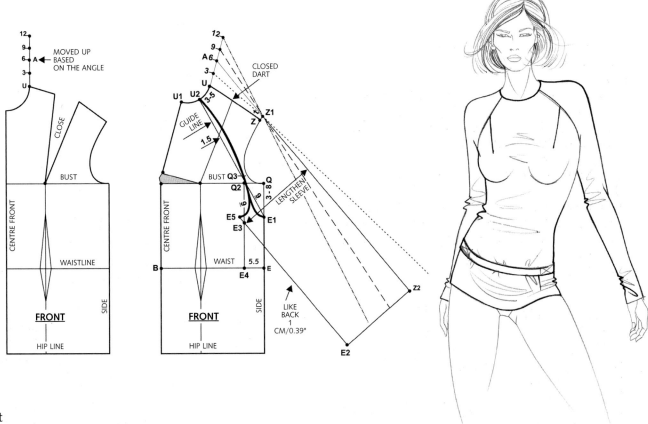

Front
- Draw the vertical line U-A as desired, depending on the angle of the sleeve.
- For the moment, close the shoulder bust dart, and open it on the centre front.
- Draw a straight line A-Z2, passing through Z1 at 1 cm/0.39" from point Z, with Z1-Z2 equal to the sleeve length taken from the centre shoulder, as on the back.

- Q-E1 equals 3-8 cm/1.18"-3.15", depending on the depth desired, as on the back.
- E-E4 equals 5.5 cm/2.17". Draw the vertical line E4-Q2.
- U-U2 3-5 cm/1.18"-1.97". - Draw the guideline U2-E1.
- From E1 to U2 equals 9 cm/3.54", for the intersection of the curves at Q3.
- Trace off the outline E1-Q3-U2.

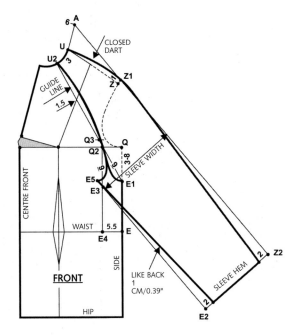

- Draw Q3-E5 like Q3-E1.
- Draw E2-E3 parallel to Z1-Z2, equal in measure to E2-E5 on the back, minus 1 cm/0.39".
- Adjust the sleeve hem depending on the style.
- Adjust the inner and outer lines of the sleeve and bodice.

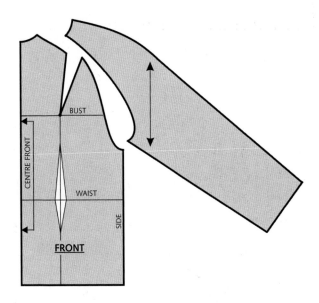

- Carefully copy the sleeve and the bodice onto another sheet of paper.
- Open the bust dart, and close the one in the centre front that had been temporarily opened.

BASIC RAGLAN BLOCK WITH FITTED SLEEVES

This type of sleeve is recommended for all garments made with elasticized or knit fabrics, since they are figure-hugging. Instead, it is poorly suited to stiff fabrics or for loose-fitting sleeves, unless an alteration is made to widen it.

- Draw the basic shirt or dress bodice block with the necessary measurements and ease allowance.
- For the moment, close the shoulder bust dart, moving it to the side.
- Draw the raglan sleeve line from the armhole to the neck, with the desired shape.
- Draw the basic fitted sleeve with ease in accordance with the bodice and desired length.
- Shift about 2.5 cm/0.98" from the back to the front, as shown in the figure, to make the seam correspond to the bodice side seam.
- Copy the two parts of the raglan drawn on the bodice and position them on the sleeve head, detaching them by about 1.5 cm/0.59" from the sleeve centre and raised by 1 cm/0.39", to eliminate some of the looseness of the fitted sleeve.
- Connect lines accordingly, as shown in the figure, and check that the bodice and sleeve lines correspond in length.

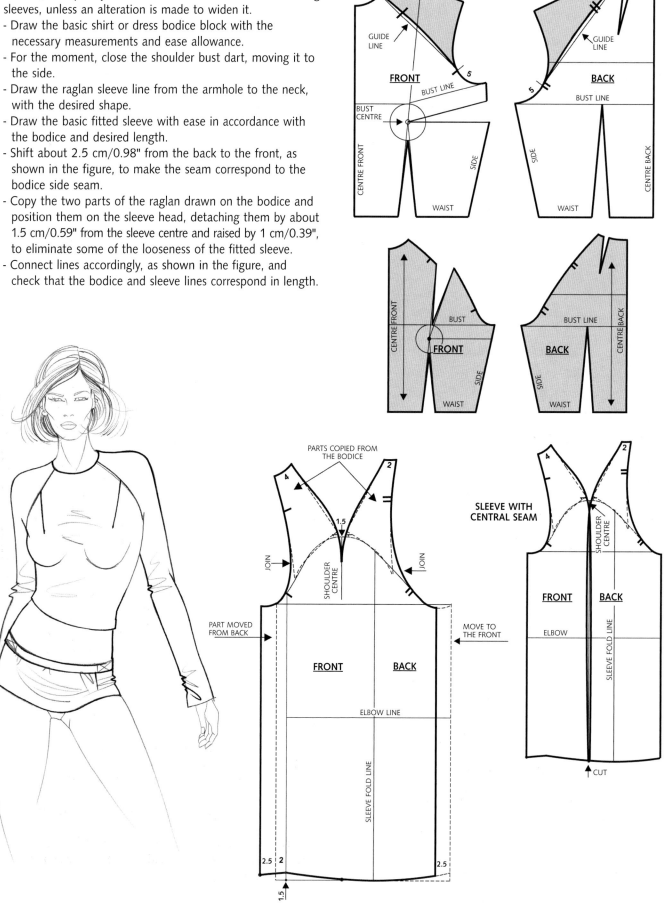

BASIC RAGLAN BLOCK WITH SIDE PANELS

T-SHAPED BODICE WITH SLEEVES

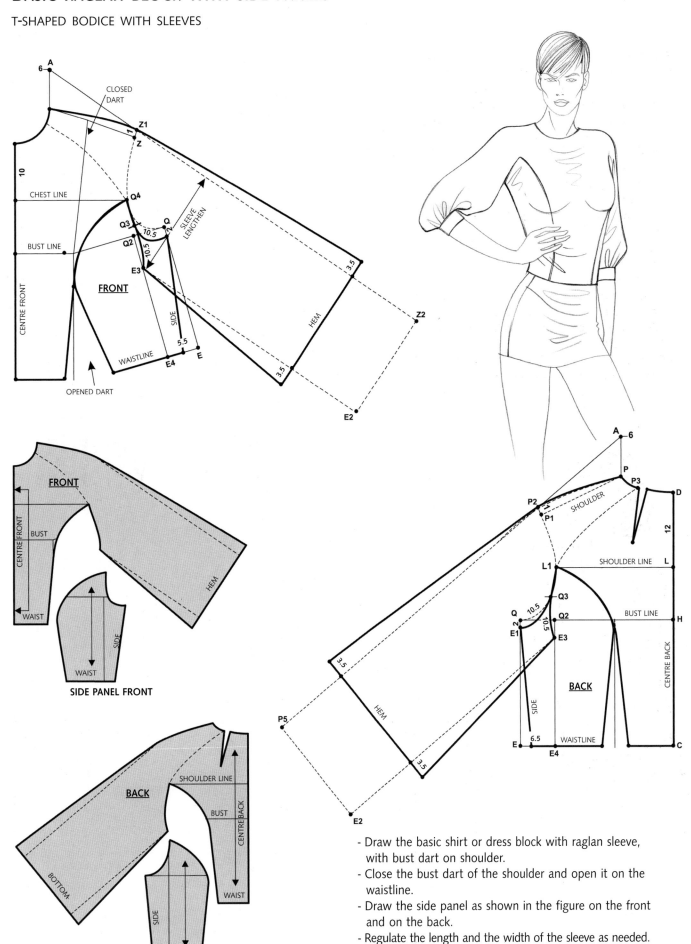

- Draw the basic shirt or dress block with raglan sleeve, with bust dart on shoulder.
- Close the bust dart of the shoulder and open it on the waistline.
- Draw the side panel as shown in the figure on the front and on the back.
- Regulate the length and the width of the sleeve as needed.
- Trace off the pattern pieces and put the front side piece on the straight of grain.

ALTERATION FOR PADDED SHOULDERS

SHOULDER PAD FOR FITTED SLEEVE

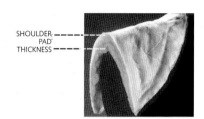

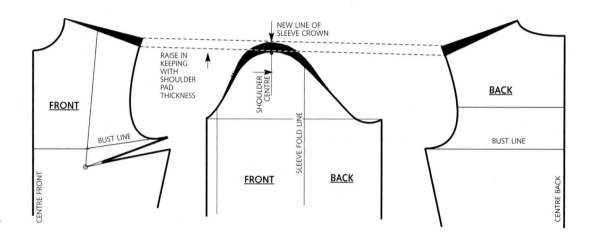

SHOULDER PAD FOR RAGLAN AND KIMONO SLEEVES

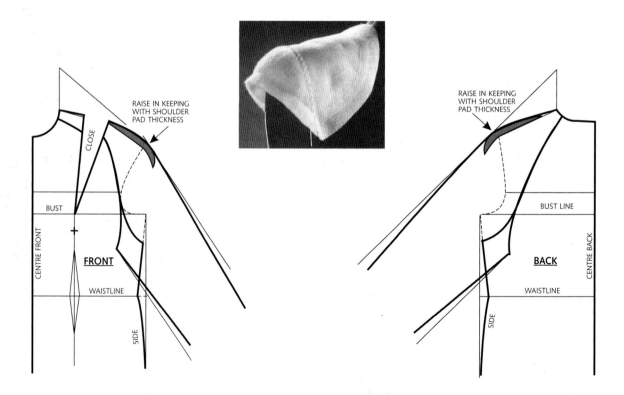

Garments with shoulder pads require alteration of the bodice shoulder line and the sleeve crown, as follows:
- Raise the bodice shoulder point and the sleeve crown in keeping with the thickness of the shoulder pad.
- Smooth the sleeve crown lines appropriately.

- Do not raise the shoulder point or the sleeve crown in the lining.
- For raglan and kimono sleeves, rounded shoulder pads are used, but they also require adjustment to the outer shoulder point in keeping with their thickness.

SLEEVE ASSEMBLY

After sewing the sleeve and the bodice, we proceed to their assembly.

- With the front laid out on the table with the inside facing up, insert the righthand sleeve in the righthand armhole, laid face to face.
- Fasten the sleeve with pins on the bodice side seam, in the lower part of the armscye, offsetting the sleeve seam by 2-3 cm/0.79"-1.18" (this measurement is only indicative and subject to variation, depending on the pattern and the subject's figure, to achieve perfect drape).
- Fasten the centre sleeve with pins to the shoulder seam (sometimes this centre must be shifted slightly forwards or backwards, for reasons of body shape). Baste with small running stitches along the lower part of the sleeve, without leaving any ease.
- Continue basting, aligning the notches, uniformly distributing any extra over the sleeve crown, taking care that the sleeve and armscye seamlines are perfectly matched, keeping the armscye and the sleeve rolled softly over the fingertips of the other hand.
- Carry on in the same way for the lefthand sleeve.

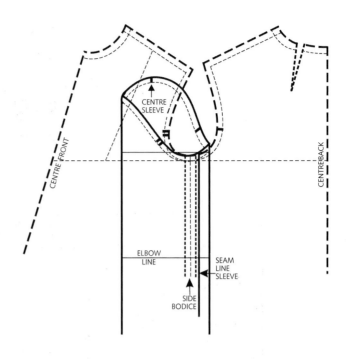

SLEEVE ASSEMBLY

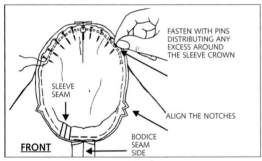

Fasten the sleeve with pins offsetting the sleeve seam by 2-3 cm/0,79"-1,18" with respect to the armscye seam.

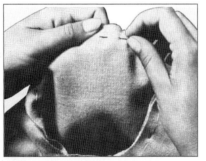

Baste, keeping the armscye rolled softly over the fingertips.

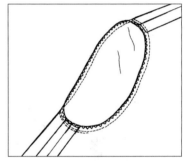

Sew and eliminate the excess fabric in the seams, finishing the edges.

DRAPE OF THE SLEEVE

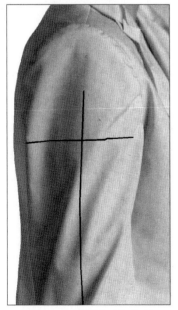

Bad drape caused diagonal wrinkling on both the front and back.

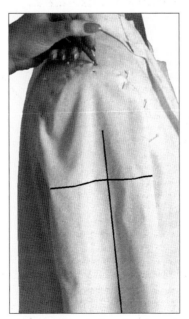

Rotate the sleeve backwards or forwards until the wrinkles are gone.

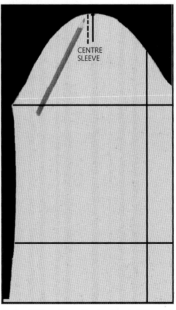

Correct the pattern by positioning the new shoulder centre properly for the individual.

FITTED SHIRT

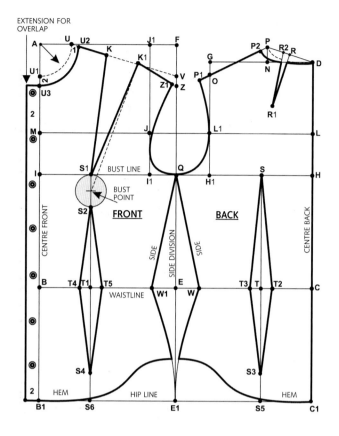

- Draw the basic block with darts and 6-8 cm/2.36"-3.15" ease.
- Extend the centre back, centre front and side division lines, as desired (15-20 cm/5.91"-7.87").
- Draw the extension for the overlap of the button placket.
- Lower the neckline as desired (2 cm/0.79").
- Move U-U2 and P-P2 1 cm/0.39".
- Finish the hem with desired shape.

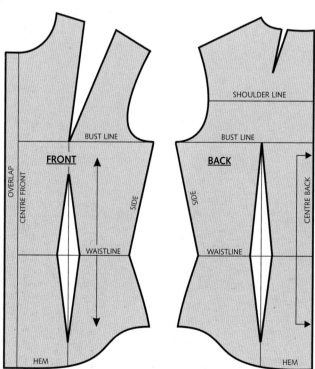

Basic shirt block without darts

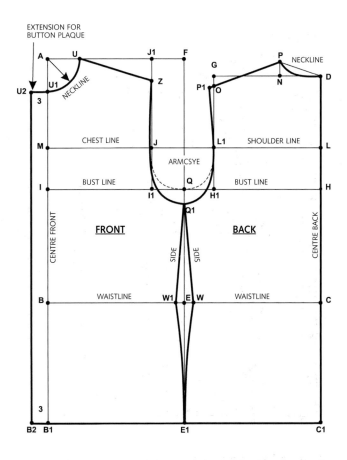

- Make the basic bodice without darts.
- C-C1 = 15-20 cm/5.91"-7.87" (or as desired).
- B-B1 like C-C1.
- B1-B2 = 3 cm/1.18".
- E-W and E-W1 = 1.5 cm/0.59" (as needed).
- Carefully draw the shape of the tails.
- Lower the armscye as needed and check the sleeve crown measurements.

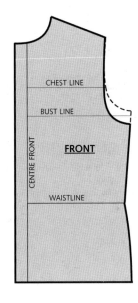

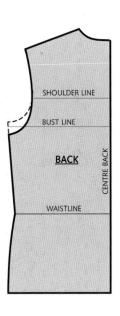

BLOUSON

MADE FULL BY ELIMINATING THE DARTS

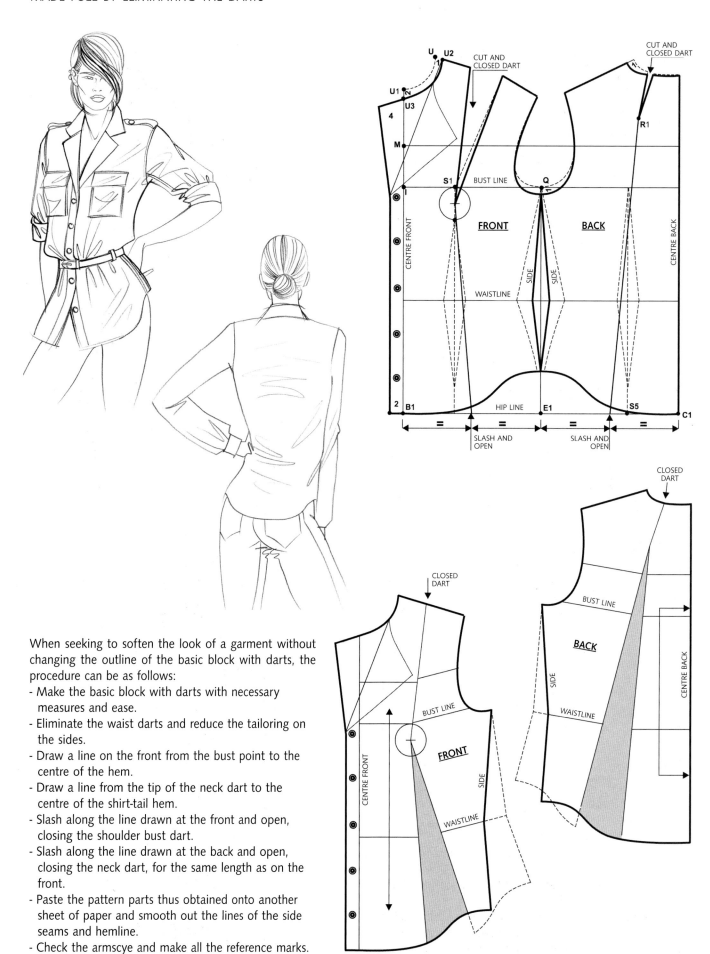

When seeking to soften the look of a garment without changing the outline of the basic block with darts, the procedure can be as follows:
- Make the basic block with darts with necessary measures and ease.
- Eliminate the waist darts and reduce the tailoring on the sides.
- Draw a line on the front from the bust point to the centre of the hem.
- Draw a line from the tip of the neck dart to the centre of the shirt-tail hem.
- Slash along the line drawn at the front and open, closing the shoulder bust dart.
- Slash along the line drawn at the back and open, closing the neck dart, for the same length as on the front.
- Paste the pattern parts thus obtained onto another sheet of paper and smooth out the lines of the side seams and hemline.
- Check the armscye and make all the reference marks.

SHIRT WITH RIBBING ON THE SHOULDERS

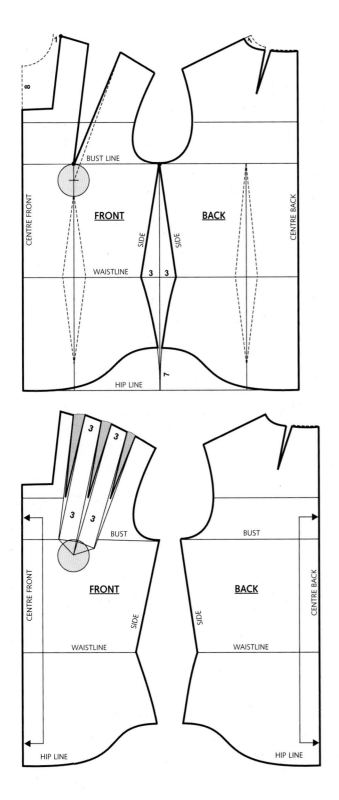

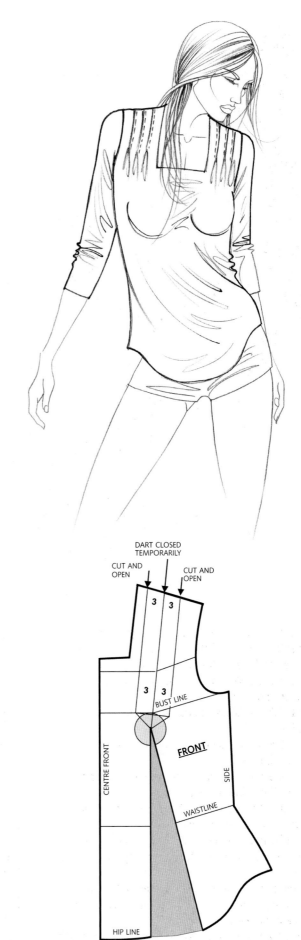

- Draw the basic bodice.
- Move the tip of the shoulder dart to the bust point.
- Momentarily close the shoulder dart, opening the one at the waist.
- Draw two equidistant lines parallel to the closed shoulder dart line, as shown in the figure.
- Cut along these lines and reopen, subdividing the opening in three equal parts, matching the sides of the waist dart.
- Smoothly finish the waistline and the shoulder line.

THE CARRÉ OR YOKE

CARRÉ BASICS

The carré (from the French), or yoke, is a shaped part of a pattern that is cut out and adapted to the individual form. The carré is usually made on the front and back shoulders, but may also be found in other positions, such as, for example, in the side panel of a bodice.

There are various kinds of carré, used for classical blouses, shirt dresses, sportswear, men's shirts, suits, jackets, and so forth. The carré can be straight or squared, tilted up or down, pointed or curved, overlaid, etc. Its dimensions can range from a narrow strip of the shoulders to a rather deep yoke extending half-way or even more down the bodice.

It may involve the upper section of the bodice only in part, or fully, or extend beyond the shoulders.

On the front, it may be joined to pieces of various size and shape, and may show many different styles.

The number of variations possible for the yoke is practically infinite. The section beneath it may be fitted or full, or loose, and can have gathers, pleats, smocking, or other kinds of folds or draping.

THE FRONT CARRÉ

Before drawing the yoke shape, if the bodice block with darts is used, close the shoulder dart.

Then, the yoke can be given any shape, completely regardless of the darts, using the lines and the construction points determined by the style.

The simplest yoke style is straight across, so it can be used as a general example.

Height - the yoke height is usually determined based on the lines of the centre front and not the armscye, and it is referenced as a portion of the front.

To establish the yoke height, it is very helpful to draw on the sketch a horizontal line at the shoulders, one at the bust, and one at the waist, and the height is determined starting from the first line.

Reference marks - to determine the position of the yoke during the assembly of the garment, reference marks must be made. These markers, made of one or more notches, must be made about 4-5 cm/1.57"-1.97" from the centre front and about 4 cm/1.57" from the armscye.

The markers are especially important when the part below the yoke is fuller than the part above.

The fullness is distributed more or less evenly on either side of the closed dart, having it coincide with the circle of the bust point.

Procedure

Cut the carré and close the part of the dart that is left in this area of the pattern, using tape or glue.

In the lower area, now separated by the yoke, the dart is usually left open to increase the fullness below the yoke, or in any case, it is suppressed into the seam.

The markers ensure that when the two sections are assembled, the fullness falls in the right place.

The upper edge of the lower section must be adjusted to obtain a uniform curve, and sometimes it is raised slightly in correspondence with the armscye to avoid pulling in that area.

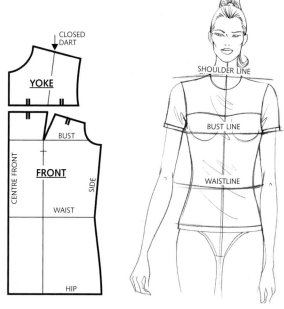

If the pattern calls for further fullness in the lower part, distributed in gathers or pleats, the fullness of the darts is added to it.

If, instead, the lower part is smooth, the fullness of the unwanted dart is made to be absorbed in the seam line of the yoke on the armscye. This can be done beforehand, when closing the dart.

THE BACK CARRÉ

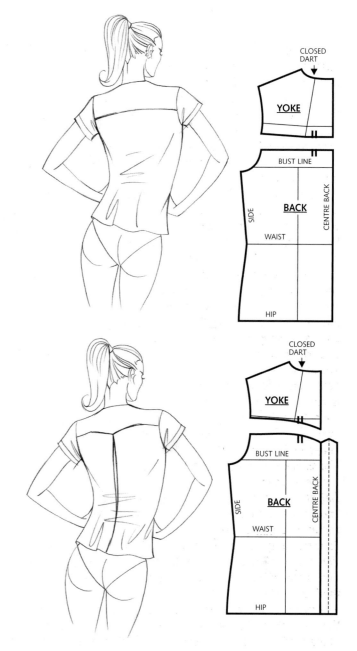

For the carré on the upper back, close the neckline dart.

If the carré ends even with the tip of the dart, it can be cut directly and then closed at a later moment, keeping the straight of grain aligned with the centre back.

If the carré line falls above or below the tip of the neckline dart, the tip must be adjusted to coincide with the line, before cutting the carré.

The shape of the neckline dart is shifted to the seam joining the carré and the armscye. So when the dart is closed, the carré slants up from the neckline dart tip to the armscye.

If a straight yoke is desired, as in most patterns, the dart must be closed before drawing the line of the yoke, so that it remains straight, with the lower part of bodice slanting down towards the armscye.

Most men's shirts and women's blouses have a yoke in the upper part of the back, and the shoulder line is shifted slightly towards the front.

The lines of the back carré do not necessarily have to be horizontal or vertical at the centre back. They can also form a V-shape, or be curved or modelled, Western-style.

The V-shaped yoke can be given curves and a box pleat at the centre, added to the centre back of the pattern.

SHOULDERS FORWARD

Moving the shoulder line forward extends the back of the bodice passing through the shoulder line and drawing a new one in the upper part of the front bodice.

The shoulder line brought forward becomes an integral and permanent part of the pattern piece for the bodice back. This device is often used in shirts and shirt-dresses.

Because of the shoulder's slant from the neckline to the armscye, the shoulder line brought forward is usually not drawn parallel to the original line, otherwise it would seem to rise toward the neckline.

Instead, it is further away on the neckline (5-5.5 cm/1.97"-2.17") than on the armscye (3-3.5 cm/1.18"-1.38"), with respect to the original shoulder line.

Often the shoulders forward line becomes an integral part of the yoke on the back.

The shoulders forward line is also often used to hold the gathers or small pleats replacing the shoulder darts.

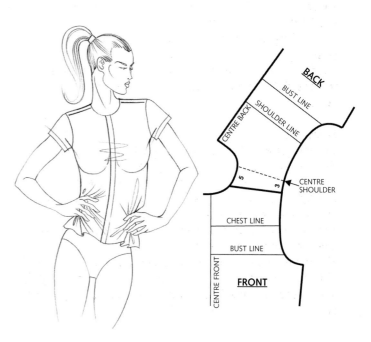

BLOUSE WITH SQUARED YOKE

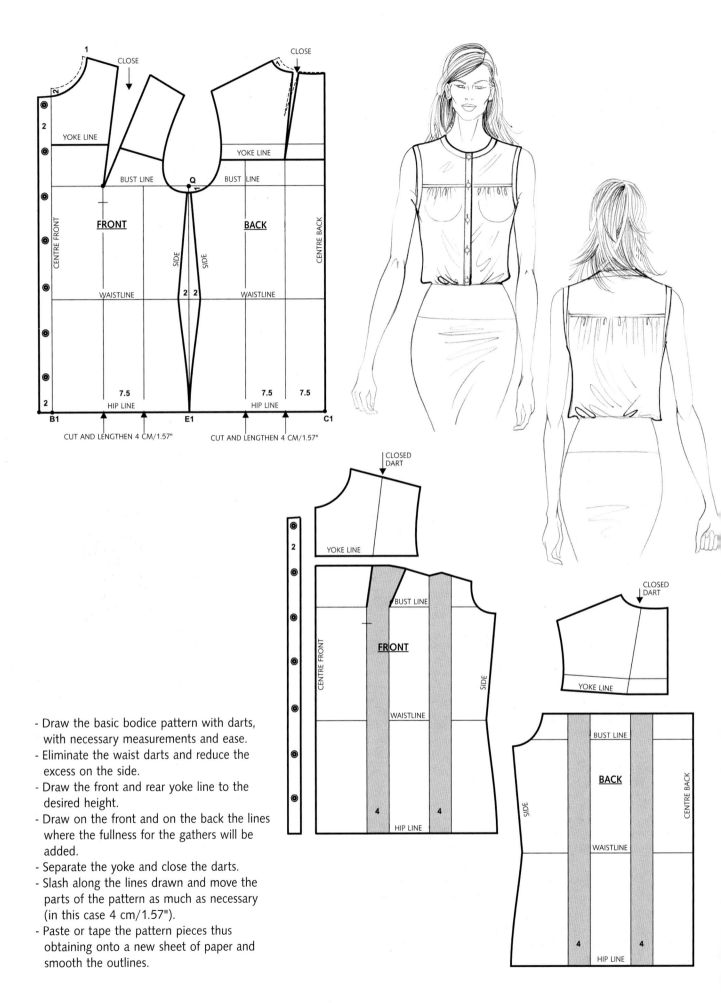

- Draw the basic bodice pattern with darts, with necessary measurements and ease.
- Eliminate the waist darts and reduce the excess on the side.
- Draw the front and rear yoke line to the desired height.
- Draw on the front and on the back the lines where the fullness for the gathers will be added.
- Separate the yoke and close the darts.
- Slash along the lines drawn and move the parts of the pattern as much as necessary (in this case 4 cm/1.57").
- Paste or tape the pattern pieces thus obtaining onto a new sheet of paper and smooth the outlines.

SHIRT WITH PLEATED YOKE

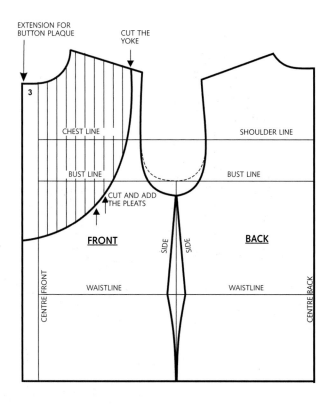

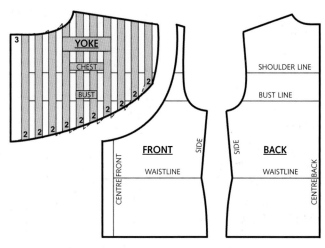

- Make the basic bodice without darts, with the necessary measurement and ease.
- Draw the extension of the centre front for the button plaque.
- Draw the outline of the front yoke with the desired dimensions.
- Within the yoke, draw the number of lines corresponding to the number of pleats desired.
- Separate the yoke from the rest of the pattern and cut along the lines drawn to create additional fullness for the pleats.

The fullness to be added depends on the width and the number of pleats. For small, 1/0.39"- to 1.5 cm/0.59" pleats, add double that width (2-3 cm/0.79"-1.18") for each pleat.

- After cutting out all the yoke pattern pieces, glue them perfectly aligned on another sheet of paper, separated by 2-3 cm/0.79"-1.18".

CRISS-CROSS FRONT CROP TOP

- Draw the basic bodice pattern with darts, with necessary measurements and ease.
- Draw the front in one piece.
- Draw the shape of desired neckline.
- Make the desired length.
- Draw the short kimono sleeve.
- Draw the front extension for the back fastening, with measure equal to back waist less 1 cm/0.39".
- Copy all the parts of the pattern onto another sheet of paper.
- Close front shoulder dart, suppressing it in the centre front for the fullness, as shown in the figure.
- Draw the back as in the figure.

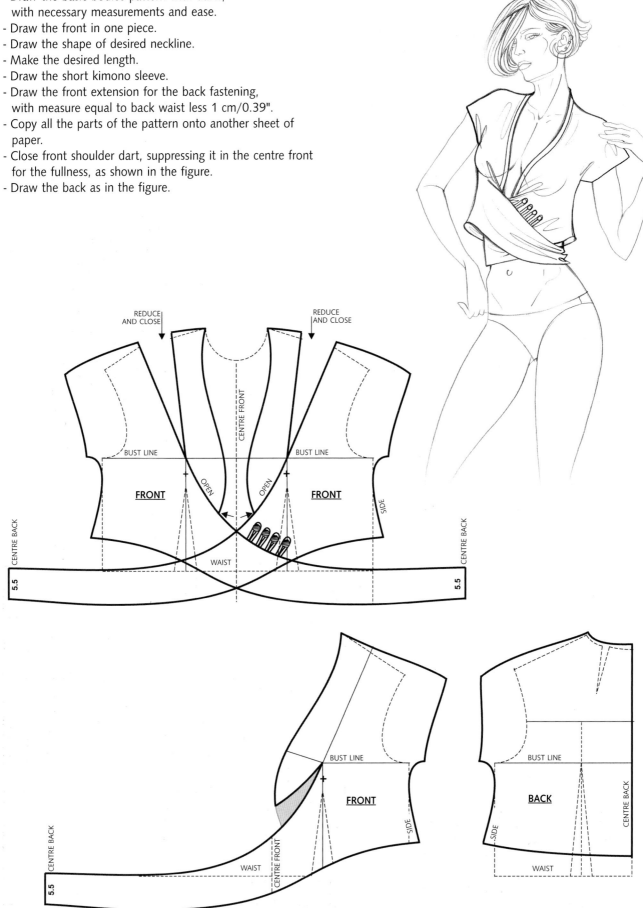

SHIRT WITH PLEATED FRONT

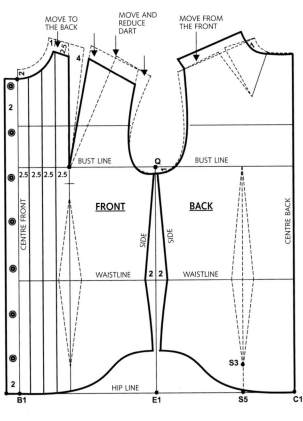

- Draw the basic bodice pattern with darts, with necessary measurements and ease.
- Eliminate the waist darts and reduce the excess on the side.
- Pivot the shoulder bust dart towards the neck line until the inner line is vertical.
- Draw on the front the lines where the pleats are to be inserted (in this case, four).
- Cut along the lines drawn and move the parts of the pattern to insert the small tucks.
- Copy the patterns obtained onto another sheet of paper and connect the lines.

MATERNITY BLOUSE

WITH STRAIGHT YOKE

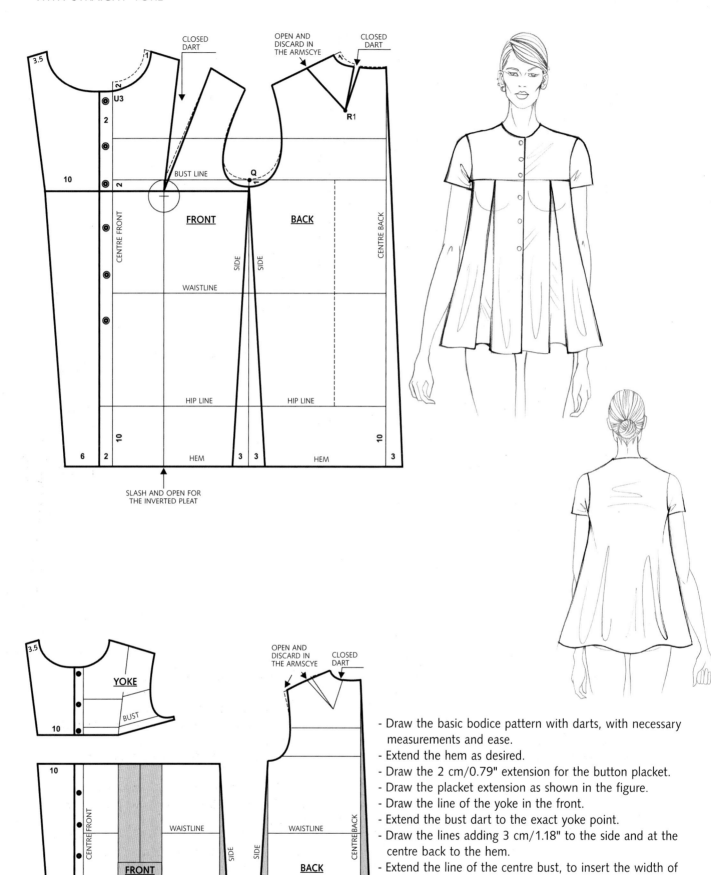

- Draw the basic bodice pattern with darts, with necessary measurements and ease.
- Extend the hem as desired.
- Draw the 2 cm/0.79" extension for the button placket.
- Draw the placket extension as shown in the figure.
- Draw the line of the yoke in the front.
- Extend the bust dart to the exact yoke point.
- Draw the lines adding 3 cm/1.18" to the side and at the centre back to the hem.
- Extend the line of the centre bust, to insert the width of the inverted pleat.
- Separate the front from the back.
- Separate the yoke and close the bust dart.
- Cut and expand the front for the inverted pleats.
- Close the back neckline dart and suppress it in the armscye.

MATERNITY BLOUSE
WITH ROUNDED YOKE

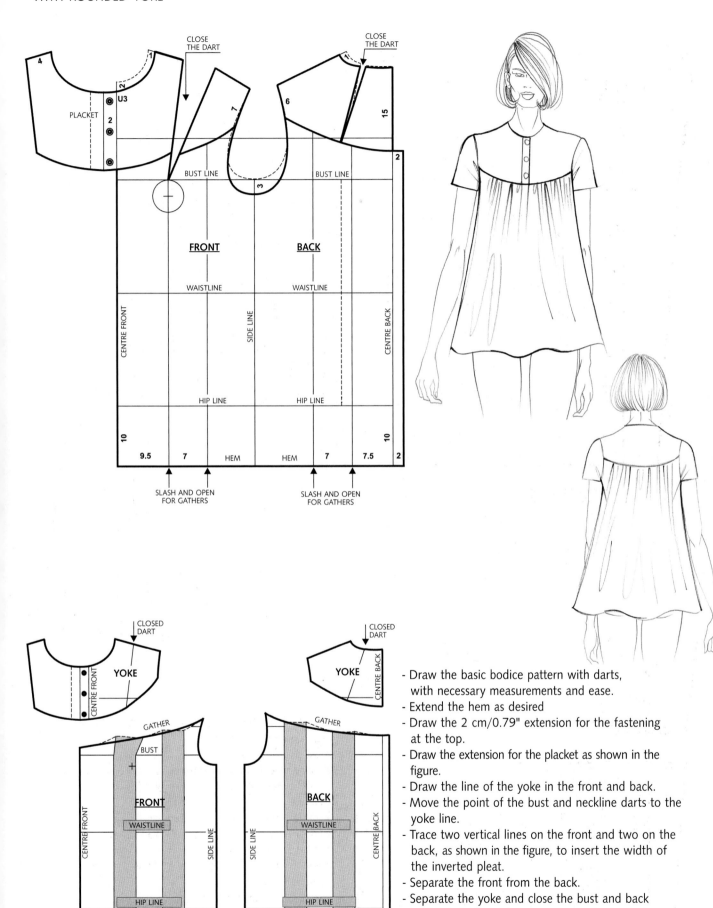

CLOSE THE DART

CLOSE THE DART

4

2

U3

PLACKET

2

1

7

6

15

2

BUST LINE

BUST LINE

3

FRONT

BACK

CENTRE FRONT

SIDE LINE

CENTRE BACK

WAISTLINE

WAISTLINE

HIP LINE

HIP LINE

10

10

9.5

7

HEM

HEM

7

7.5

2

SLASH AND OPEN FOR GATHERS

SLASH AND OPEN FOR GATHERS

CLOSED DART

CLOSED DART

YOKE

CENTRE FRONT

YOKE

CENTRE BACK

GATHER

GATHER

BUST

FRONT

BACK

CENTRE FRONT

WAISTLINE

SIDE LINE

SIDE LINE

WAISTLINE

CENTRE BACK

HIP LINE

HIP LINE

4

HEM

4

4

HEM

4

- Draw the basic bodice pattern with darts, with necessary measurements and ease.
- Extend the hem as desired
- Draw the 2 cm/0.79" extension for the fastening at the top.
- Draw the extension for the placket as shown in the figure.
- Draw the line of the yoke in the front and back.
- Move the point of the bust and neckline darts to the yoke line.
- Trace two vertical lines on the front and two on the back, as shown in the figure, to insert the width of the inverted pleat.
- Separate the front from the back.
- Separate the yoke and close the bust and back neckline darts.
- Cut along the lines drawn on the front and back for the gathers and widen by 4 cm/1.57".

RAGLAN SLEEVE BLOUSE WITH RUFFLE COLLAR

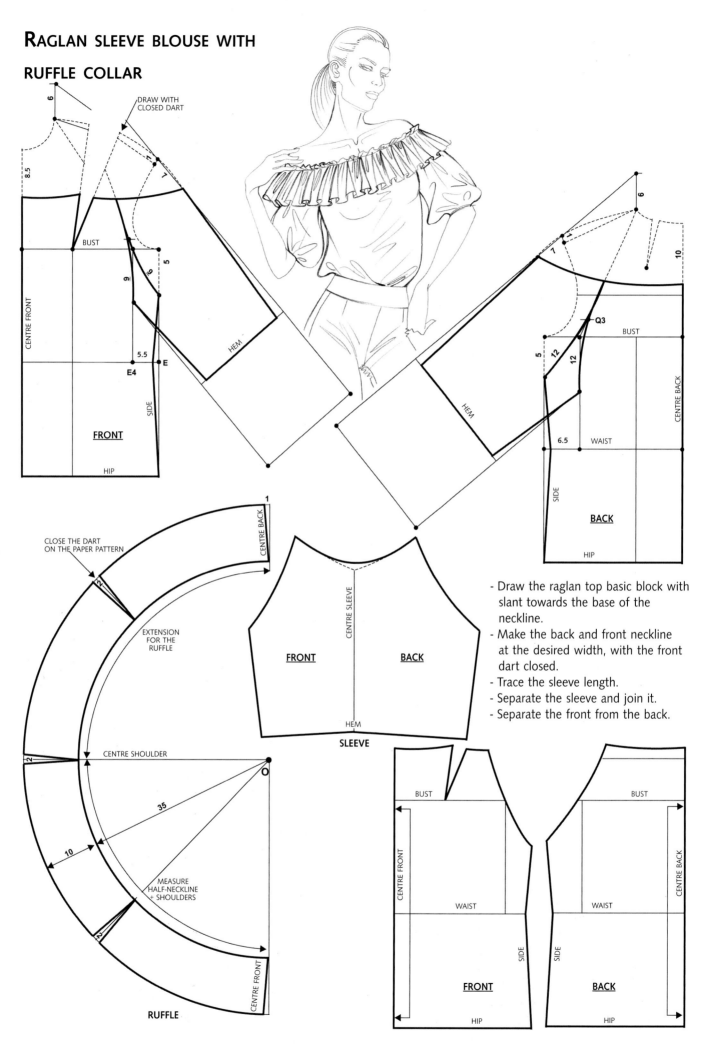

DRAW WITH CLOSED DART

8.5

6

BUST

CENTRE FRONT

5

9
6

5.5

E4   E

HEM

SIDE

FRONT

HIP

6

7
7

Q3   BUST

5   12
12

CENTRE BACK

6.5   WAIST

SIDE

10

BACK

HIP

1

CENTRE BACK

CLOSE THE DART
ON THE PAPER PATTERN

2

EXTENSION
FOR THE
RUFFLE

CENTRE SLEEVE

FRONT   **BACK**

HEM

SLEEVE

2

CENTRE SHOULDER

O

35

10

MEASURE
HALF-NECKLINE
+ SHOULDERS

2

CENTRE FRONT

RUFFLE

- Draw the raglan top basic block with
  slant towards the base of the
  neckline.
- Make the back and front neckline
  at the desired width, with the front
  dart closed.
- Trace the sleeve length.
- Separate the sleeve and join it.
- Separate the front from the back.

BUST

BUST

CENTRE FRONT

WAIST

SIDE

FRONT

HIP

CENTRE BACK

WAIST

SIDE

BACK

HIP

Gathered raglan top

WITH BOAT NECKLINE

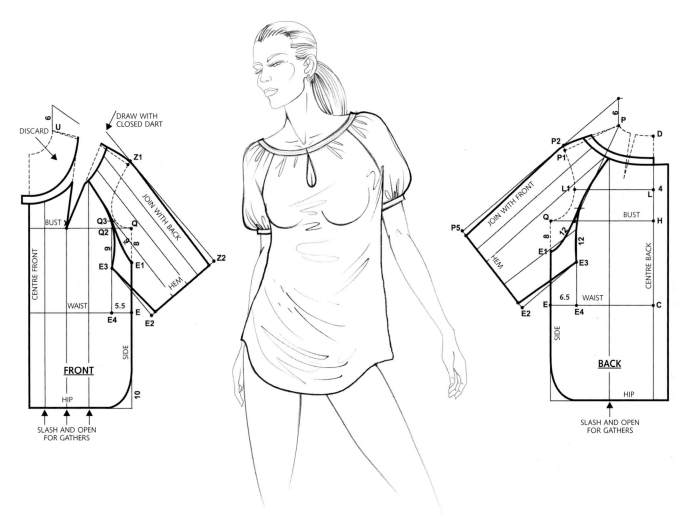

- Draw the raglan top basic block of the darted shirt and eliminate the waist darts.
- Draw the back and front necklines as desired.
- Extend the centre back and trace the vertical lines on the front and back to insert the gathers.
- Trace some longitudinal lines on the sleeves for the gathers.
- Draw the border of collar, to insert the tape.
- Copy the parts, slash along the lines drawn and make the extension as shown in the figure.

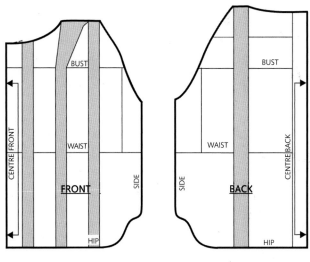

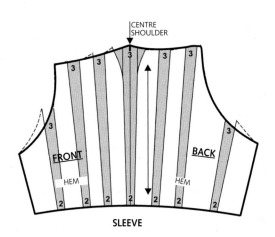

SLEEVE

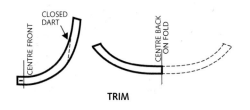

TRIM

FANCY RAGLAN BLOUSE

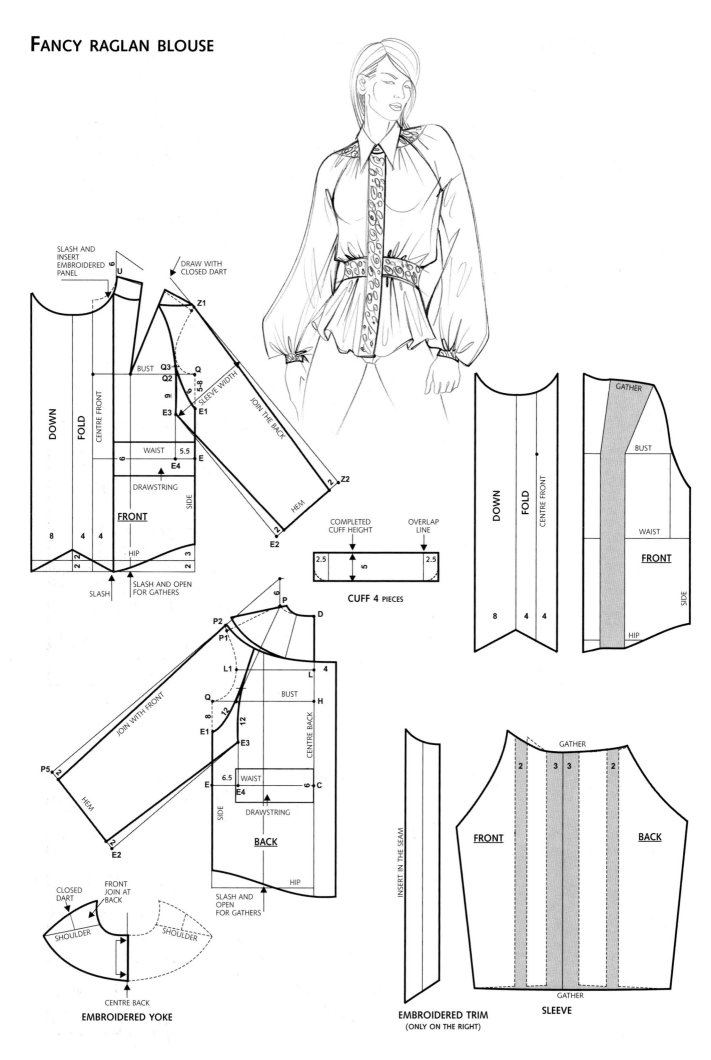

SLASH AND INSERT EMBROIDERED PANEL

DRAW WITH CLOSED DART

6
U

DOWN

FOLD

CENTRE FRONT

BUST Q3 Q Q2

SLEEVE WIDTH

5-8
9
6

E3 E1

JOIN THE BACK

Z1

WAIST 5.5
6 E E4

DRAWSTRING

SIDE

FRONT

8 4 4

2 2 HIP 3
2 2 2

Z2

HEM

E2

SLASH

SLASH AND OPEN FOR GATHERS

COMPLETED CUFF HEIGHT

OVERLAP LINE

2.5 5 2.5

CUFF 4 PIECES

DOWN

FOLD

CENTRE FRONT

8 4 4

GATHER

BUST

WAIST

FRONT

HIP

SIDE

JOIN WITH FRONT

P5 2

HEM

E2

P2
P1
P
D
L1 4 L
Q 12 BUST H
8 12
E1
E3

CENTRE BACK

E 6.5 WAIST 6 C
E4

DRAWSTRING

SIDE

BACK

HIP

SLASH AND OPEN FOR GATHERS

CLOSED DART

FRONT JOIN AT BACK

SHOULDER

SHOULDER

CENTRE BACK

EMBROIDERED YOKE

INSERT IN THE SEAM

EMBROIDERED TRIM
(ONLY ON THE RIGHT)

GATHER

2 3 3 2

FRONT

BACK

GATHER

SLEEVE

Fancy kimono top

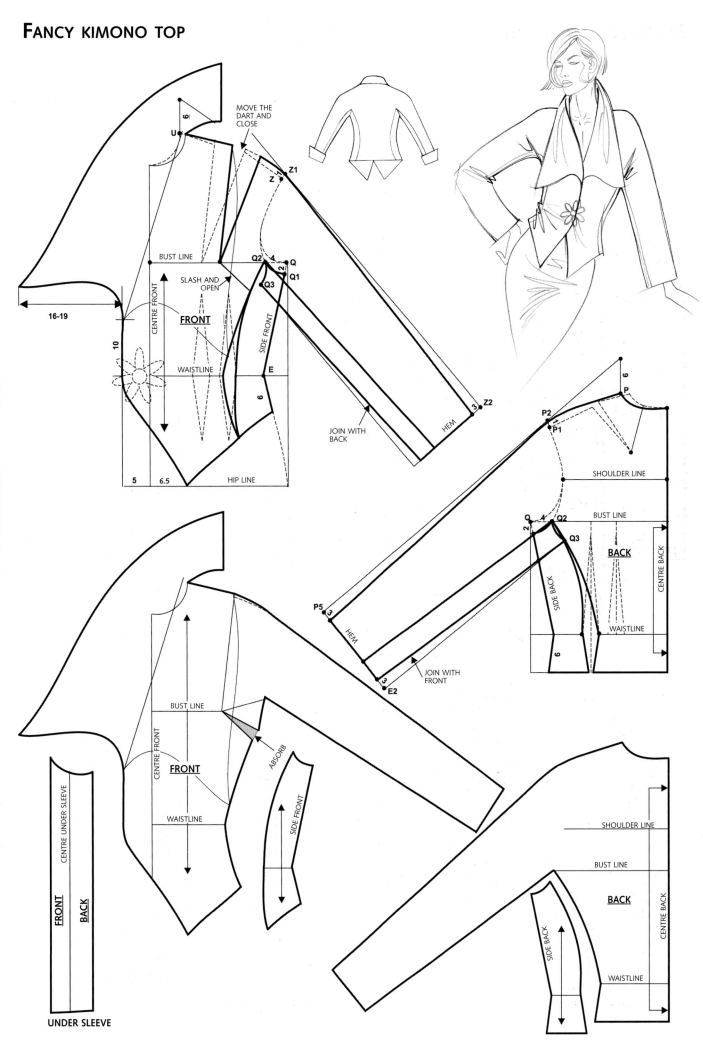

MOVE THE DART AND CLOSE

U

6

Z1

Z

BUST LINE

Q2   4   Q

2   Q1

Q3

SLASH AND OPEN

CENTRE FRONT

FRONT

SIDE FRONT

16-19

10

WAISTLINE

E

6

5   6.5   HIP LINE

JOIN WITH BACK

HEM

3   Z2

P

6

P2

P1

SHOULDER LINE

BUST LINE

Q   4   Q2

2

Q3

BACK

CENTRE BACK

SIDE BACK

WAISTLINE

P5   3

HEM

6

3

JOIN WITH FRONT

E2

BUST LINE

CENTRE FRONT

FRONT

ABSORB

SIDE FRONT

WAISTLINE

FRONT

BACK

CENTRE UNDER SLEEVE

FRONT   **BACK**

SHOULDER LINE

BUST LINE

BACK

CENTRE BACK

SIDE BACK

WAISTLINE

UNDER SLEEVE

BATWING BLOUSE

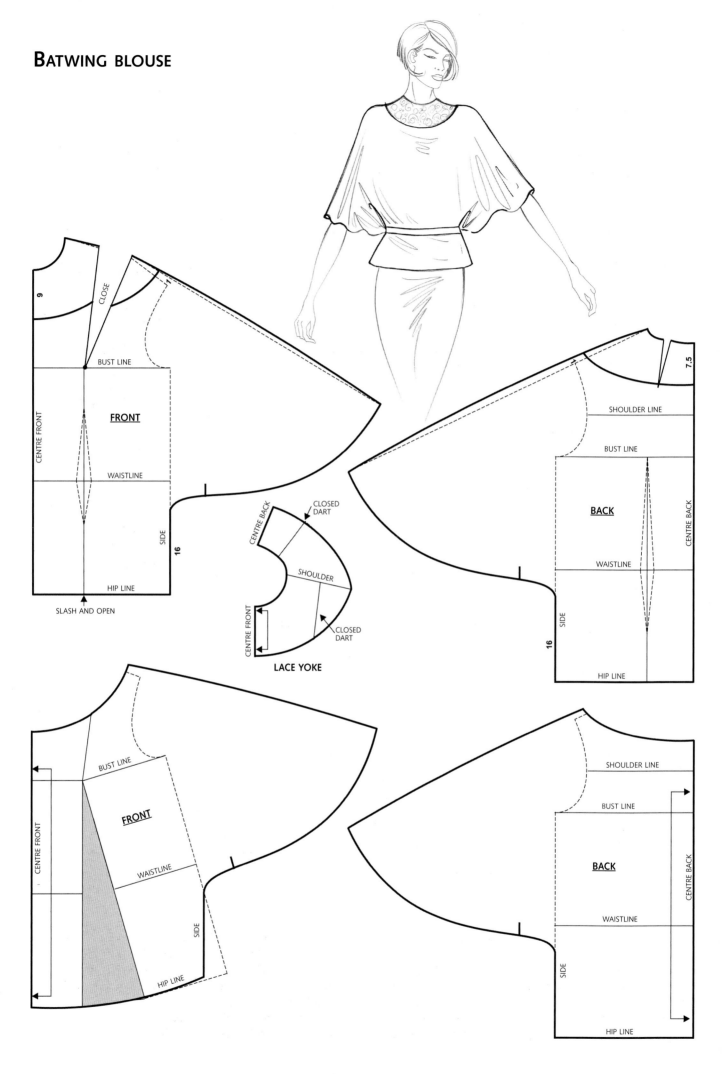

FRONT

9

CLOSE

BUST LINE

CENTRE FRONT

WAISTLINE

SIDE

16

HIP LINE

SLASH AND OPEN

CENTRE BACK

CLOSED DART

SHOULDER

CENTRE FRONT

CLOSED DART

LACE YOKE

7.5

SHOULDER LINE

BUST LINE

BACK

CENTRE BACK

WAISTLINE

SIDE

16

HIP LINE

BUST LINE

CENTRE FRONT

FRONT

WAISTLINE

SIDE

HIP LINE

SHOULDER LINE

BUST LINE

BACK

CENTRE BACK

WAISTLINE

SIDE

HIP LINE

BLOUSE WITH GATHERED FRONT

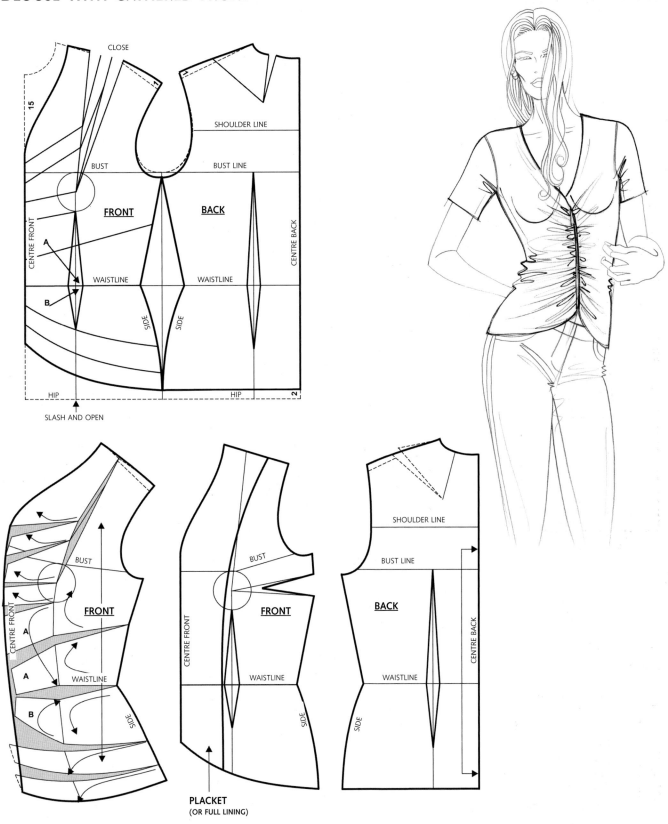

- Draw the basic shirt block with darts, with necessary measurements and ease.
- Draw the neckline with desired shape.
- Divide the shoulder dart in three parts as show in the figure.
- Draw the lines for the gathers from the front centre to the edges of the darts and of the sides, as shown in the figure.
- Slash along these lines and open them rotating clockwise the upper parts and down to the waist (except the part indicated with the letter "A", to be rotated counter clockwise), while rotating in an anticlockwise direction the lower parts (except the part marked with the letter "B", to be rotated clockwise).
- Adjust the centre front accordingly.
- Discard the neckline dart in the armscye.

Knotted raglan sleeve top

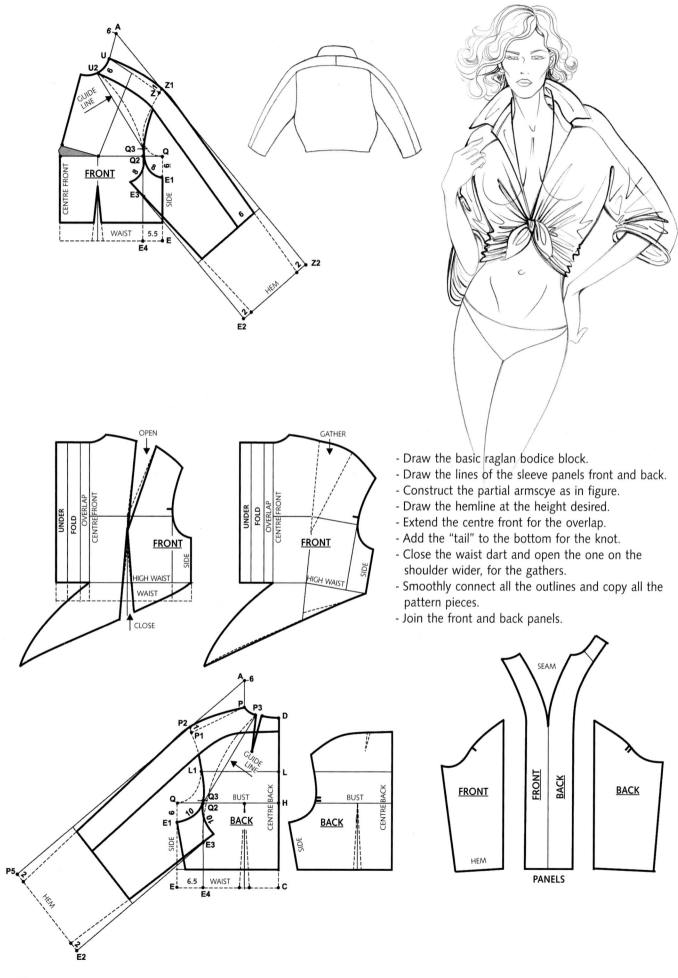

- Draw the basic raglan bodice block.
- Draw the lines of the sleeve panels front and back.
- Construct the partial armscye as in figure.
- Draw the hemline at the height desired.
- Extend the centre front for the overlap.
- Add the "tail" to the bottom for the knot.
- Close the waist dart and open the one on the shoulder wider, for the gathers.
- Smoothly connect all the outlines and copy all the pattern pieces.
- Join the front and back panels.

58

JUMPSUITS AND OVERALLS

Darted basic jumpsuit block

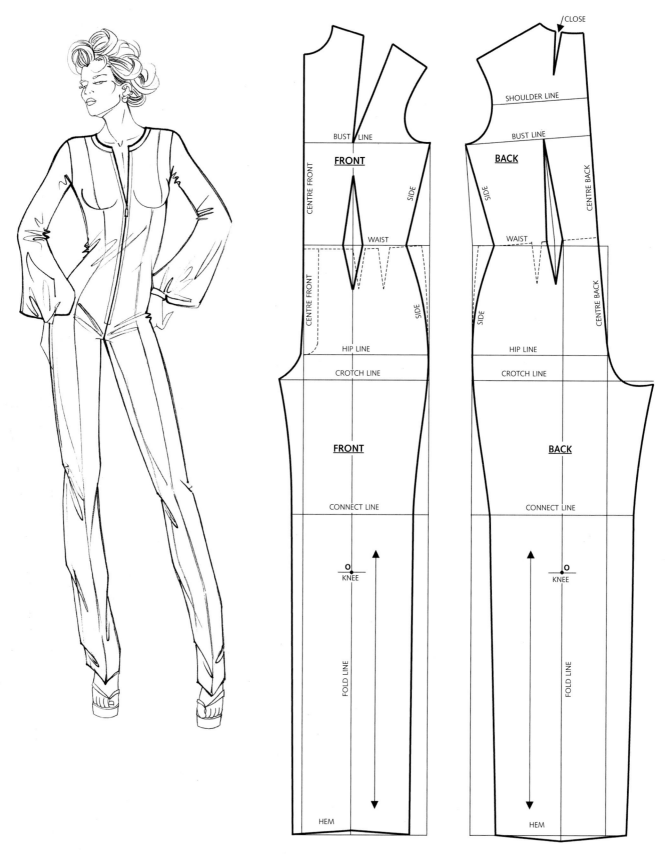

- Draw the basic bodice block with darts, with adequate ease.
- Draw the basic trouser block with darts, with adequate ease.
- Join the bodice front and back to the pants overlapping the waistpoint.
- The rear basic bodice block should be inclined slightly like the trousers to allow movement.
- Shift the waist darts of the trousers to match up with the bodice darts.
- Connect the side lines of the bodice and of the trousers, making sure that the total measurement half the waist circumference.
- Adjust the hem as desidered.

FULL-LENGTH, BLOUSED JUMPSUIT

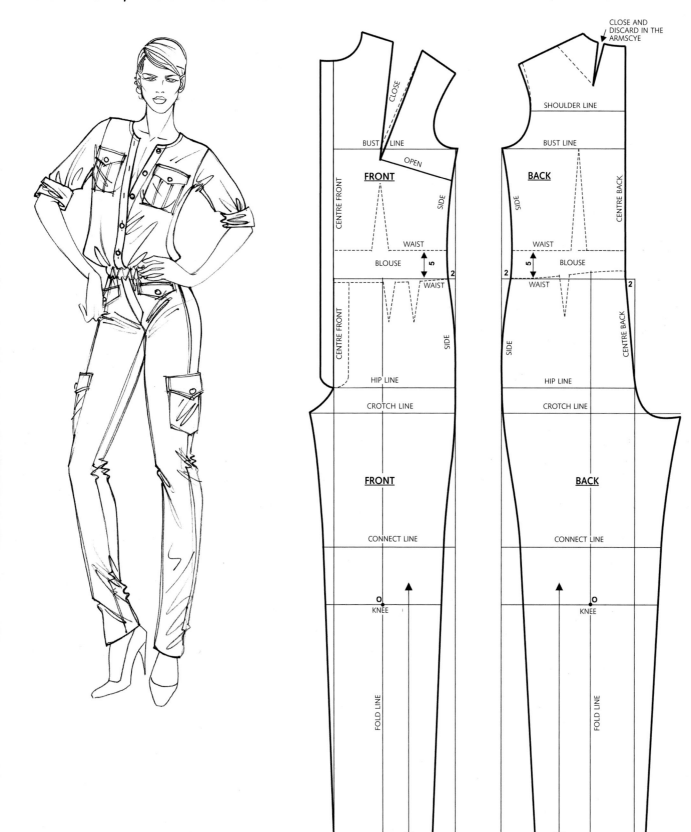

- Draw the basic bodice block with darts, with adequate ease.
- Draw the basic trouser block with the same ease of the bodice.
- Join the bodice front and back to the pants allowing 5 cm/1.97" for the blousing, as shown in the figure.

- Eliminate the darts of both the bodice and the pants and reduce the excess on the side as needed.
- Finish the lines of the front and side.
- Move the bust dart to the side if the style calls for it, as in this case.

Slinky jeans jumpsuit

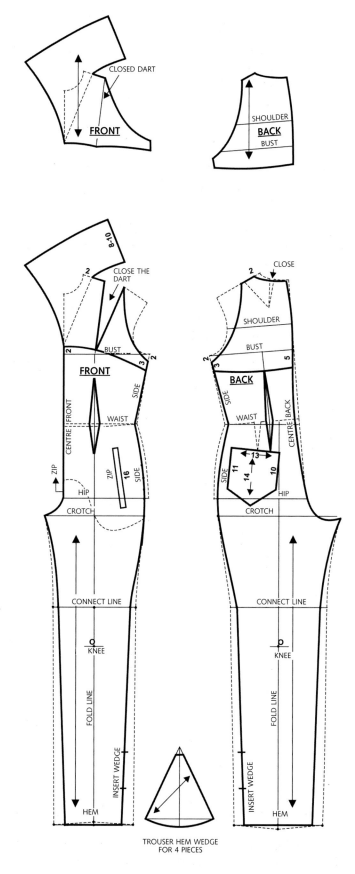

CLOSED DART

FRONT

SHOULDER

BACK

BUST

8-10

2

CLOSE THE DART

2

BUST

2

3

FRONT

CENTRE FRONT

SIDE

ZIP

WAIST

ZIP

16

SIDE

HIP

CROTCH

CONNECT LINE

KNEE

FOLD LINE

INSERT WEDGE

HEM

2

CLOSE

2

SHOULDER

BUST

5

BACK

2

3

SIDE

WAIST

CENTRE BACK

11

13

14

10

SIDE

HIP

CROTCH

CONNECT LINE

KNEE

FOLD LINE

INSERT WEDGE

HEM

TROUSER HEM WEDGE
FOR 4 PIECES

- Draw the basic jeans trousers, with desired measures and fit.
- Draw the basic bodice block with darts, with measurement and fit equal to a close-fitting top.
- Position the bodice front on the front of the trousers, matching up the line of the centre front and the waist line.
- Position the bodice back over the back of the trousers, matching up the centre back line and the slightly inclined waist line.
- Connect the bodice side line smoothly with the trousers side line.
- Adjust the waist line according to the exact measurements, trimming the excess from the side and adding a dart.
- Copy all the pattern motifs, as shown in the figure.

Overalls

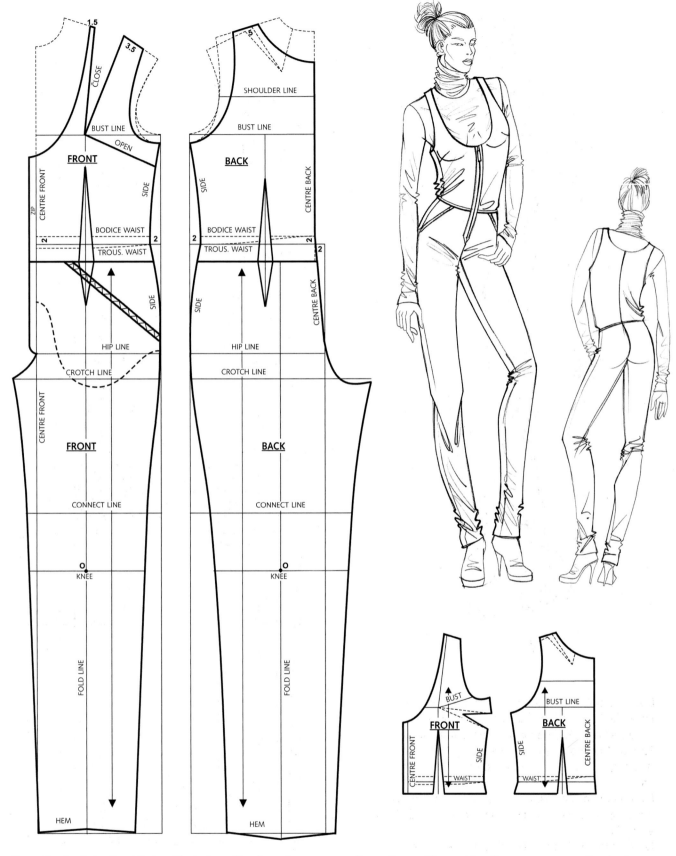

- Draw the basic bodice block with darts, with adequate ease.
- Draw the basic trouser block with darts, with adequate ease.
- Join the bodice front and back to the pants, separating them by 2 cm/0.79". for ease of movement, and lower the waist point, as shown in figure.

- Draw the neckline, widen the armscye according to the style, and use darts to adjust the measure of the waist.
- Connect all the lines of the front and side.
- Move the bust dart to the side, if the style calls for it, as in this case.

Bib-and-brace overall

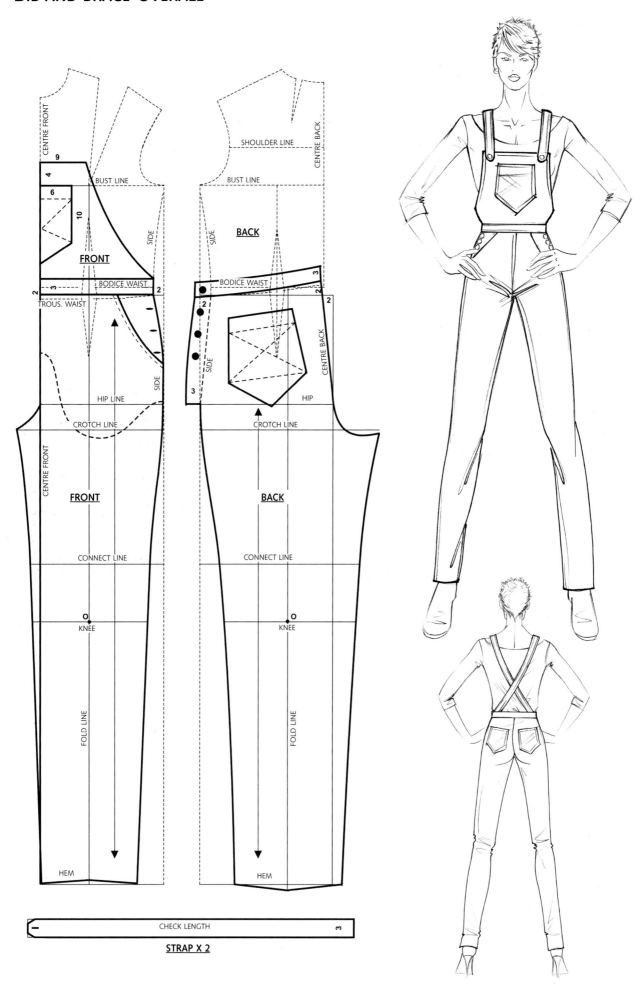

CENTRE FRONT

SHOULDER LINE

CENTRE BACK

9

4

6

BUST LINE

BUST LINE

10

SIDE

SIDE

BACK

FRONT

BODICE WAIST

BODICE WAIST

3

2

3

2

3

TROUS. WAIST

SIDE

SIDE

CENTRE BACK

HIP LINE

HIP

SIDE

3

CROTCH LINE

CROTCH LINE

CENTRE FRONT

FRONT

BACK

CONNECT LINE

CONNECT LINE

O

O

KNEE

KNEE

FOLD LINE

FOLD LINE

HEM

HEM

CHECK LENGTH

3

STRAP X 2

SHORTALLS WITH DARTS

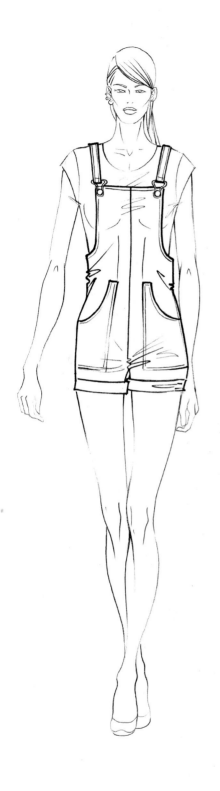

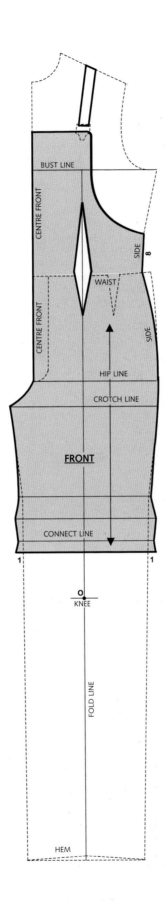

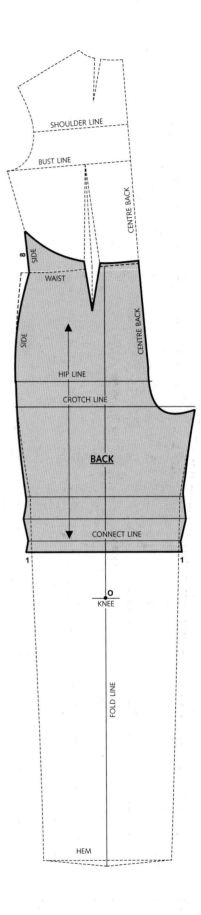

- Draw the basic overall without darts, with adequate ease.
- Move the front dart to the side seam.
- Make the changes of basic bodice block as desired.

Halter top jumpsuit

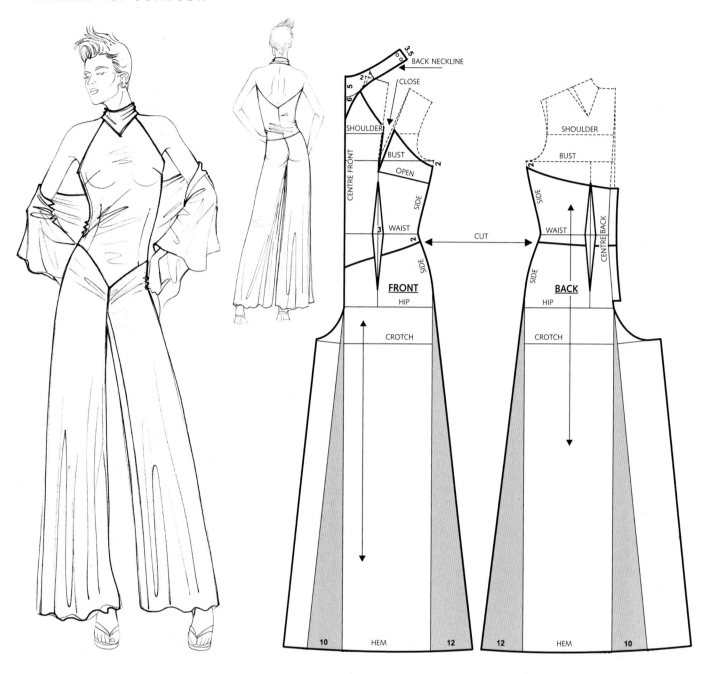

- Draw the basic dress block with darts, with adequate measurements and ease.
- Draw the crotch line at 10 cm/3.94" from the hip line. (1/10 hip circum.)
- Extend the crotch line by 7-8 cm/2.76"-3.15" on the front and 12-13 cm/4.72"-5.12" on the back.
- Connect with curved line to the centre front and back, and with a straight line toward the hemline.
- Widen at the bottom for greater flare as shown in figure.
- Draw the neckline front and back and the cuts.
- Draw the collar.
- Separate the parts.

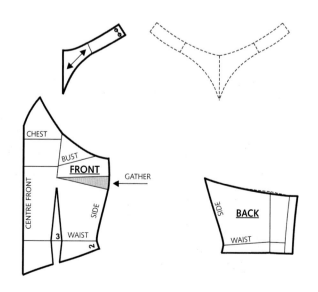

FANCY JUMPSUIT

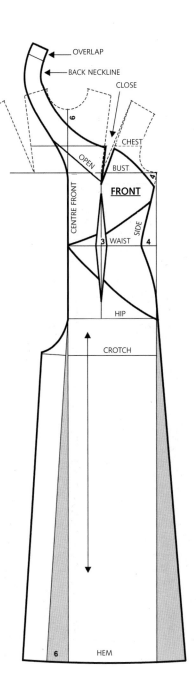

OVERLAP
BACK NECKLINE
CLOSE
OPEN
CHEST
BUST
6
CENTRE FRONT
FRONT
SIDE
4
3 WAIST 4
HIP
CROTCH
6 HEM

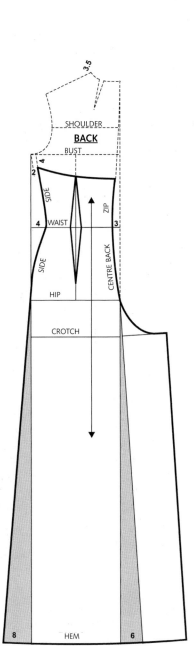

3.5
SHOULDER
BACK
BUST
4
2
SIDE
ZIP
4 WAIST 3
SIDE
CENTRE BACK
HIP
CROTCH
8 HEM 6

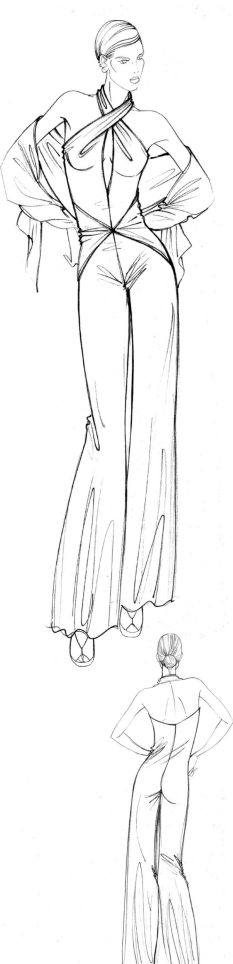

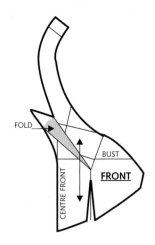

FOLD
BUST
CENTRE FRONT
FRONT

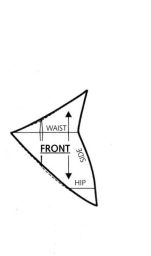

WAIST
FRONT
SIDE
HIP

67

DRESSES

DRESSES

A woman's dress is a one-piece garment that clothes the entire figure, from the shoulders to the legs, and it wraps the torso, the hips, and both legs.

It can be tight-fitting or loose; with horizontal or vertical cuts, or without cuts at all; with the opening in the front or in the back; symmetrical or asymmetrical; with various lengths, mini, midi, maxi, or to the ground.

The dress has primordial origins, and in fact, the most recent research has shown that women of antiquity were not dressed as we imagine them, that is, with a woven fabric fastened with a clasp, but also with complete outfits, cut out and sewn together. An example of this is preserved in the Copenhagen National Museum.

The oldest "model" (1700 years before Christ) unearthed in Crete and known as "La Parisienne", wears a dress with a bodice revealing the breasts and a flared skirt with flounces.

The Egyptians wore a long tunic that covered the figure down to the ankles.

In ancient Greece, the national garment was the peplos, a sort of shawl held up with two clasps and open on one side, falling to the ankles in undulating folds.

In the course of the centuries, women's attire has undergone the most unthinkable changes in every culture and at all levels of society: close-fitting at the top with tightly laced bodices, and full skirts in the 1700s; shirt-dresses with low necklines in the early 1800s, and then in the second half of the 1800s, those with crinolines or bustles, to increase the fullness of the skirt; in the early 1900s, dresses with "corolla" skirts, flared at the hem; the boyish 1920s, the New Look, etc., up to the acceleration of the recent decades, where female attire has taken on more practical and defined characteristics. The dress, while no longer with the rigidity of the past, can be catalogued according to the various occasions of the day, or the events. Thus, we have the daytime dress, cocktail dress, evening dresses and gowns, formal attire and wedding gowns.

Nowadays, every season, stylists propose new lines, new fabrics, new styles, and new volumes and women are increasingly courted and prompted to go with this trend or that fashion.

THE MAIN SHAPES AND STYLES OF DRESSES

A dress's line or shape is defined and indicated on the basis of a criterion of the garment's similarity with: letters of the alphabet; geometric figures; period styles; kinds of cuts, and other.
The main lines referred to letters are:
"A"-line, .and "H"-, "I"-, "T"-, "V"-, "X"- and "Y"- lines.

The lines referred to geometrical shapes are:
the Trapezoid and the Triangle.
The lines referred to objects or styles of other times are: "Bell-shaped", "Balloon", "Amphora", "Princesse", "Empire", "Charleston", "Flou", "Mermaid", and "Asymmetrical".

X-line   Trapezoid-shaped   Charleston   Princesse   Empire

Amphora   Triangle-shaped   Asymmetrical   Flou   Balloon

Bell-shaped   H-line   Y-line   I-line   Mermaid

PATTERN TERMINOLOGY

FOR THE DRESS

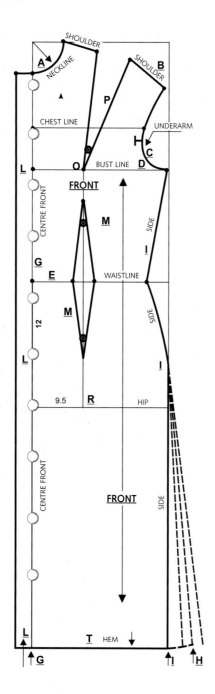

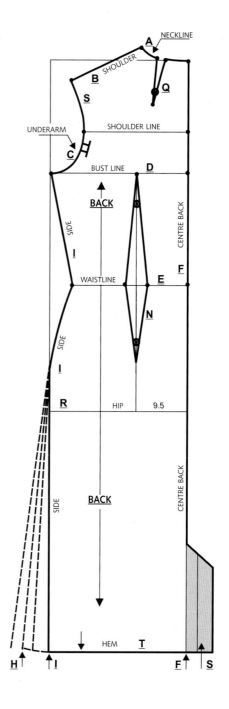

PATTERN TERMINOLOGY OF THE BODICE

A) Décolleté - Round neckline - Collar stand.
B) Shoulder - Dropped shoulder - Shoulder slope.
C) Armhole - Sleeve head - Armscye.
D) Bust line
E) Waist - Waist circumference - Waistline.
F) Centre back - Back half.
G) Centre front - Front half.
I) Side - Side panel - Side seam.
L) Button plaque overlap.
M) Pleat - Tuck - Front dart.
N) Pleat - Tuck - Rear dart.
O) Centre bust - Bust point.
P) Bust dart - Bust tuck.
Q) Neck dart - Neck tuck.

PATTERN TERMINOLOGY OF THE SKIRT

R) Hips - Hip line
M) Pleat - Tuck - Front dart.
N) Pleat - Tuck - Rear dart.
F) Centre back - Back half.
G) Centre front - Front half.
I) Side - Side panel - Side seam.
H) Flare - Gore - Fit.
S) Shear - Inverted pleat.
L) Fastening - Closure.
T) Bottom - Bottom line - Hem.

DRESS MEASUREMENTS

For the construction of the dress, you will need to take the following measurements: Neck base circumference – Chest girth – Bust circumference – Waist circumference – Hips circumference – Bust point height – Front waist length – Front chest width – Bust divergence – Neck to shoulder width – Back shoulder width – Back waist length – Waist-to-hip length – Total dress length – Abdomen circumference – Waist height-to-armscye – Armscye depth.

Before taking the measures, tie a ribbon or a tape around the waist and one around the hips.

The measurements have to be noted down immediately on the client's personal data sheet, along with the date and the person's weight, in order to avoid mistakes and inaccuracy. Then, these measurements should be double-checked against the pattern before laying it out and cutting the fabric.

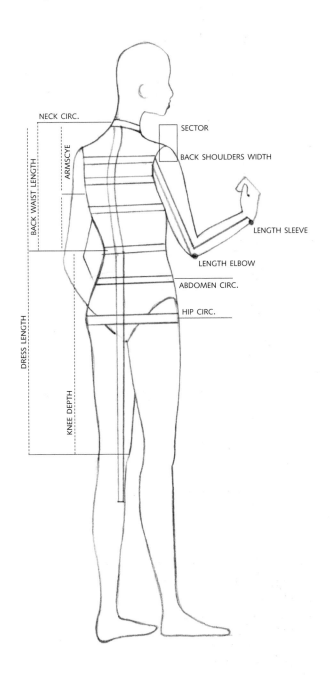

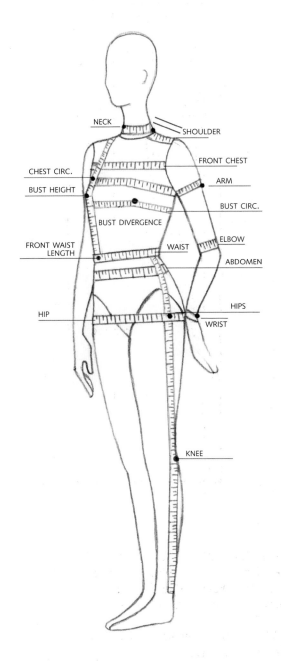

Note: *The measurements should be taken carefully, making sure that the tape measure is neither too tight nor too loose.*
Increase these measurements by the wearing ease, which varies depending on the type of garment, the kind of fabric, and the style, as shown in the table published in the first volume.
The circumference/girth and width measurements, plus the ease, should be divided by 2, because the pattern is halved.

DARTED DRESS

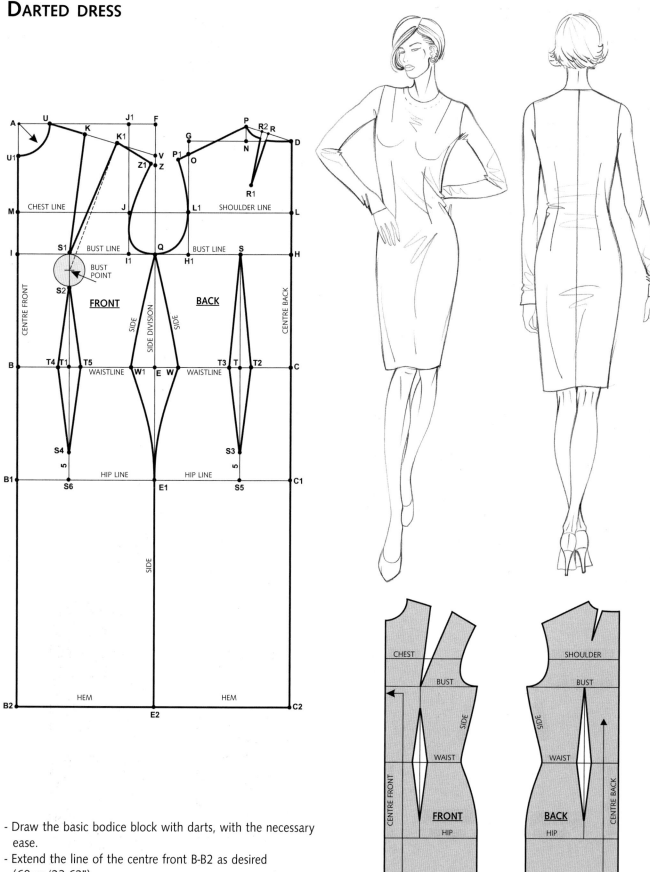

- Draw the basic bodice block with darts, with the necessary ease.
- Extend the line of the centre front B-B2 as desired (60cm/23.62")
- Extend the line of the centre back C-C2 like B-B2.
- Extend the division line E-E2.
- B2-C2 like B-C hemline.
- Join W-E1 and W1-E1 with a curved line.
- Draw the front dart T4-S4-T5 with the necessary depth, based on waist circumference.
- Draw the back darts T3-S3-T2.

LOOSE-FITTING DARTLESS SHIFT

"I"-LINE STYLE

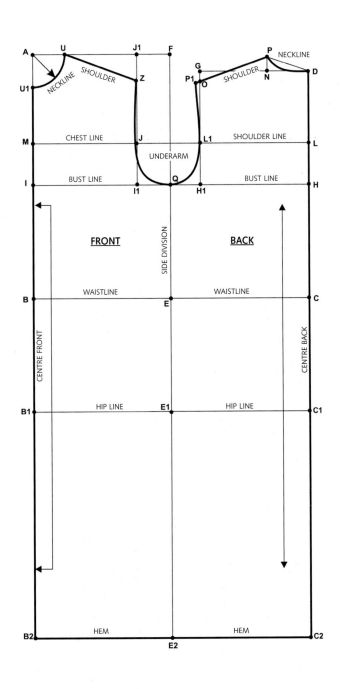

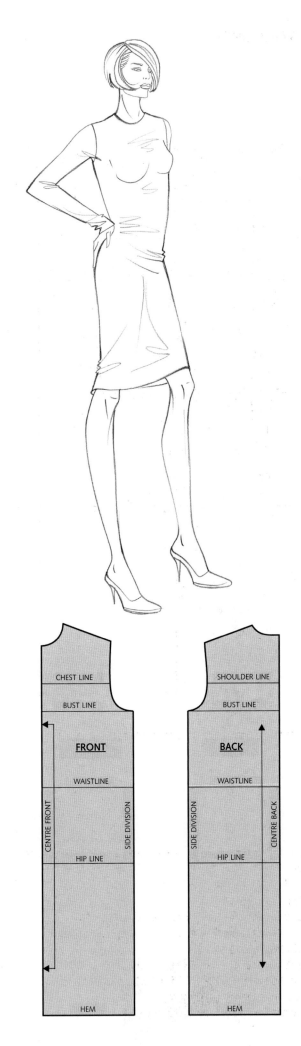

- Draw the basic bodice block without darts.
- Extend the line of the centre front B-B2 as desired.
- Extend the line of the centre back C-C2 like B-B2.
- Extend the division Line E-E2.
- B2-C2 like B-C hem line.
- Copy the back and front of the pattern.

WIDE-HEMMED DRESS

A-LINE STYLE

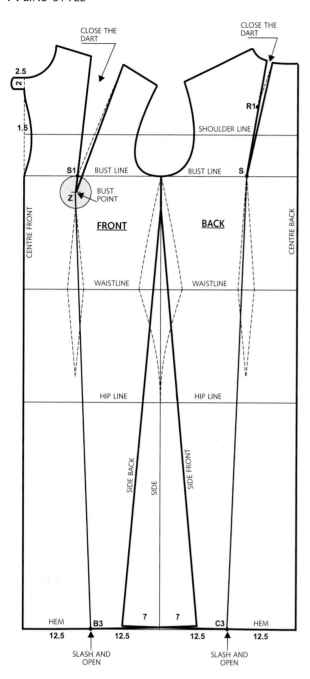

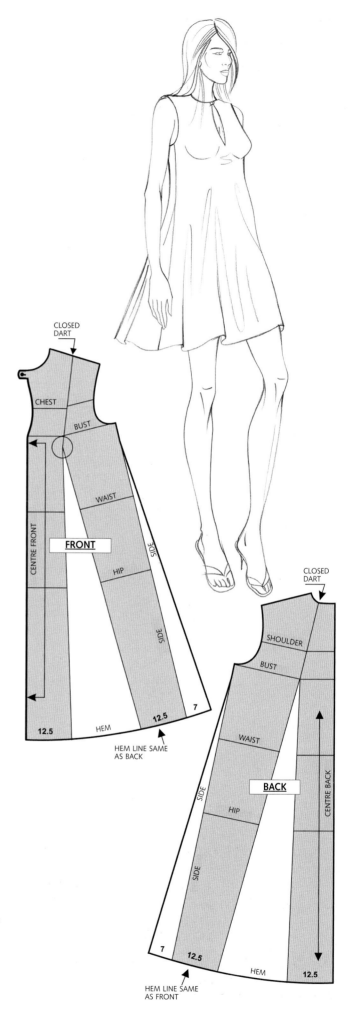

- Draw a pattern block for a dress with darts, with adequate ease.
- Draw the keyhole neckline and the tab for the fastening.
- Extend the line of the front bust dart to the bust point.
- Draw a straight line X-B3 on the front.
- Extend the lines of the back neck dart to point S.
- Draw a straight line S-C3 on the back.
- Cut along the lines and open at the hemline, closing the shoulder darts.
- Check that the width of the front hem is equal to the back.
- Smoothly finish the side line.

FLARED SLEEVELESS DRESS

WITH BUTTON-DOWN FRONT

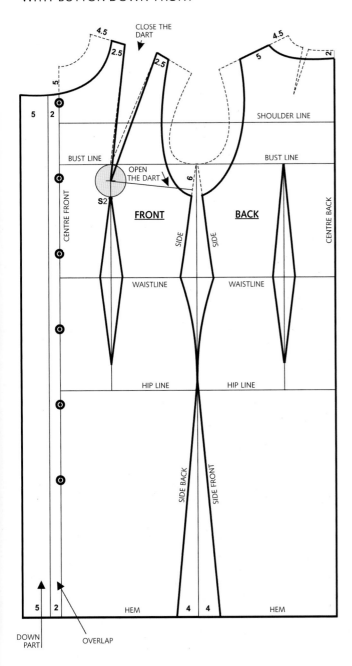

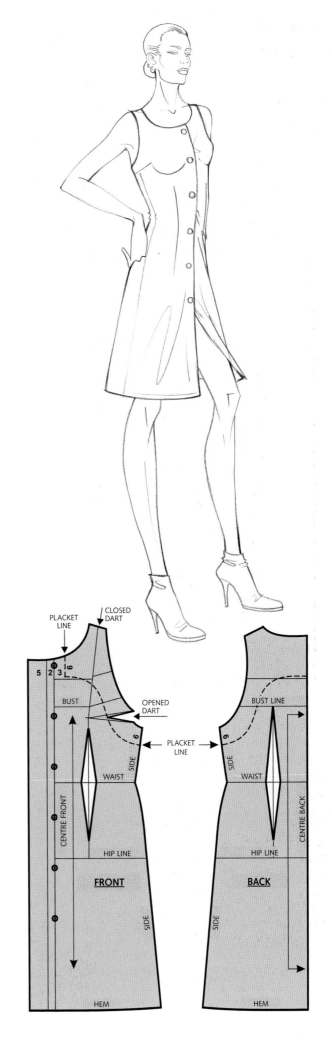

- Draw a pattern block for a dress with darts, with adequate ease.
- Make the neckline and the depth of the armscye and the shoulder as desired, for both the front and the back, as shown in the figure.
- Add 2 cm to the centre front for the button plaque, plus 5-6 cm for the facing.
- Close the shoulder bust dart and open it on the side.
- Flare the hemline as desired.
- Draw the bodice facing as shown.

Double-breasted dress

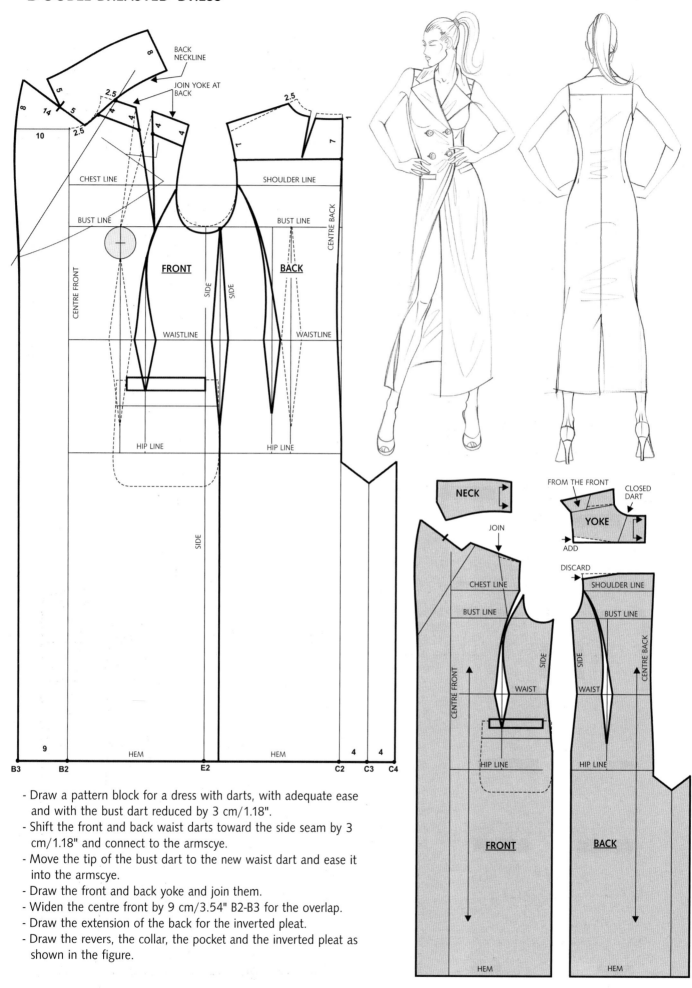

- Draw a pattern block for a dress with darts, with adequate ease and with the bust dart reduced by 3 cm/1.18".
- Shift the front and back waist darts toward the side seam by 3 cm/1.18" and connect to the armscye.
- Move the tip of the bust dart to the new waist dart and ease it into the armscye.
- Draw the front and back yoke and join them.
- Widen the centre front by 9 cm/3.54" B2-B3 for the overlap.
- Draw the extension of the back for the inverted pleat.
- Draw the revers, the collar, the pocket and the inverted pleat as shown in the figure.

PRINCESS-LINE DRESS

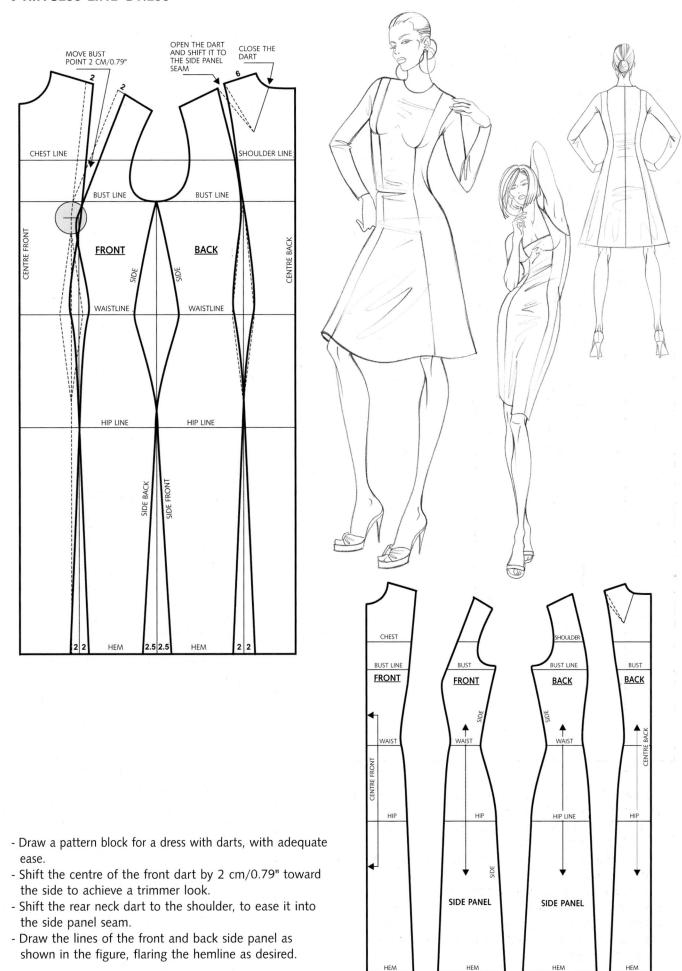

MOVE BUST POINT 2 CM/0.79"

OPEN THE DART AND SHIFT IT TO THE SIDE PANEL SEAM

CLOSE THE DART

CHEST LINE

SHOULDER LINE

BUST LINE

BUST LINE

CENTRE FRONT

FRONT

BACK

SIDE

SIDE

CENTRE BACK

WAISTLINE

WAISTLINE

HIP LINE

HIP LINE

SIDE BACK

SIDE FRONT

2 2 HEM 2.5 2.5 HEM 2 2

- Draw a pattern block for a dress with darts, with adequate ease.
- Shift the centre of the front dart by 2 cm/0.79" toward the side to achieve a trimmer look.
- Shift the rear neck dart to the shoulder, to ease it into the side panel seam.
- Draw the lines of the front and back side panel as shown in the figure, flaring the hemline as desired.

CHEST

SHOULDER

BUST LINE

BUST

BUST LINE

BUST

FRONT

FRONT

SIDE

BACK

BACK

CENTRE FRONT

WAIST

WAIST

WAIST

CENTRE BACK

HIP

HIP

HIP LINE

HIP

SIDE

SIDE PANEL

SIDE PANEL

HEM

HEM

HEM

HEM

Flared frock coat

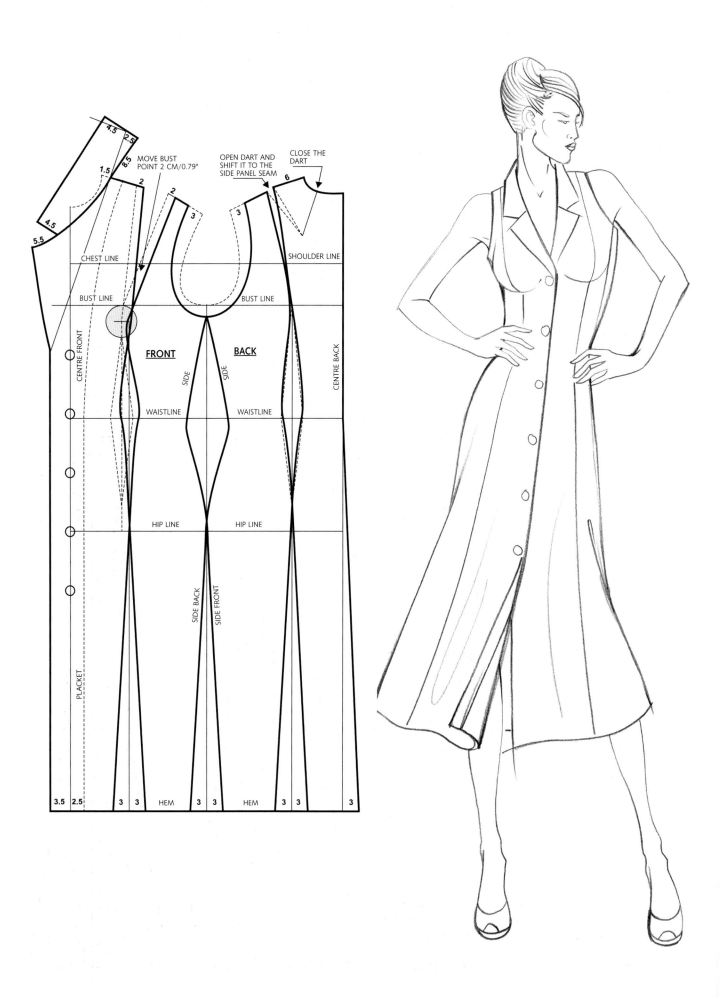

MOVE BUST
POINT 2 CM/0.79"

OPEN DART AND
SHIFT IT TO THE
SIDE PANEL SEAM

CLOSE THE
DART

4.5
2.5
1.5
8.5
2
4.5
5.5

CHEST LINE

SHOULDER LINE

BUST LINE

BUST LINE

CENTRE FRONT

FRONT

BACK

SIDE

SIDE

CENTRE BACK

WAISTLINE

WAISTLINE

HIP LINE

HIP LINE

SIDE BACK

SIDE FRONT

PLACKET

3.5   2.5   3   3   HEM   3   3   HEM   3   3   3

2

2

3

3

6

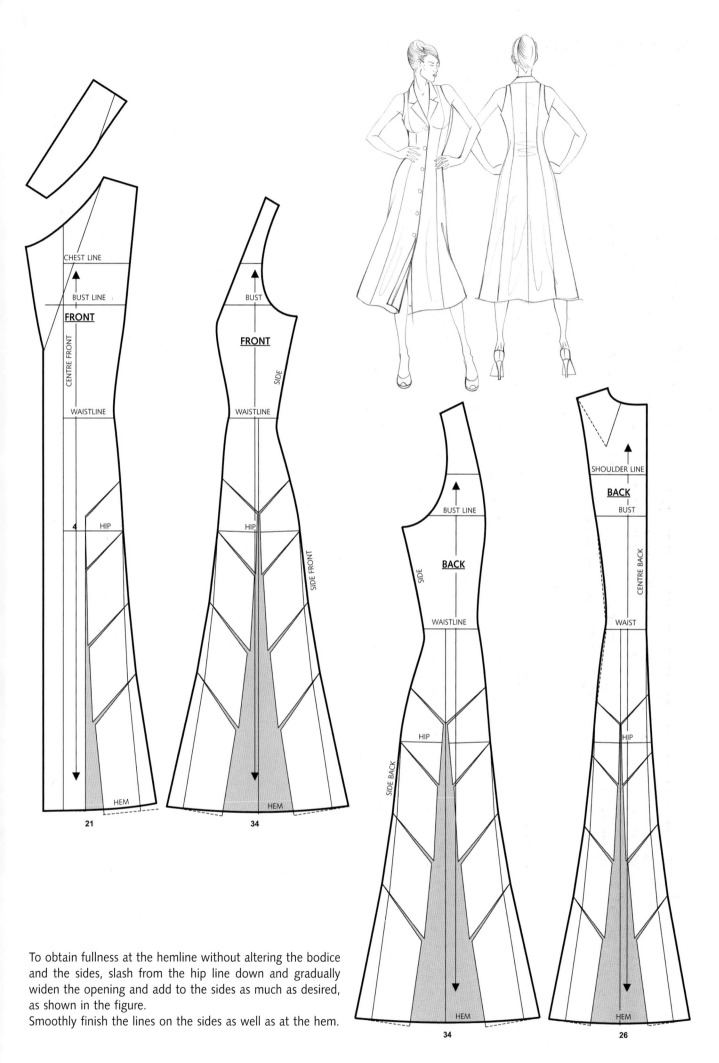

CHEST LINE

BUST LINE

FRONT

CENTRE FRONT

WAISTLINE

4   HIP

HEM

21

BUST

FRONT

SIDE

WAISTLINE

HIP

SIDE FRONT

HEM

34

BUST LINE

BACK

SIDE

WAISTLINE

SIDE BACK

HIP

HEM

34

SHOULDER LINE

BACK

BUST

CENTRE BACK

WAIST

HIP

HEM

26

To obtain fullness at the hemline without altering the bodice and the sides, slash from the hip line down and gradually widen the opening and add to the sides as much as desired, as shown in the figure.

Smoothly finish the lines on the sides as well as at the hem.

DRESS WITH SIDE PANELS

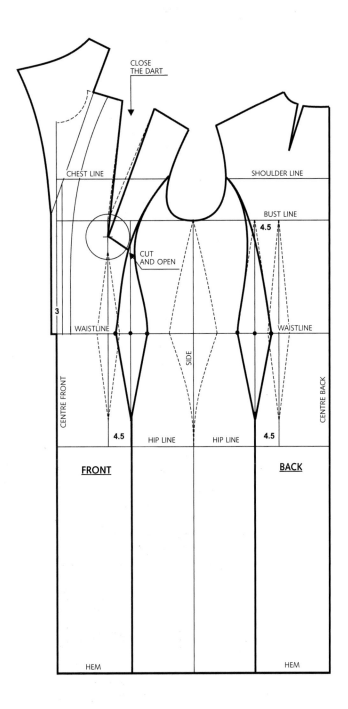

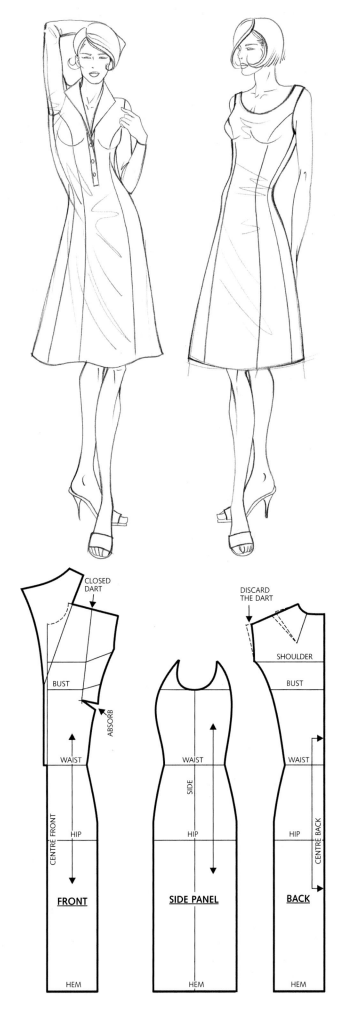

- Draw a pattern block for a dress with darts, with adequate ease and measurements.
- Draw the desired collar.
- Shift the front and back waist darts to the side by 4-5 cm/1.57"-1.97" and discard the excess in the side seam.
- Draw the side panel lines from the darts to the armscye.
- Draw a line from the tip of the front shoulder dart to side seam, to suppress the shoulder dart.
- Copy the pattern parts onto another sheet of paper.
- Close the shoulder bust dart, suppressing it in the side seam.
- Close the back neck dart and discard it in the armscye.

DRESS WITH SEAM UNDER BUSTLINE

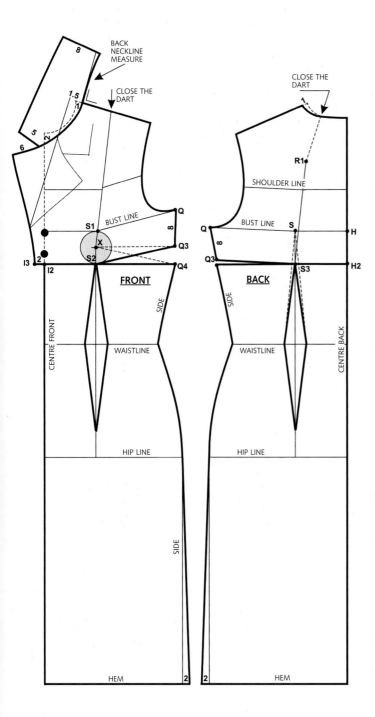

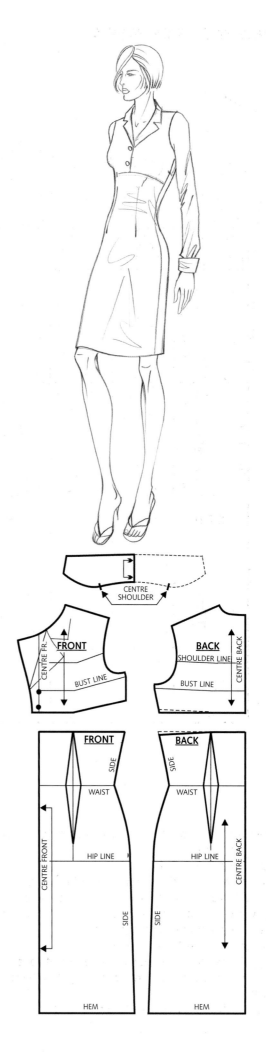

- Draw a pattern block for a dress with darts, with adequate ease.
- Draw the seam line I2-H2 by 8 cm/3.15" from the bust line.
- Separate the front and the back.
- Close the shoulder bust dart and open it momentarily (x-Q4 line).
- Shift that dart to the seam in S2-Q3-Q4.
- Draw the lapel, lengthening by 2 cm/0.79" the seam line under the bust.
- Draw the collar as shown in the figure.
- On the back, shorten the tip of the waist dart to S3.
- Joint the neck dart with the tip of S3.
- Close the neck dart, opening it on the seam line under the bust Q3.
- Widen the hemline as desired (2 cm/0.79").

EMPIRE-STYLE DRESS

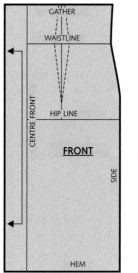

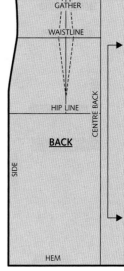

- Draw a pattern block for a dress with darts, with adequate ease.
- Move the shoulder dart to the side.
- Draw the seam line and the neck line.
- Widen the waist line dart by 1 cm/0.39" on the front yoke, for a snugger fit.
- Close the bust dart on the side, shifting it to the front yoke waist dart.
- Extend the line I2-I3 and B1-B2 on the front and H2-H3 and C1-C2 on the back for the gathers.
- Close the back yoke waist dart.

BASIC BLOCK FOR MATERNITY DRESS

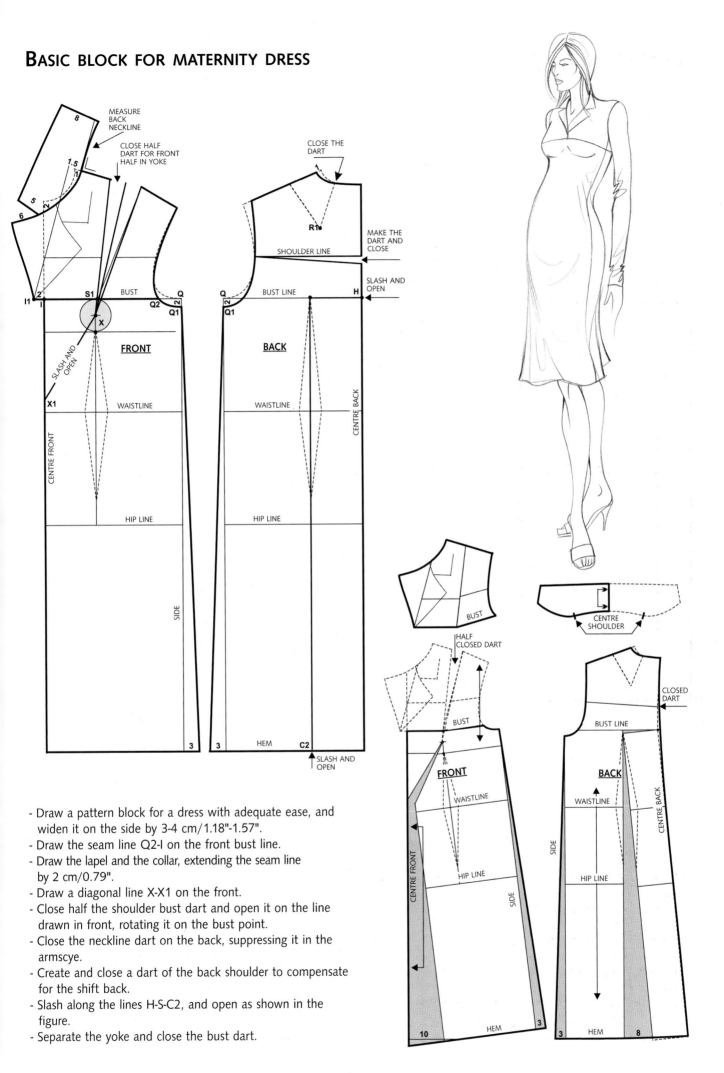

- Draw a pattern block for a dress with adequate ease, and widen it on the side by 3-4 cm/1.18"-1.57".
- Draw the seam line Q2-I on the front bust line.
- Draw the lapel and the collar, extending the seam line by 2 cm/0.79".
- Draw a diagonal line X-X1 on the front.
- Close half the shoulder bust dart and open it on the line drawn in front, rotating it on the bust point.
- Close the neckline dart on the back, suppressing it in the armscye.
- Create and close a dart of the back shoulder to compensate for the shift back.
- Slash along the lines H-S-C2, and open as shown in the figure.
- Separate the yoke and close the bust dart.

DRESS WITH POCKET MOTIF

X-LINE STYLE

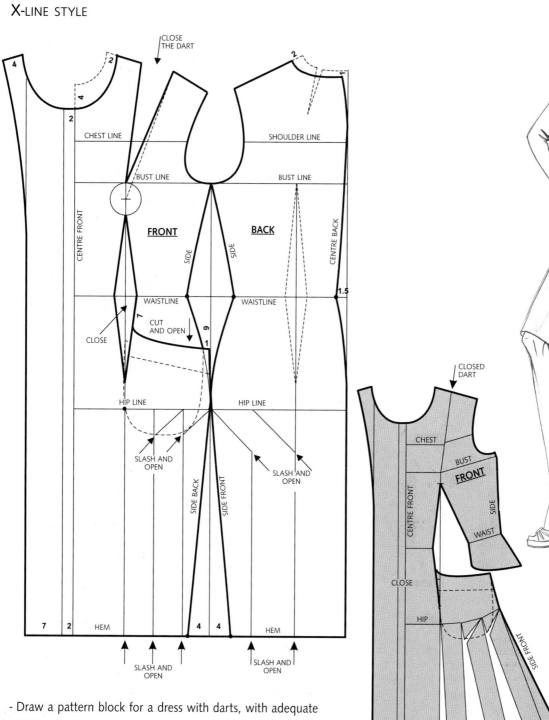

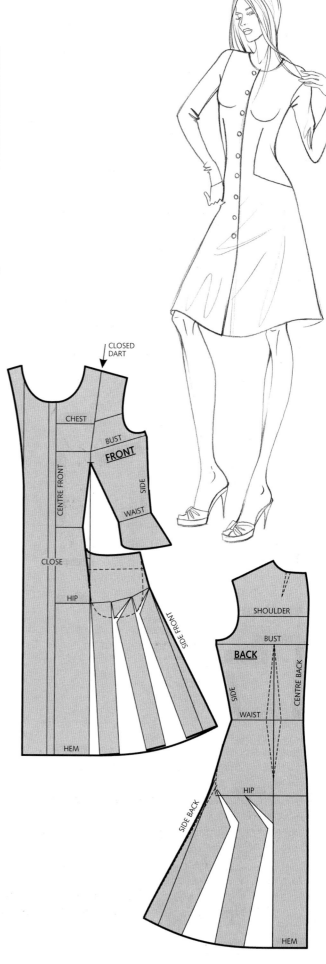

- Draw a pattern block for a dress with darts, with adequate ease.
- Draw the extension for the overlap of the button placket and the facing.
- Draw the position and the shape of the pocket.
- Close the bust dart of the shoulder and shift it to the waist dart.
- Trace the front and back neckline.
- Make the flare in the front and back, slashing from the hem to the hip, as shown in figure.
- Eliminate the dart of the back making an indent in the centre back
- Smoothly join all the lines checking that hem is equal in the front and back.
- Draw the flap and the pocket lining as desired.

DRESS WITH DROPPED WAIST LINE

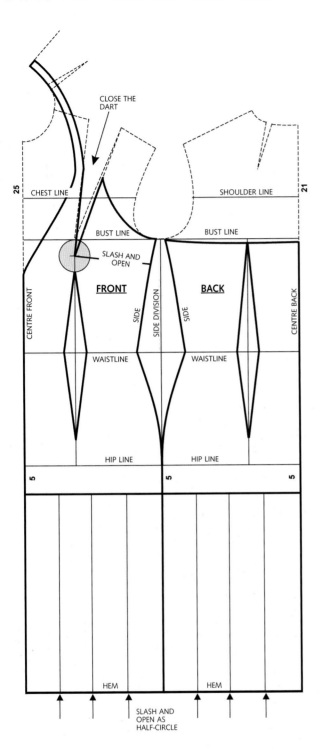

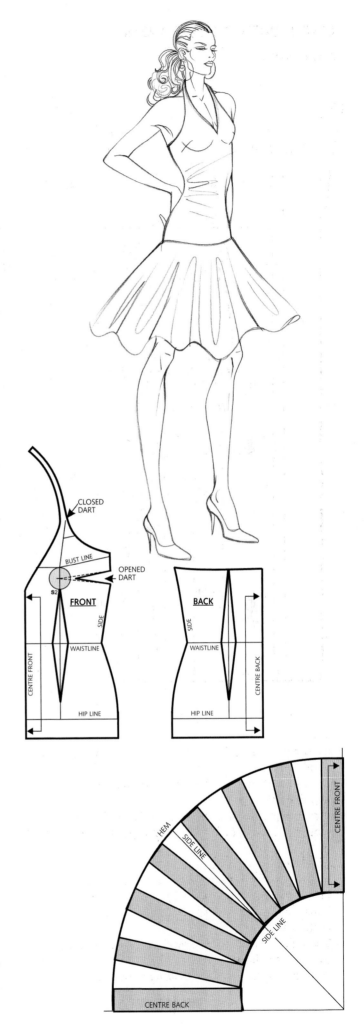

- Draw a pattern block for a dress with darts, with adequate ease.
- Draw the lines of the armscye and of the neckline of the front and the back as desired.
- Trace the seam line under the hips at desired height (5 cm/1.97").
- From that line trace some parallel vertical lines to the hemline to create volume.
- Close the bust dart on the shoulder and open it on the side.
- Slash the hem line and spread in the lower part as desired. (8 cm/3.15").

DRESS WITH PLEATED SKIRT

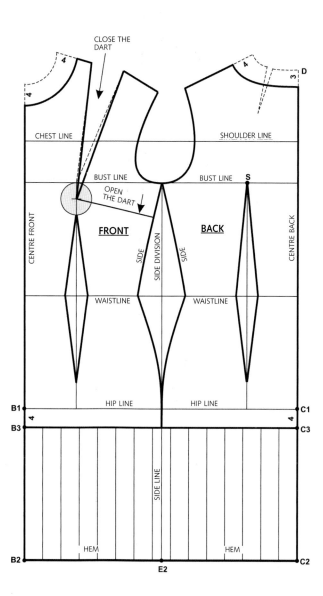

- Draw a pattern block for a dress with darts, with adequate ease.
- Move the bust dart from the shoulder to the side.
- Modify front and back neckline as needed.
- Draw the line B3-C3 for the pleats, at the desired height.
- Draw the vertical lines for the pleats, as many as desired.
- Draw the pattern for the pleats as explained above.

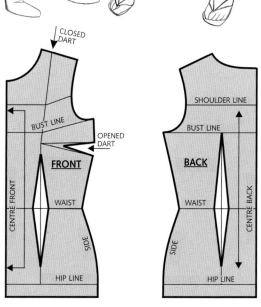

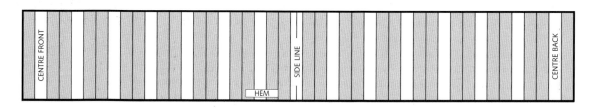

Mermaid style dress

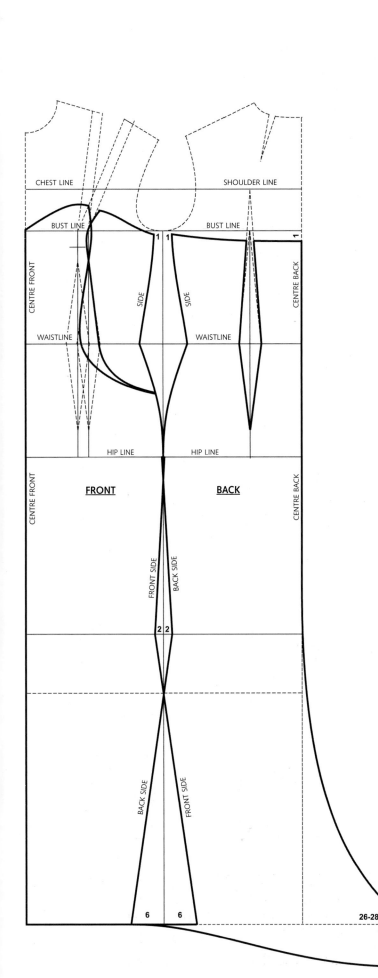

CHEST LINE
SHOULDER LINE
BUST LINE
BUST LINE
CENTRE FRONT
SIDE
SIDE
CENTRE BACK
WAISTLINE
WAISTLINE
HIP LINE
HIP LINE
CENTRE FRONT
FRONT
BACK
CENTRE BACK
FRONT SIDE
BACK SIDE
BACK SIDE
FRONT SIDE
26-28

- Draw a pattern block for a dress with darts, with adequate ease and measurements.
- Extend the bottom to the desired length.
- Make a 2-3 cm/0.79"-1.18" indent on the side seam at knee level.
- Widen the hem at the side seam by 6-7 cm/2.36"-2.76" and at the centre back by 26-28 cm/10.24"-11.02" (or as desired).
- Draw the neckline front and back as desired.
- Shift the bust dart by 2-3 cm/0.79"-1.18" toward the side and draw the outline of the side panels.
- Reduce the bodice top (neckline) by 1 cm/0.39" on each side for a snugger fit, and shape the bust point.

ASYMMETRICAL EMPIRE-STYLE DRESS

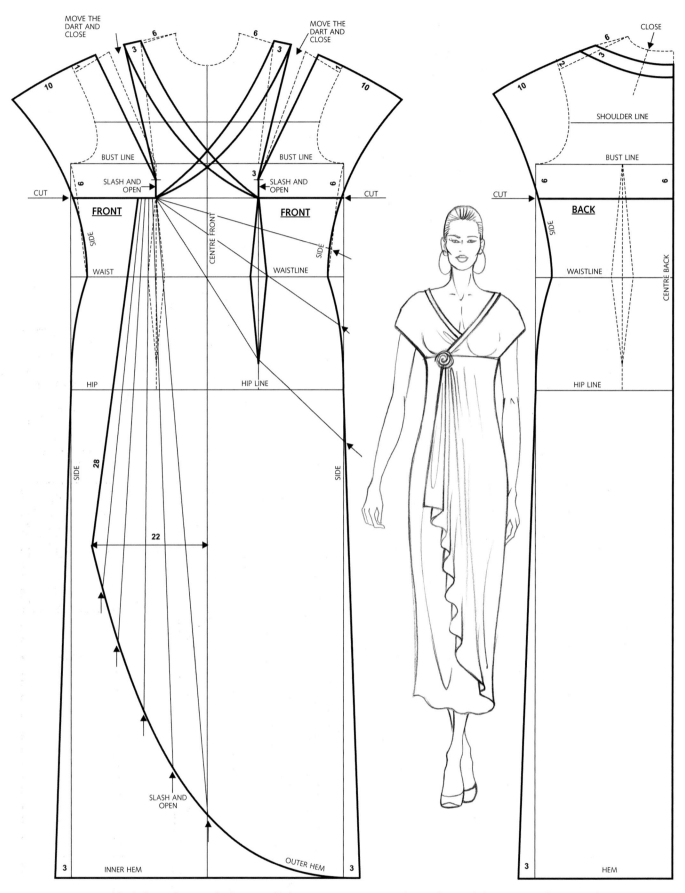

MOVE THE DART AND CLOSE

MOVE THE DART AND CLOSE

CLOSE

6   6

3   3

10   10

6   3

SHOULDER LINE

BUST LINE   BUST LINE

BUST LINE

CUT   SLASH AND OPEN   SLASH AND OPEN   CUT

6   3   6

CUT   6   6

FRONT   **FRONT**   **BACK**

SIDE   CENTRE FRONT   SIDE   SIDE   CENTRE BACK

WAIST   WAISTLINE   WAISTLINE

HIP   HIP LINE   HIP LINE

SIDE   28   SIDE

22

SLASH AND OPEN

3   INNER HEM   OUTER HEM   3   3   HEM

- Draw a pattern block for a dress with darts, with the the front in one piece and make the desired length.
- Move the bust dart on the shoulder about 3 cm/1.18" toward the outside.
- Draw the kimono sleeves as desired.

- Draw the outlines of the inner and outer sides.
- Draw the high waistline and the neckline in the front and back.
- Draw some lines on the outer side of the front for the gathered fullness.
- Draw the neckline edging.

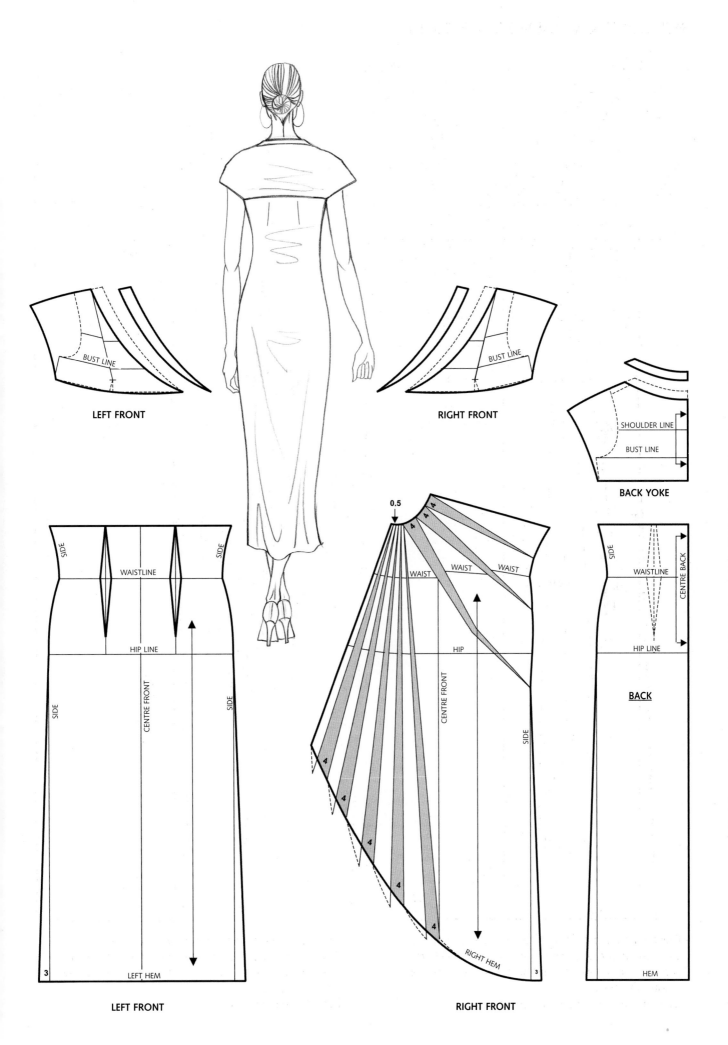

LEFT FRONT

RIGHT FRONT

BUST LINE

BUST LINE

BACK YOKE

SHOULDER LINE

BUST LINE

SIDE

WAISTLINE

SIDE

HIP LINE

SIDE

CENTRE FRONT

SIDE

LEFT HEM

3

LEFT FRONT

0.5

4 4 4

4

WAIST

WAIST

WAIST

HIP

CENTRE FRONT

SIDE

4

4

4

4

4

RIGHT HEM

3

RIGHT FRONT

SIDE

WAISTLINE

CENTRE BACK

HIP LINE

BACK

HEM

BALLOON DRESS

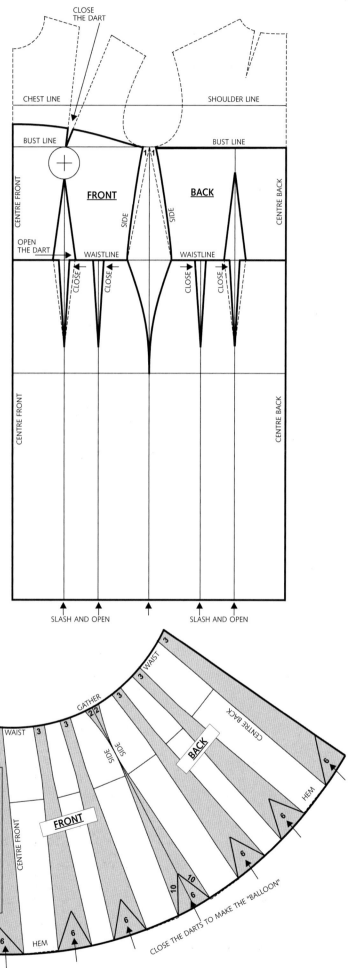

- Draw a pattern block for a dress with darts, with adequate ease.
- Draw the front and back neckline as desired.
- Divide the waist dart of the skirt in two equal parts and lengthen the lines of the dart centre down to the hem.
- Copy on separate sheets the pattern for the bodice and the skirt, front and back.
- Close the bust dart, opening one at the waist.
- Slash along the lines drawn on the skirt and open them at the bottom, closing the darts.
- Spread the cut parts for the gathers.
- Finish and smooth the outlines for the skirt pattern.
- Make some darts at the hem to create the balloon effect.

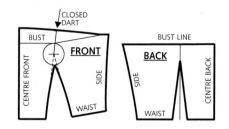

92

FLOU-STYLE DRESS

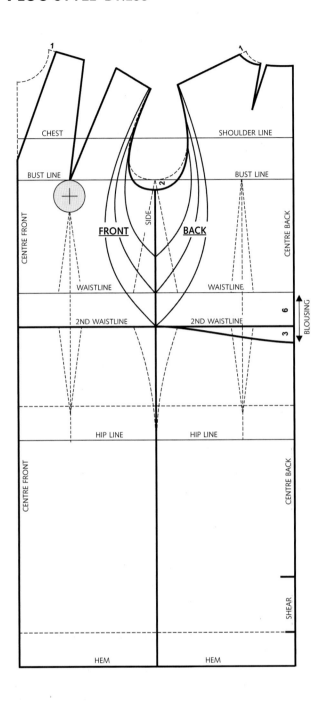

CHEST

SHOULDER LINE

BUST LINE

BUST LINE

CENTRE FRONT

CENTRE BACK

SIDE

FRONT   **BACK**

WAISTLINE

WAISTLINE

2ND WAISTLINE

2ND WAISTLINE

6

3

BLOUSING

HIP LINE

HIP LINE

CENTRE FRONT

CENTRE BACK

SHEAR

HEM

HEM

1

1

2

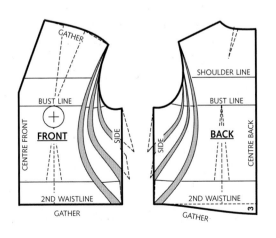

GATHER

SHOULDER LINE

BUST LINE

BUST LINE

CENTRE FRONT

SIDE

SIDE

CENTRE BACK

FRONT

BACK

2ND WAISTLINE

2ND WAISTLINE

GATHER

GATHER

3

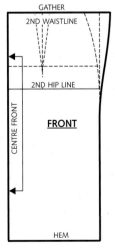

GATHER

2ND WAISTLINE

2ND HIP LINE

CENTRE FRONT

FRONT

HEM

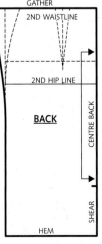

GATHER

2ND WAISTLINE

2ND HIP LINE

BACK

CENTRE BACK

SHEAR

HEM

DRESS WITH PUFFED AMPHORA SKIRT

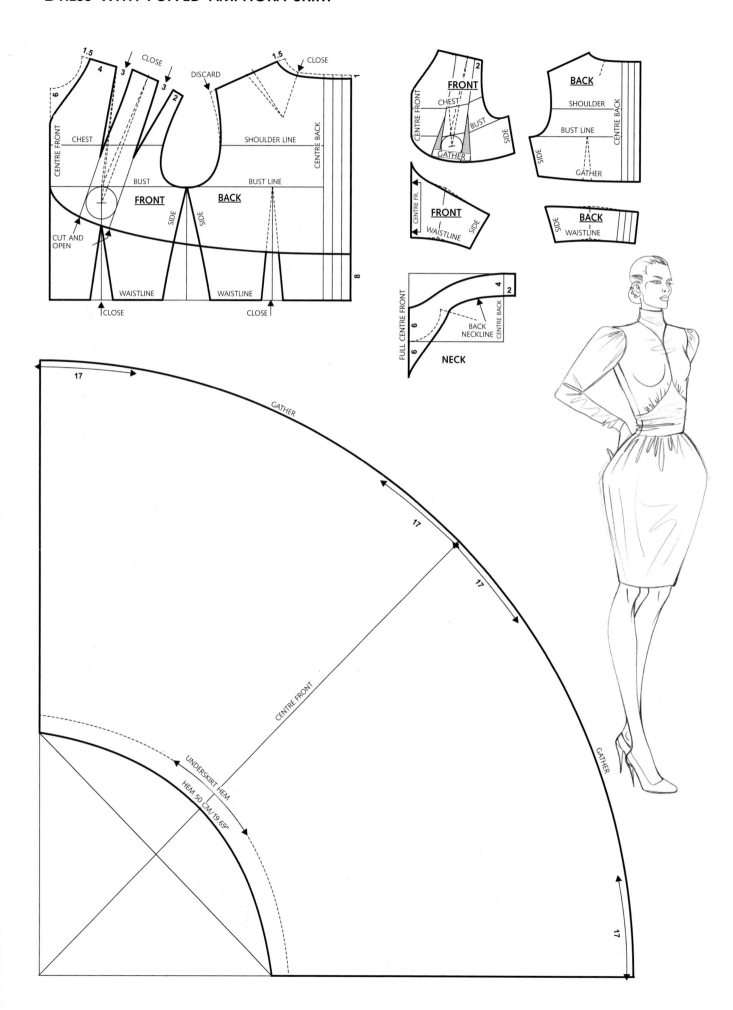

Dress with neckline darts

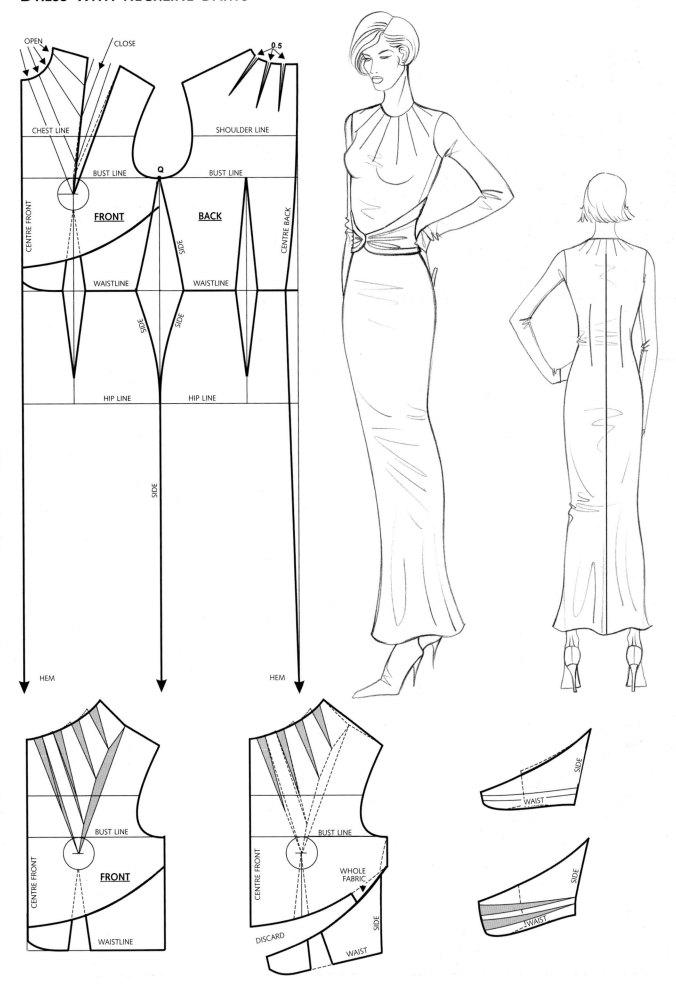

OPEN   CLOSE

0.5

CHEST LINE   SHOULDER LINE

BUST LINE   Q   BUST LINE

CENTRE FRONT

FRONT   **BACK**

SIDE

CENTRE BACK

WAISTLINE   WAISTLINE

SIDE   SIDE

HIP LINE   HIP LINE

SIDE

SIDE

HEM   HEM

BUST LINE

CENTRE FRONT

FRONT

WAISTLINE

BUST LINE

CENTRE FRONT

WHOLE FABRIC

DISCARD   WAIST   SIDE

SIDE
WAIST

SIDE
WAIST

DRESS WITH ASYMMETRICAL SEAM UNDER BUST

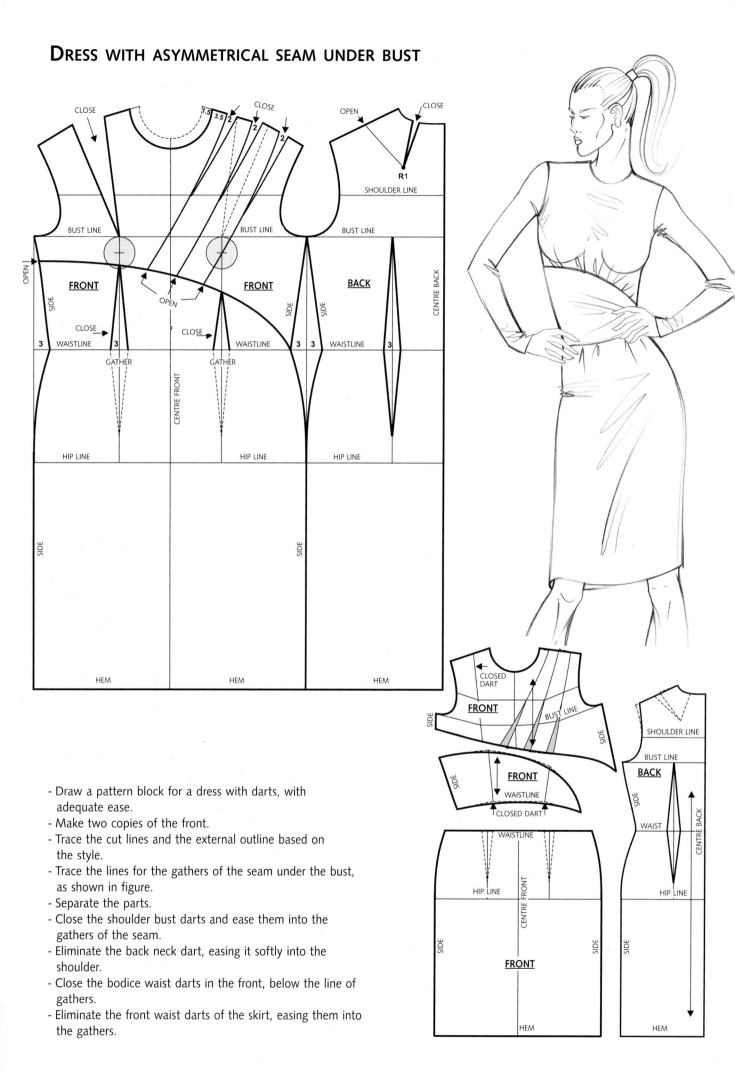

- Draw a pattern block for a dress with darts, with adequate ease.
- Make two copies of the front.
- Trace the cut lines and the external outline based on the style.
- Trace the lines for the gathers of the seam under the bust, as shown in figure.
- Separate the parts.
- Close the shoulder bust darts and ease them into the gathers of the seam.
- Eliminate the back neck dart, easing it softly into the shoulder.
- Close the bodice waist darts in the front, below the line of gathers.
- Eliminate the front waist darts of the skirt, easing them into the gathers.

Dress with gathers at side panels

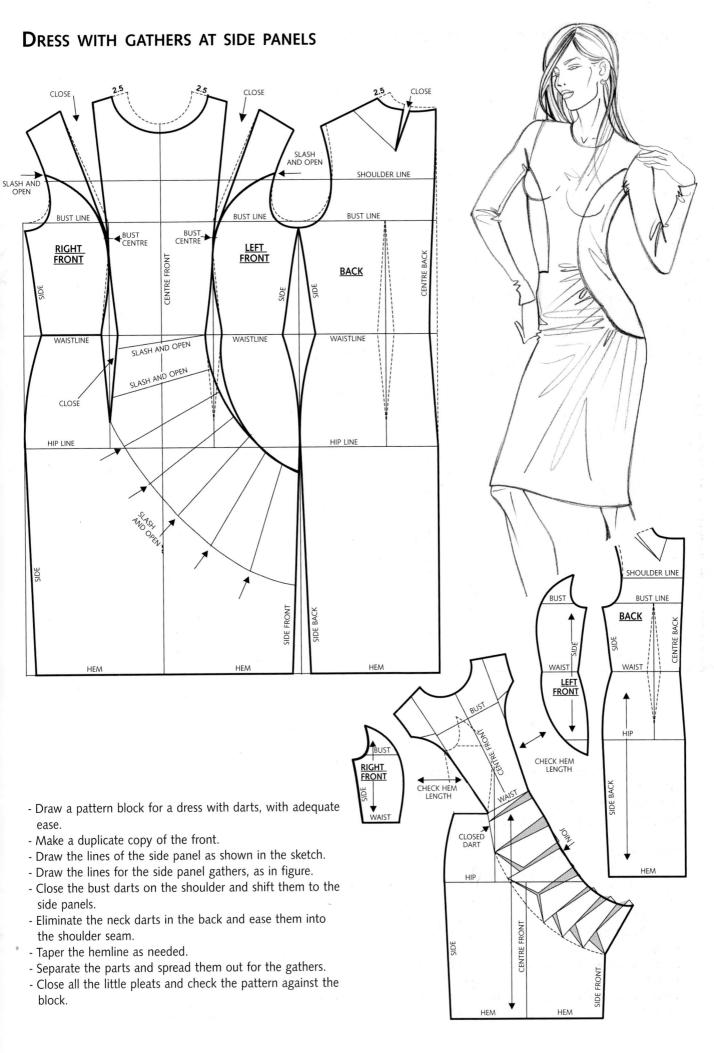

- Draw a pattern block for a dress with darts, with adequate ease.
- Make a duplicate copy of the front.
- Draw the lines of the side panel as shown in the sketch.
- Draw the lines for the side panel gathers, as in figure.
- Close the bust darts on the shoulder and shift them to the side panels.
- Eliminate the neck darts in the back and ease them into the shoulder seam.
- Taper the hemline as needed.
- Separate the parts and spread them out for the gathers.
- Close all the little pleats and check the pattern against the block.

DRESS WITH GATHERS DOWN FRONT

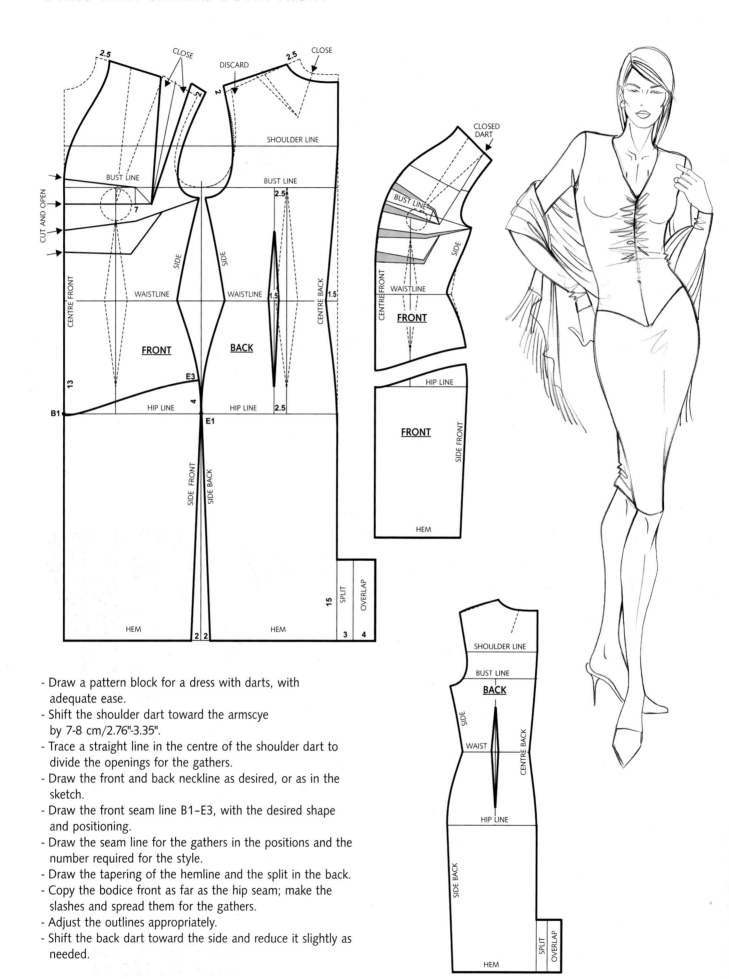

- Draw a pattern block for a dress with darts, with adequate ease.
- Shift the shoulder dart toward the armscye by 7-8 cm/2.76"-3.35".
- Trace a straight line in the centre of the shoulder dart to divide the openings for the gathers.
- Draw the front and back neckline as desired, or as in the sketch.
- Draw the front seam line B1–E3, with the desired shape and positioning.
- Draw the seam line for the gathers in the positions and the number required for the style.
- Draw the tapering of the hemline and the split in the back.
- Copy the bodice front as far as the hip seam; make the slashes and spread them for the gathers.
- Adjust the outlines appropriately.
- Shift the back dart toward the side and reduce it slightly as needed.

Dress with gathered motif in centre

NO CENTRAL SEAM

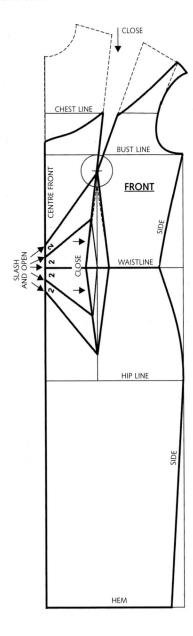

- Draw a pattern block for a dress with darts, with adequate measurements and ease.
- Draw the neckline front and back as desired.
- Draw the length and the desired hemline.
- Draw five lines from the centre front to the tips of the bust darts and waist darts, to make the gathers.
- Slash and spread as shown in figure.
- Correct the centre front and side lines
- Place the pattern on the fold, matching the centre front of the pattern piece with the folded edge, pinning it as you go along.

Note: This system only works with soft fabrics that can adapt to the pattern outline.

Dress with front panel and gathers

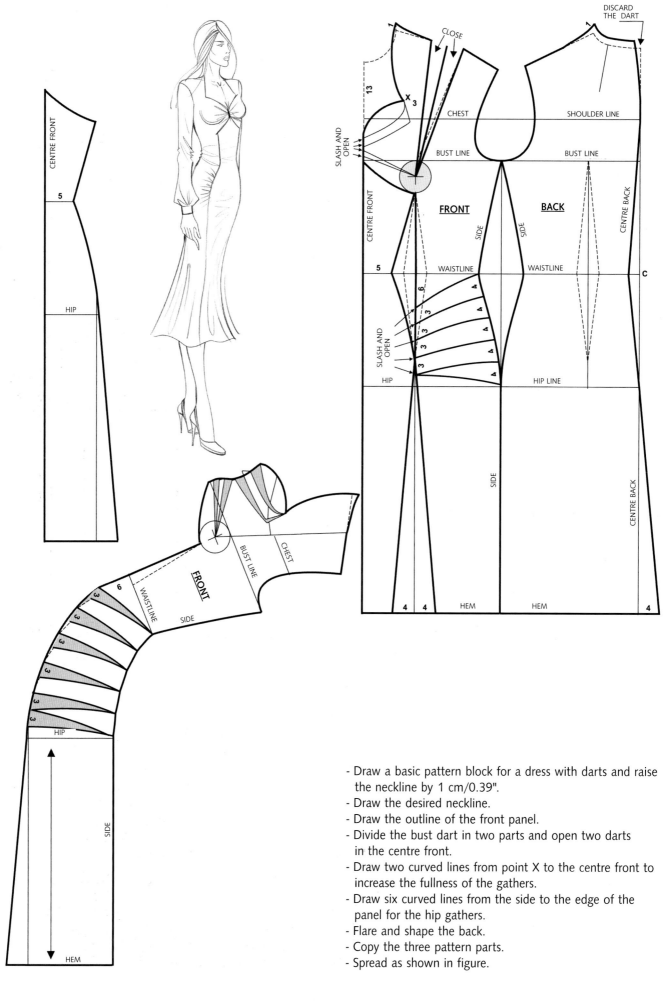

- Draw a basic pattern block for a dress with darts and raise the neckline by 1 cm/0.39".
- Draw the desired neckline.
- Draw the outline of the front panel.
- Divide the bust dart in two parts and open two darts in the centre front.
- Draw two curved lines from point X to the centre front to increase the fullness of the gathers.
- Draw six curved lines from the side to the edge of the panel for the hip gathers.
- Flare and shape the back.
- Copy the three pattern parts.
- Spread as shown in figure.

DRESS WITH GATHERS IN BACK

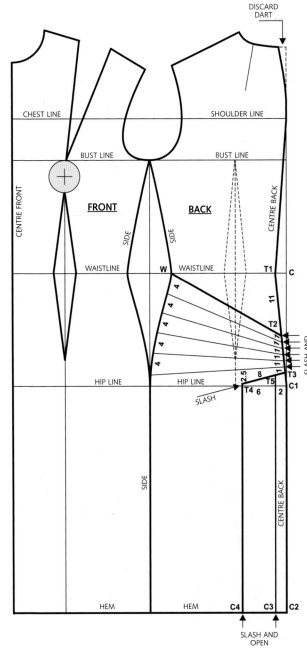

- Draw a basic pattern block for a dress with darts.
- T1–T2 = 11–12 cm/4.33"-4.72".
- Draw six lines crossing from the side to the centre back, as shown in figure.
- Draw the line T3–T4, 8 cm/3.15".
- C2–C4 = 8 cm/3.15", and C2–C3 = 2 cm/0.79". Join C4–T4 and C3–T5.
- Copy the three pattern parts.
- Spread out the lower part as shown in figure.

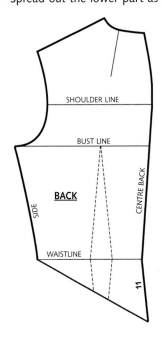

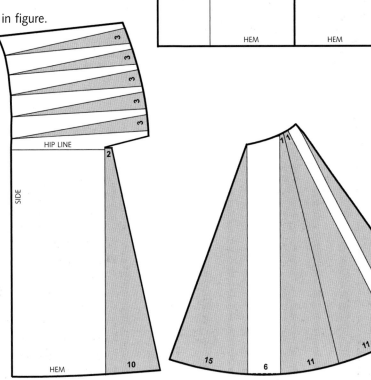

KIMONO DRESS WITH WRAP FRONT

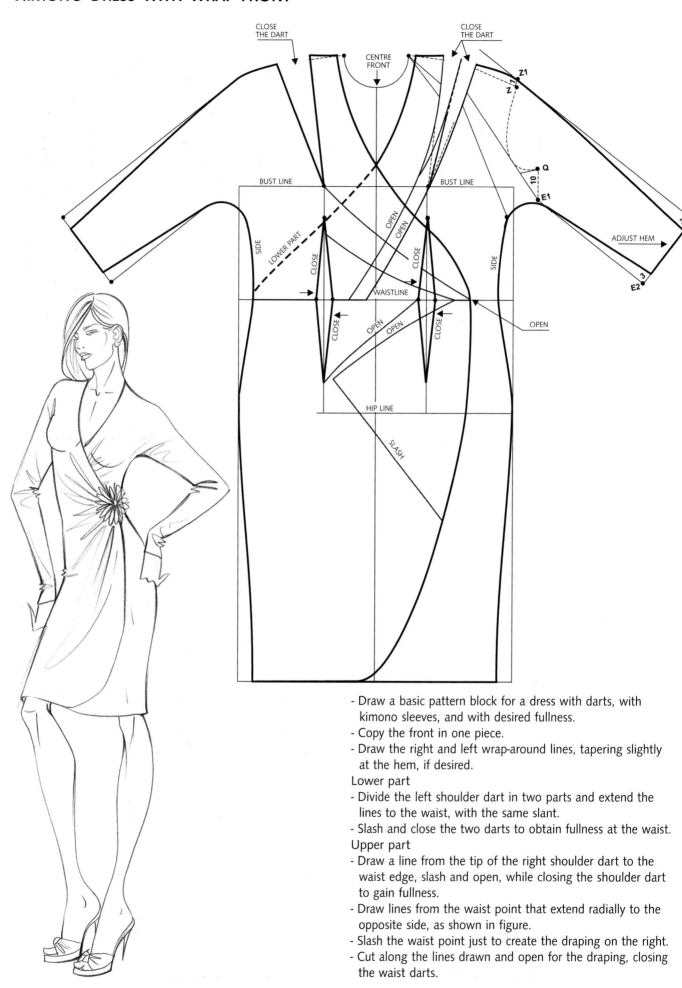

- Draw a basic pattern block for a dress with darts, with kimono sleeves, and with desired fullness.
- Copy the front in one piece.
- Draw the right and left wrap-around lines, tapering slightly at the hem, if desired.

Lower part
- Divide the left shoulder dart in two parts and extend the lines to the waist, with the same slant.
- Slash and close the two darts to obtain fullness at the waist.

Upper part
- Draw a line from the tip of the right shoulder dart to the waist edge, slash and open, while closing the shoulder dart to gain fullness.
- Draw lines from the waist point that extend radially to the opposite side, as shown in figure.
- Slash the waist point just to create the draping on the right.
- Cut along the lines drawn and open for the draping, closing the waist darts.

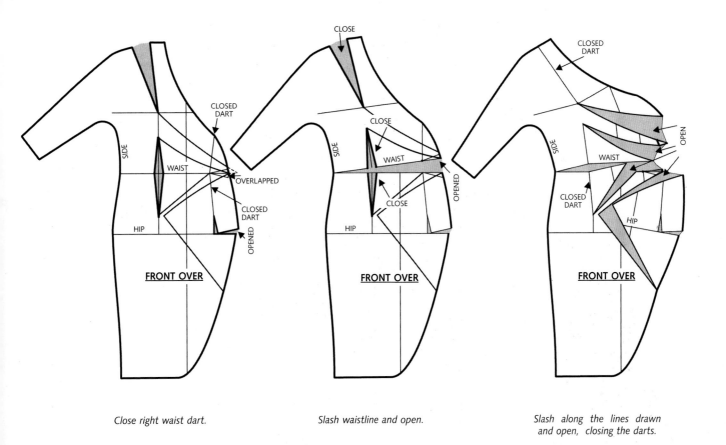

Close right waist dart.

Slash waistline and open.

Slash along the lines drawn and open, closing the darts.

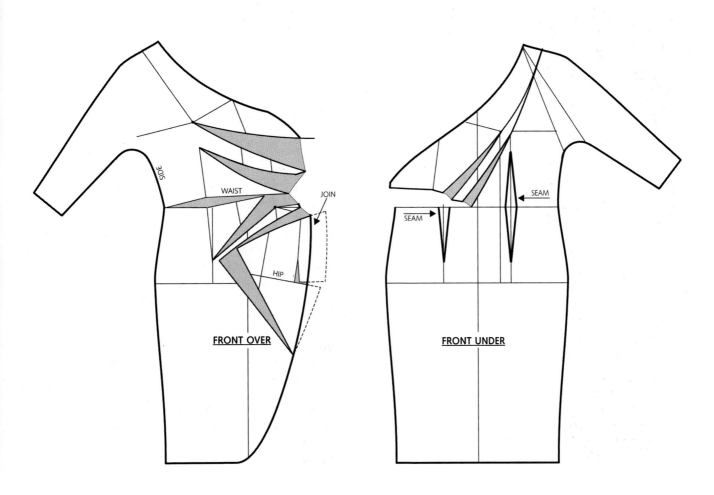

Dress with crossed halter bodice

WITH FRONT CENTRE SEAM GATHERS

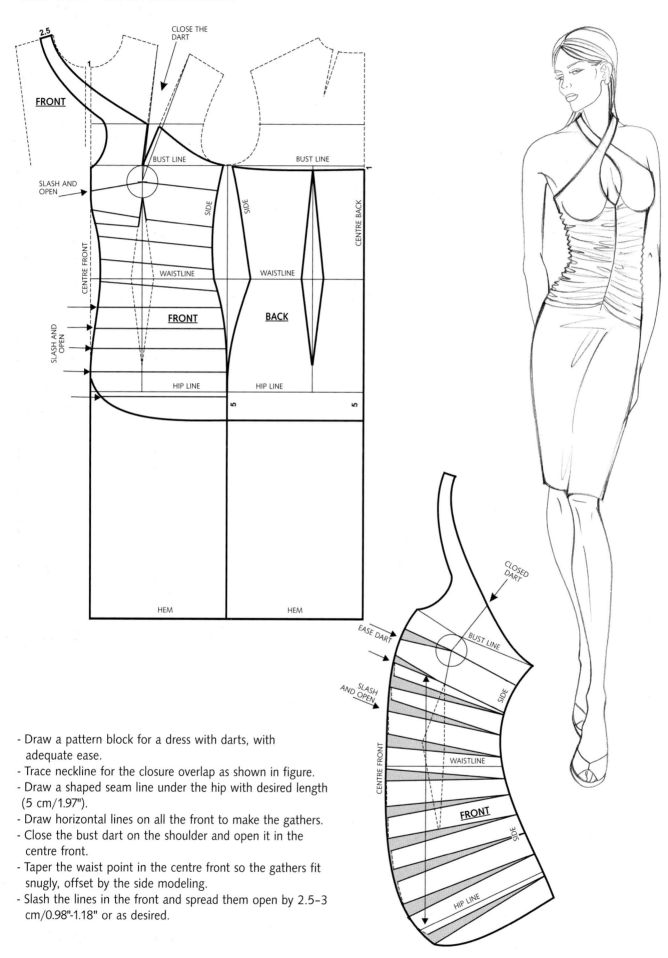

- Draw a pattern block for a dress with darts, with adequate ease.
- Trace neckline for the closure overlap as shown in figure.
- Draw a shaped seam line under the hip with desired length (5 cm/1.97").
- Draw horizontal lines on all the front to make the gathers.
- Close the bust dart on the shoulder and open it in the centre front.
- Taper the waist point in the centre front so the gathers fit snugly, offset by the side modeling.
- Slash the lines in the front and spread them open by 2.5–3 cm/0.98"-1.18" or as desired.

Kimono dress with gusset

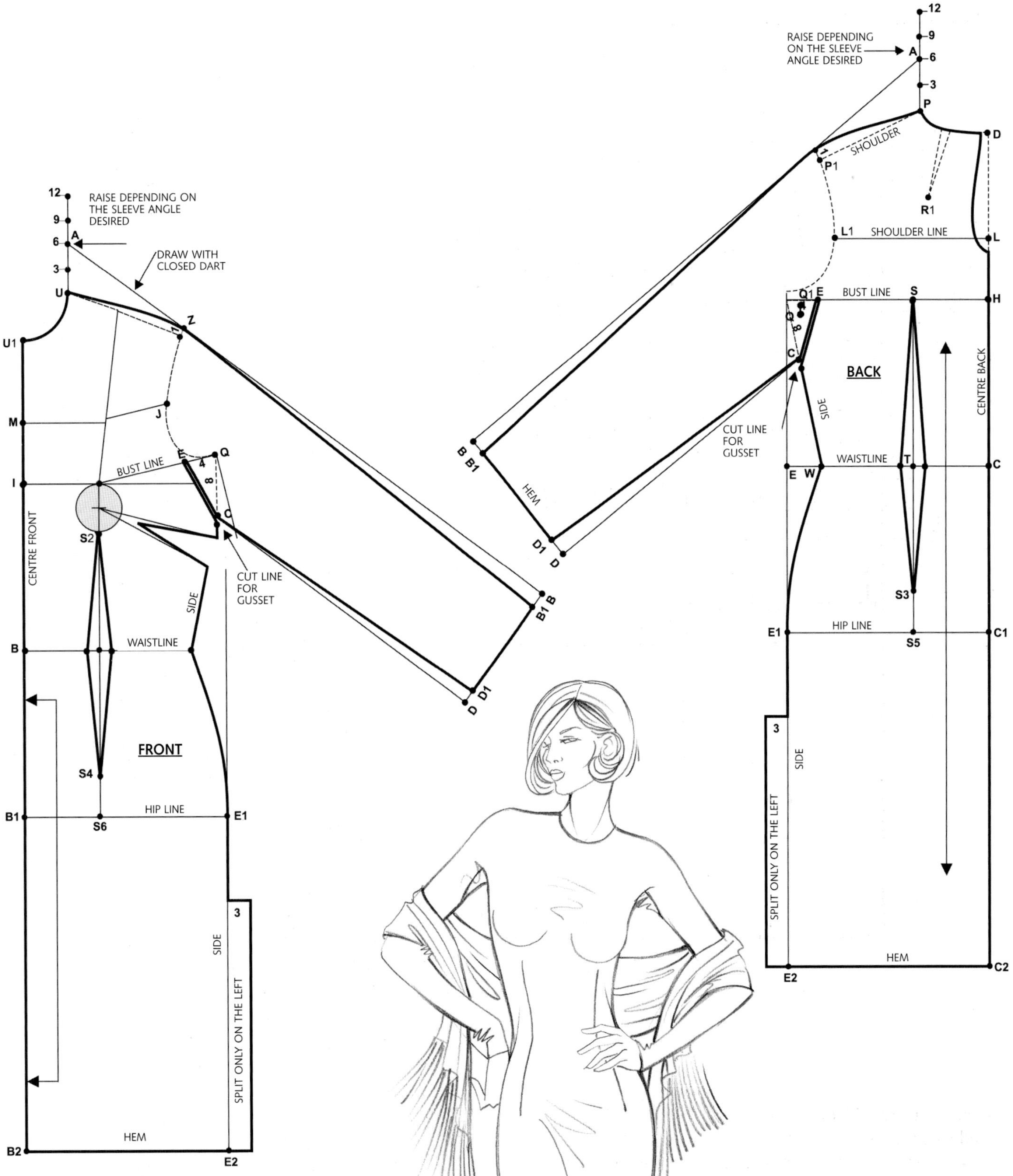

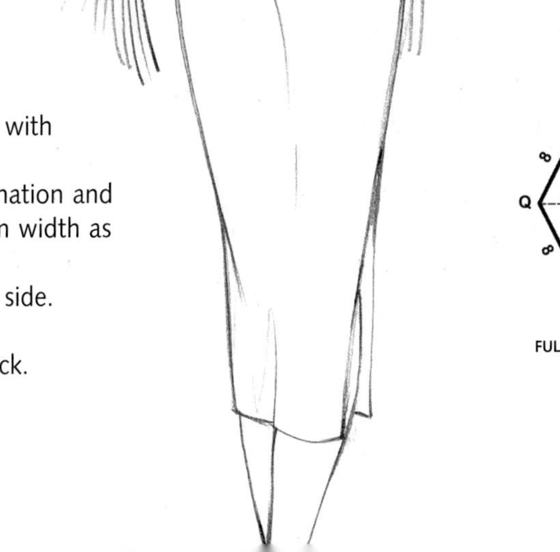

RAISE DEPENDING ON THE SLEEVE ANGLE DESIRED

RAISE DEPENDING ON THE SLEEVE ANGLE DESIRED

DRAW WITH CLOSED DART

BACK

FRONT

SHOULDER

SHOULDER LINE

BUST LINE

WAISTLINE

HIP LINE

HEM

CENTRE BACK

CENTRE FRONT

SIDE

BUST LINE

WAISTLINE

HIP LINE

HEM

CUT LINE FOR GUSSET

SPLIT ONLY ON THE LEFT

- Draw a pattern block for a dress with darts, with adequate ease.
- Draw a kimono sleeve with the desired inclination and with a cut for the gusset and the sleeve hem width as desired, as shown in figure.
- Shift the bust dart from the shoulder to the side.
- Draw the split to the desired.
- Draw the "tear-drop" shape in the centre back.
- Draw the gusset as shown in figure.

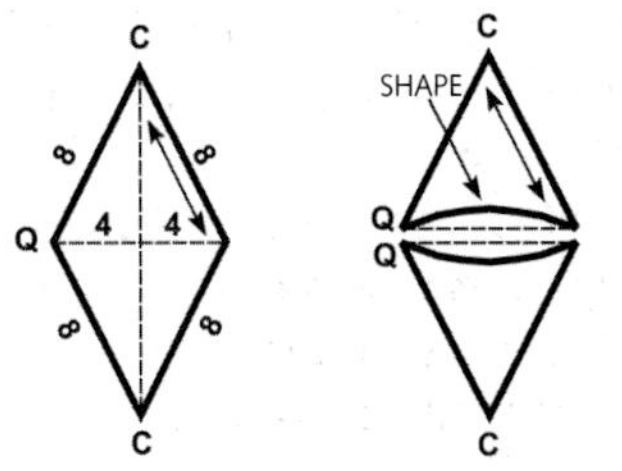

FULL GUSSET

GUSSET SPLIT HORIZONTALLY

SHAPE

Short amphora-kimono dress

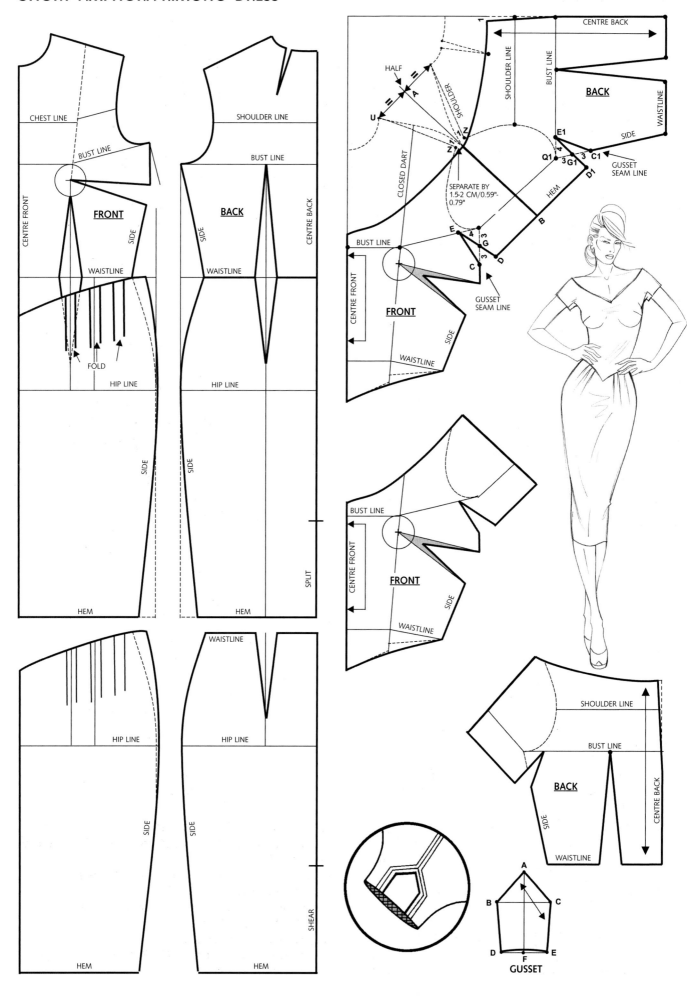

CHEST LINE

BUST LINE

CENTRE FRONT

FRONT

SIDE

WAISTLINE

FOLD

HIP LINE

SIDE

HEM

SHOULDER LINE

BUST LINE

BACK

CENTRE BACK

SIDE

WAISTLINE

HIP LINE

SIDE

SPLIT

HEM

WAISTLINE

HIP LINE

SIDE

HEM

WAISTLINE

HIP LINE

SIDE

SHEAR

HEM

HALF

SHOULDER

CLOSED DART

U

Z

Z1

1

SEPARATE BY 1.5-2 CM/0.59"-0.79"

SHOULDER LINE

BUST LINE

CENTRE BACK

BACK

WAISTLINE

SIDE

E1

Q1   3 G1   3 C1

D1

GUSSET SEAM LINE

E   4

C   3   G3

D

B

HEM

BUST LINE

CENTRE FRONT

FRONT

WAISTLINE

SIDE

GUSSET SEAM LINE

BUST LINE

CENTRE FRONT

FRONT

WAISTLINE

SIDE

SHOULDER LINE

BUST LINE

CENTRE BACK

BACK

SIDE

WAISTLINE

A

B   C

D   F   E

GUSSET

106

Minidress with dropped sleeves

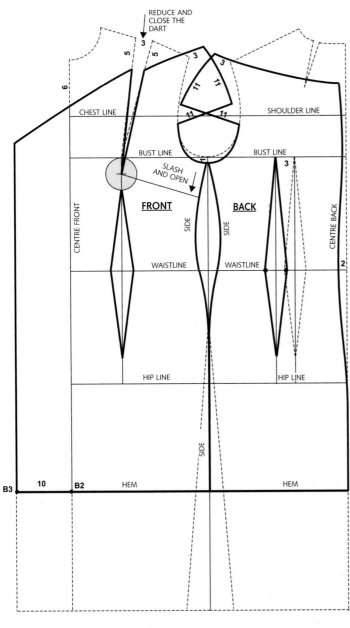

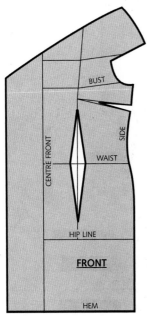

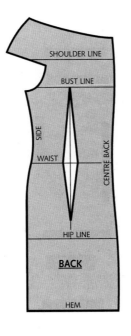

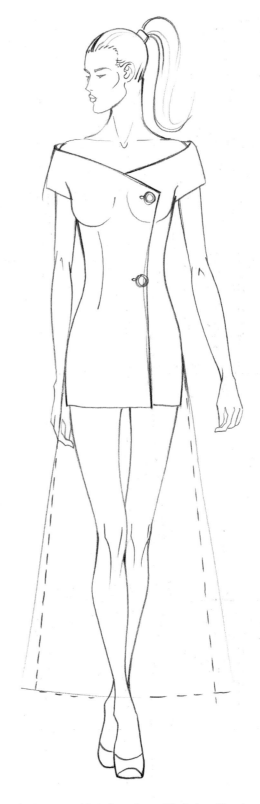

- Draw a basic pattern block for a dress with darts, with adequate ease and with the shoulder bust dart reduced by half, compared to the basic pattern.
- Close the shoulder bust dart and shift it to the side.
- Lower the armscye 2 cm/0.79".
- Draw the neckline and sleeve as shown in figure.
- Shift the back dart 3 cm/1.18".
- Reduce the waist as needed.
- Extend B2–B3 by 9-11 cm/3.54"-4.33", for the double-breast overlap.

Frock coat dress

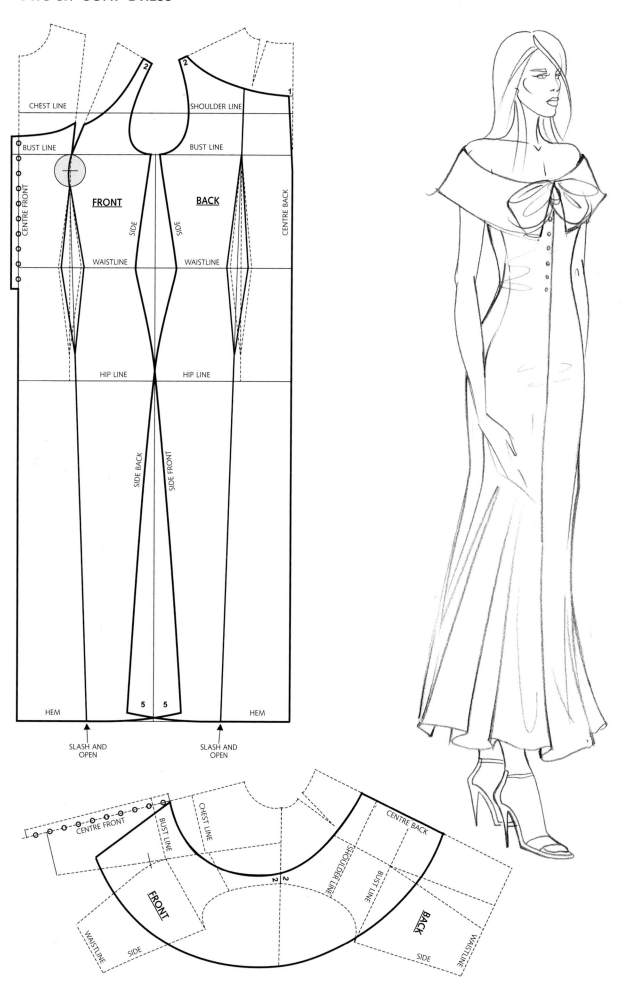

CHEST LINE | SHOULDER LINE
BUST LINE | BUST LINE

CENTRE FRONT

FRONT | BACK

SIDE | SIDE

CENTRE BACK

WAISTLINE | WAISTLINE

HIP LINE | HIP LINE

SIDE BACK | SIDE FRONT

HEM | HEM

5 | 5

SLASH AND OPEN | SLASH AND OPEN

2 | 2
1

CENTRE FRONT

BUST LINE | CHEST LINE
SHOULDER LINE

CENTRE BACK
BUST LINE

FRONT | BACK

2 | 2

WAISTLINE | SIDE | SIDE | WAISTLINE

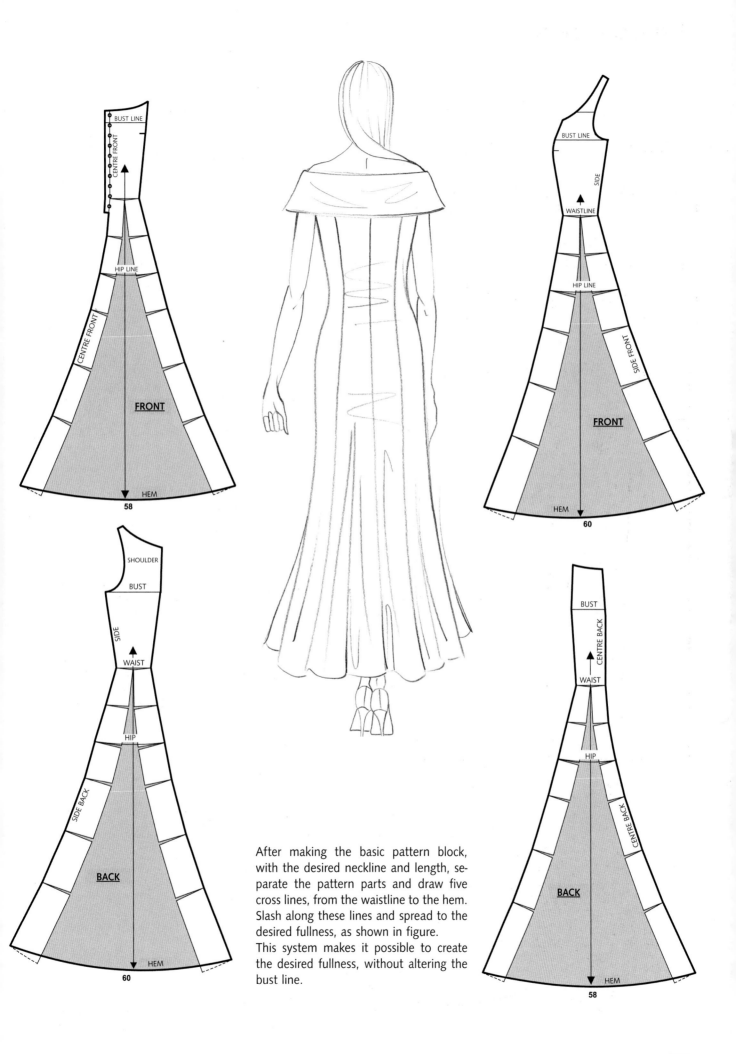

BUST LINE

CENTRE FRONT

CENTRE FRONT

HIP LINE

FRONT

HEM

58

SHOULDER

BUST

SIDE

WAIST

HIP

SIDE BACK

BACK

HEM

60

BUST LINE

SIDE

WAISTLINE

HIP LINE

SIDE FRONT

FRONT

HEM

60

BUST

CENTRE BACK

WAIST

HIP

CENTRE BACK

BACK

HEM

58

After making the basic pattern block, with the desired neckline and length, separate the pattern parts and draw five cross lines, from the waistline to the hem. Slash along these lines and spread to the desired fullness, as shown in figure.
This system makes it possible to create the desired fullness, without altering the bust line.

Raglan dress with neckline gathers

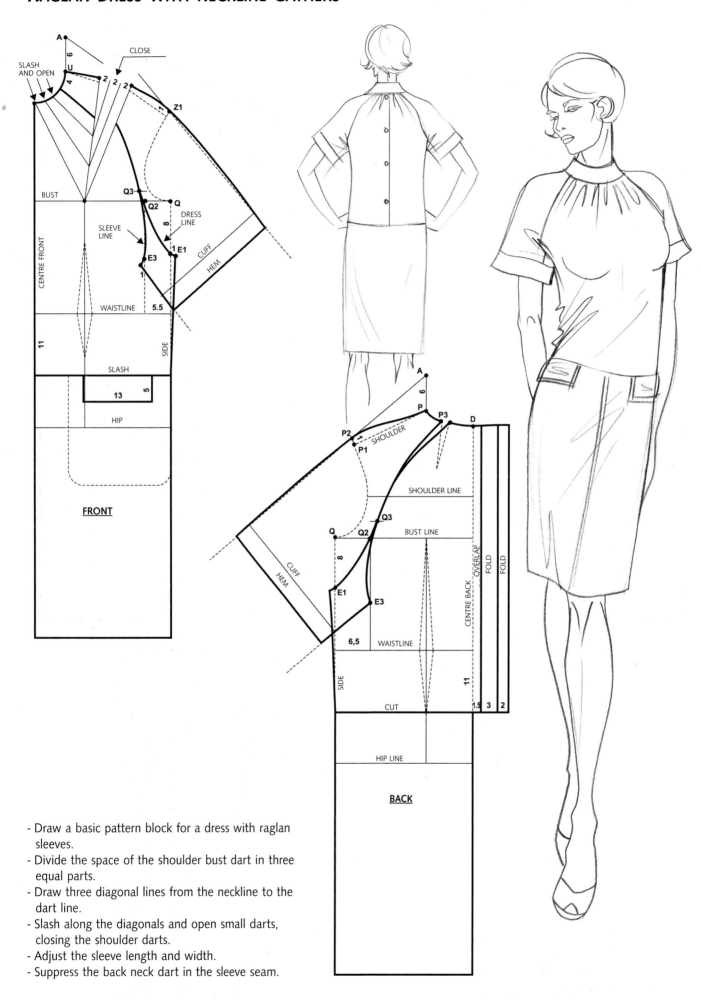

FRONT

BACK

Labels on FRONT pattern:
A, 6, U, 4, CLOSE, 2, 2, 2, SLASH AND OPEN, Z1, BUST, Q3, Q2, Q, DRESS LINE, SLEEVE LINE, 8, CENTRE FRONT, 1 E1, CUFF, HEM, E3, 1, WAISTLINE, 5.5, SIDE, 11, SLASH, 13, 5, HIP

Labels on BACK pattern:
A, 6, P, P3, D, P2, P1, SHOULDER, SHOULDER LINE, Q, Q3, Q2, BUST LINE, CUFF, HEM, 8, OVERLAP, FOLD, FOLD, CENTRE BACK, E1, E3, 11, WAISTLINE, 6,5, SIDE, CUT, 1.5, 3, 2, HIP LINE

- Draw a basic pattern block for a dress with raglan sleeves.
- Divide the space of the shoulder bust dart in three equal parts.
- Draw three diagonal lines from the neckline to the dart line.
- Slash along the diagonals and open small darts, closing the shoulder darts.
- Adjust the sleeve length and width.
- Suppress the back neck dart in the sleeve seam.

Dress with bat sleeve

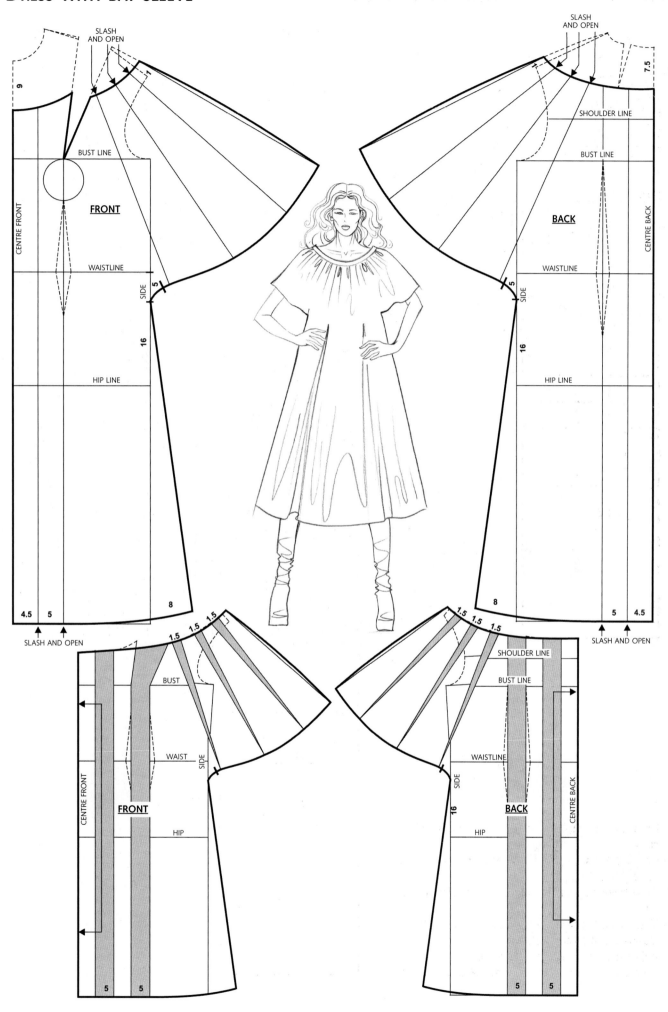

SLASH AND OPEN

SLASH AND OPEN

9

BUST LINE

CENTRE FRONT

FRONT

WAISTLINE

SIDE

5

16

HIP LINE

4.5 5

8

SLASH AND OPEN

SLASH AND OPEN

7.5

SHOULDER LINE

BUST LINE

BACK

CENTRE BACK

WAISTLINE

SIDE

5

16

HIP LINE

8

5 4.5

SLASH AND OPEN

1.5 1.5 1.5

7

BUST

CENTRE FRONT

FRONT

WAIST

SIDE

HIP

5 5

1.5 1.5 1.5

SHOULDER LINE

BUST LINE

BACK

WAISTLINE

SIDE

16

CENTRE BACK

HIP

5 5

DRESS WITH DROPPED RAGLAN SLEEVES

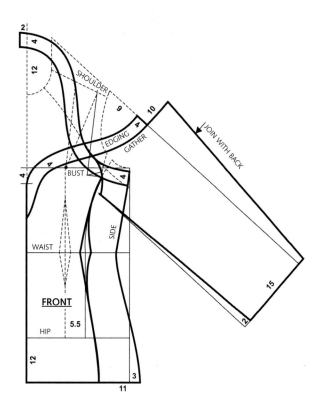

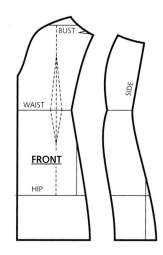

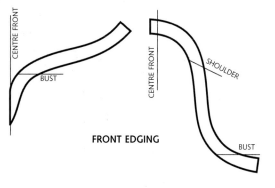

FRONT EDGING

- Draw the basic bodice with darts and extend the hem to desired length.
- Move the bust dart, draw the lines of the side panel, and close the bust dart, easing it into the side panel seam.
- Draw the raglan sleeve raised by 8-9 cm/3.15"-3.54".
- Draw the sleeve drop at the height desired, and create the 10–12 cm/3.94"-4.72" extension for the gathers.
- Draw the front and back neckline with desired shape.
- Draw the outline and the shoulder pad.
- Copy the front and back of the sleeve and join them.
- Copy the other parts of the pattern.
- Draw a circle skirt with the hip measurements equal to double the bodice, to have the necessary extension for the gathers.

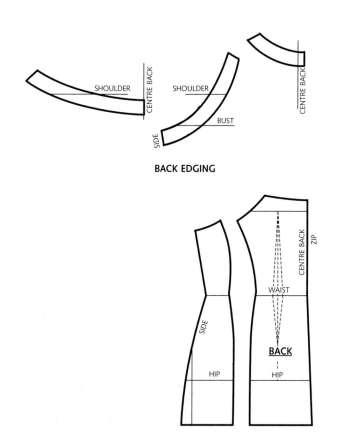

BACK EDGING

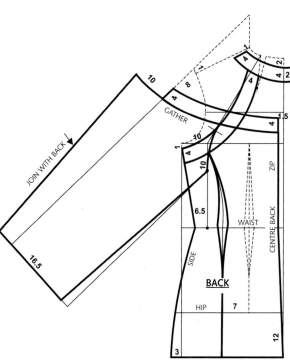

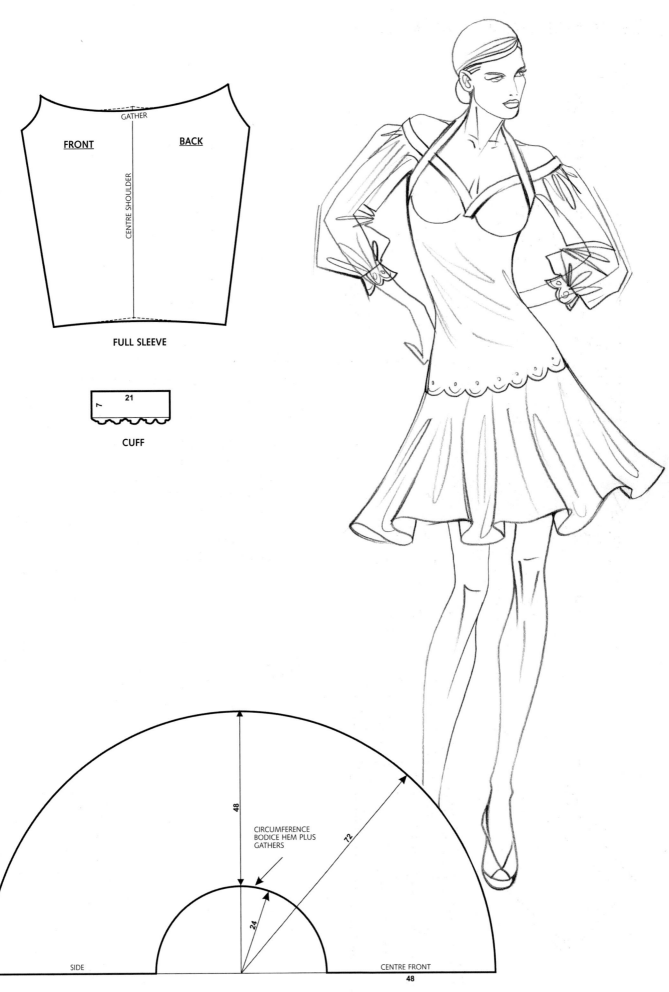

FRONT

BACK

GATHER

CENTRE SHOULDER

FULL SLEEVE

7 21

CUFF

48

72

24

CIRCUMFERENCE
BODICE HEM PLUS
GATHERS

SIDE

CENTRE FRONT

48

DOUBLE CIRCLE + GATHERS

DRESS WITH RUFFLED ASYMMETRICAL SKIRT

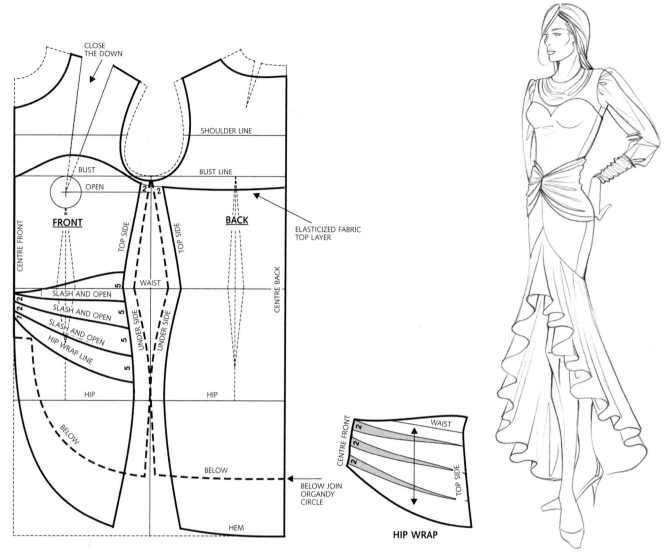

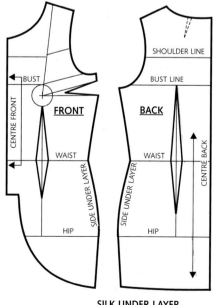

- Draw a basic pattern block for a dress with darts.
- On the same block, draw the top part of the dress for elasticized fabric, and the bottom for silk fabric.
- The stretch fabric dress is made by eliminating the darts and shifting the side seam by 1–2.5 cm/0.39"-0.98", depending on the fabric's elasticity.

- The lower part requires darts, shifting the bust dart to the side, to a position that will be hidden by the top layer.
- The skirt is created with a circle base then sewn to the part underneath.
- The hip wrap is drawn on the pattern block, then spread out.

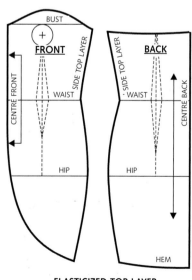

ELASTICIZED TOP LAYER

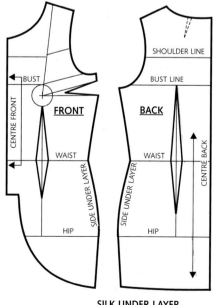

SILK UNDER LAYER

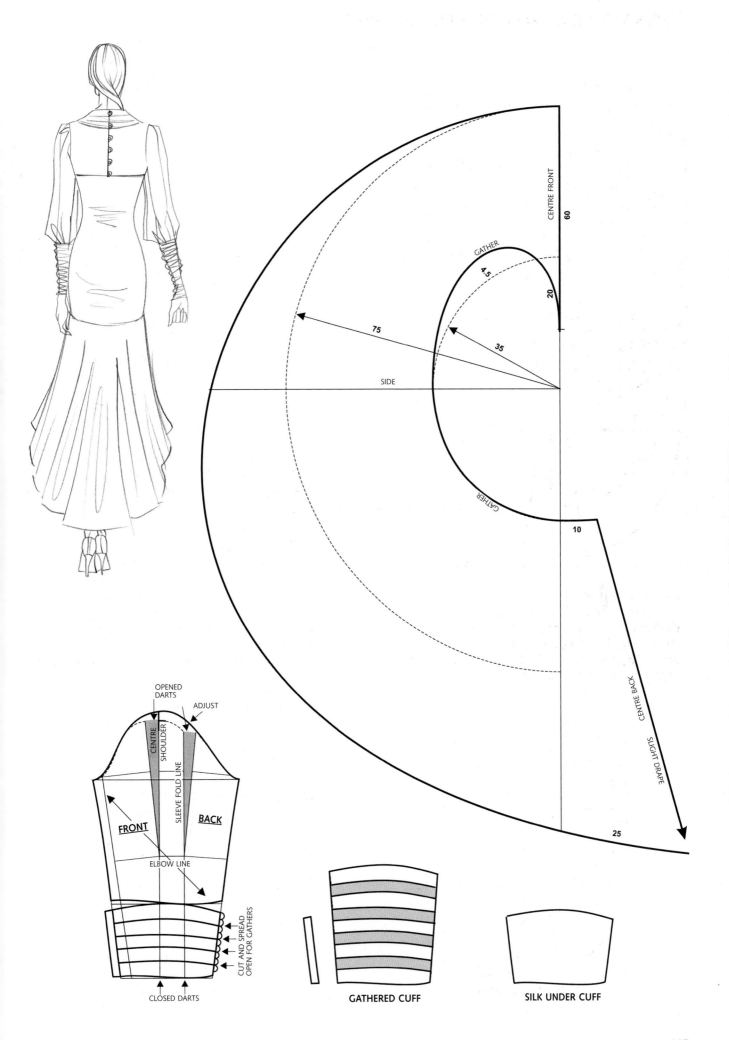

CENTRE FRONT

60

GATHER

4.5

20

75

35

SIDE

GATHER

10

CENTRE BACK

SLIGHT DRAPE

25

OPENED
DARTS

ADJUST

CENTRE SHOULDER

SLEEVE FOLD LINE

FRONT   BACK

ELBOW LINE

CUT AND SPREAD
OPEN FOR GATHERS

CLOSED DARTS

GATHERED CUFF

SILK UNDER CUFF

Dress with asymmetrical neckline

MOVE AND CLOSE

CLOSE

CHEST LINE

SHOULDER LINE

BUST

BUST

BUST LINE

SIDE

FRONT

SIDE

BACK

SIDE

WAIST

WAIST

WAIST

EDGING

EDGING

HIP

HIP

SIDE

CENTRE FRONT

SIDE

SIDE

CENTRE BACK

SIDE

HEM

HEM

SIDE

BUST LINE

CHEST

BUST

CENTRE FRONT

FRONT

SIDE

OPEN

OPEN

WAIST

OPEN

WAIST

SMOOTH THE OUTLINE

CLOSE THE DART

SMOOTH THE OUTLINE

CLOSE AND RESTORE

BUST

BUST

FRONT

FRONT

SIDE

CENTRE FRONT

SIDE

WAIST

FITTED LINING

SHOULDER LINE

BUST LINE

BACK

CENTRE BACK

BACK

SIDE

WAIST

116

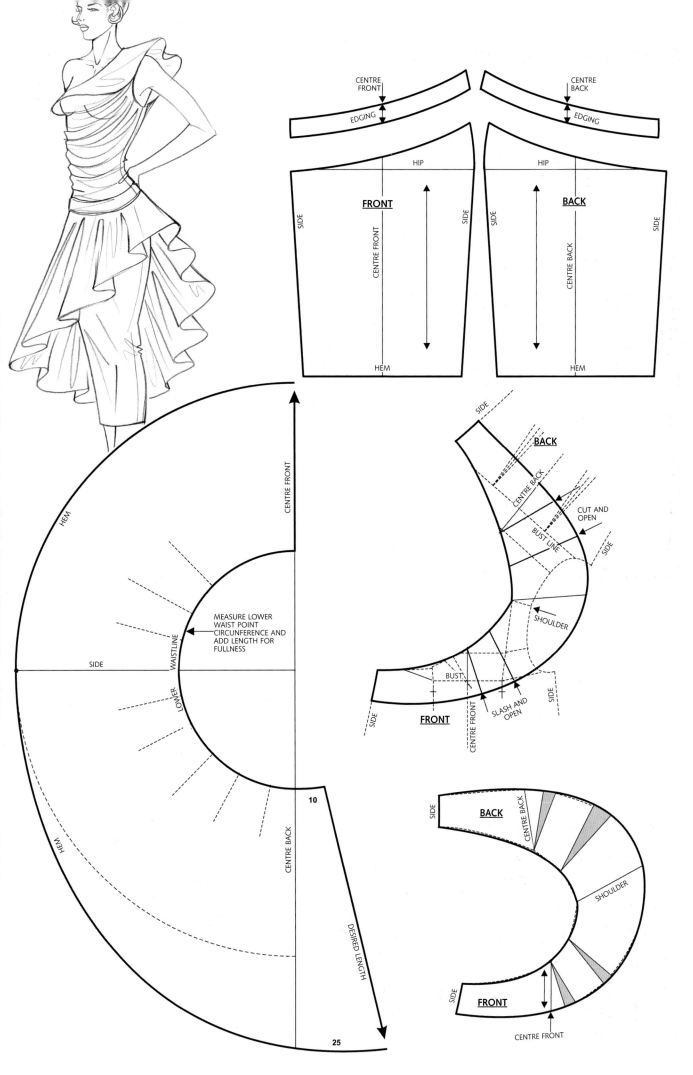

CENTRE
FRONT

EDGING

CENTRE
BACK

EDGING

HIP

HIP

FRONT

BACK

SIDE

SIDE

SIDE

SIDE

CENTRE FRONT

CENTRE BACK

HEM

HEM

SIDE

BACK

CENTRE BACK

CUT AND
OPEN

BUST LINE

SIDE

SHOULDER

BUST

SIDE

SIDE

FRONT

CENTRE FRONT

SLASH AND
OPEN

HEM

CENTRE FRONT

MEASURE LOWER
WAIST POINT
CIRCUNFERENCE AND
ADD LENGTH FOR
FULLNESS

WAISTLINE

SIDE

LOWER

HEM

CENTRE BACK

10

DESIRED LENGTH

25

SIDE

BACK

CENTRE BACK

SHOULDER

SIDE

FRONT

CENTRE FRONT

DRESS WITH DOUBLE SKIRT

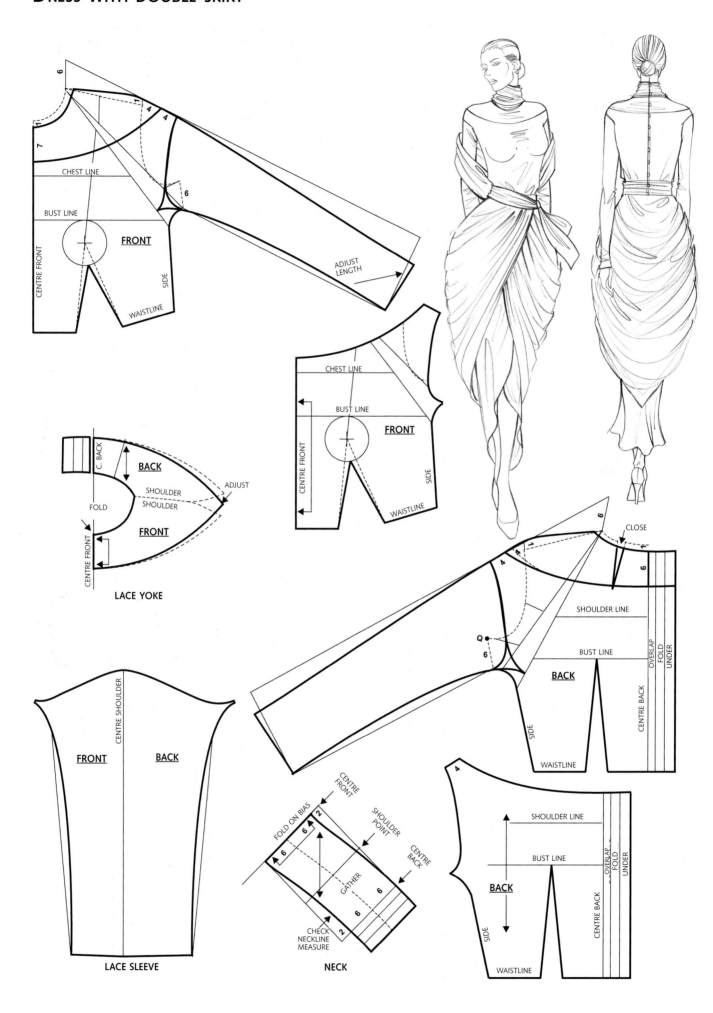

6

CHEST LINE

BUST LINE

CENTRE FRONT

FRONT

SIDE

WAISTLINE

7

4

4

1

6

ADJUST
LENGTH

CHEST LINE

BUST LINE

CENTRE FRONT

FRONT

SIDE

WAISTLINE

C. BACK

BACK

SHOULDER

SHOULDER

ADJUST

FOLD

FRONT

CENTRE FRONT

LACE YOKE

CENTRE SHOULDER

FRONT   **BACK**

LACE SLEEVE

6

4

1

CLOSE

6

SHOULDER LINE

BUST LINE

Q

6

BACK

SIDE

WAISTLINE

OVERLAP
FOLD
UNDER

CENTRE BACK

CENTRE
FRONT

FOLD ON BIAS

2

6

6

SHOULDER
POINT

CENTRE
BACK

GATHER

6

6

2

CHECK
NECKLINE
MEASURE

NECK

4

SHOULDER LINE

BUST LINE

BACK

SIDE

WAISTLINE

OVERLAP
FOLD
UNDER

CENTRE BACK

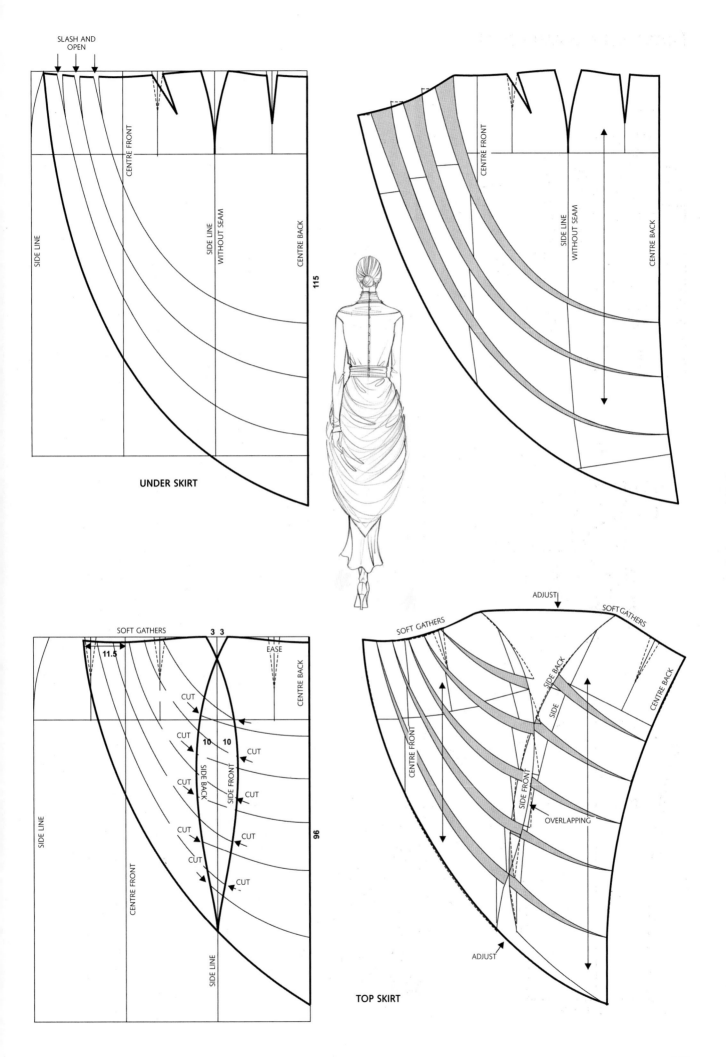

SLASH AND
OPEN

SIDE LINE

CENTRE FRONT

SIDE LINE
WITHOUT SEAM

CENTRE BACK

115

UNDER SKIRT

SIDE LINE

CENTRE FRONT

SIDE LINE
WITHOUT SEAM

CENTRE BACK

SOFT GATHERS   3 3

11.5

EASE

CENTRE BACK

CUT

CUT   10 10   CUT

CUT   CUT

CUT   CUT

CUT

SIDE BACK

SIDE FRONT

SIDE LINE

CENTRE FRONT

SIDE LINE

96

ADJUST

SOFT GATHERS   SOFT GATHERS

SIDE BACK

SIDE

CENTRE FRONT

SIDE FRONT

OVERLAPPING

CENTRE BACK

ADJUST

TOP SKIRT

RAGLAN SLEEVE DRESS WITH SASH

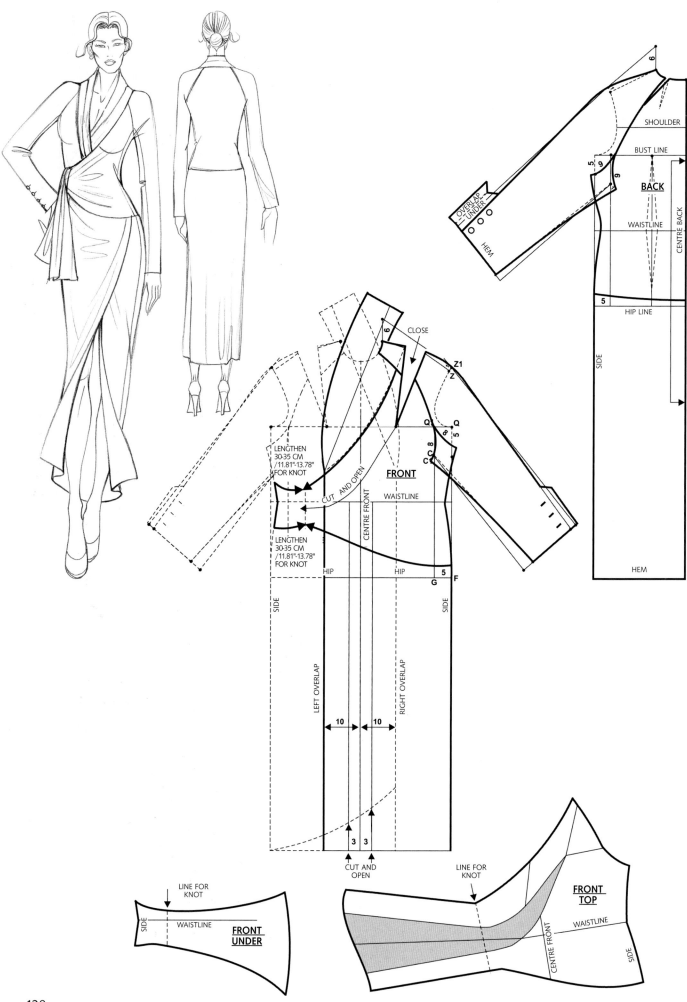

SHOULDER

BUST LINE

BACK

WAISTLINE

CENTRE BACK

HIP LINE

SIDE

OVERLAP
UNDER

HEM

6

5 9

9

5

CLOSE

6

Z1

Z

Q Q

8 5

C C 8

FRONT

WAISTLINE

LENGTHEN
30-35 CM
/11.81"-13.78"
FOR KNOT

CUT AND OPEN

CENTRE FRONT

LENGTHEN
30-35 CM
/11.81"-13.78"
FOR KNOT

HIP HIP

5 F

G

SIDE SIDE

LEFT OVERLAP

RIGHT OVERLAP

10 10

3 3

CUT AND
OPEN

HEM

LINE FOR
KNOT

SIDE WAISTLINE

**FRONT
UNDER**

LINE FOR
KNOT

**FRONT
TOP**

WAISTLINE

CENTRE FRONT

SIDE

120

PLEATED LOW NECKLINE DRESS

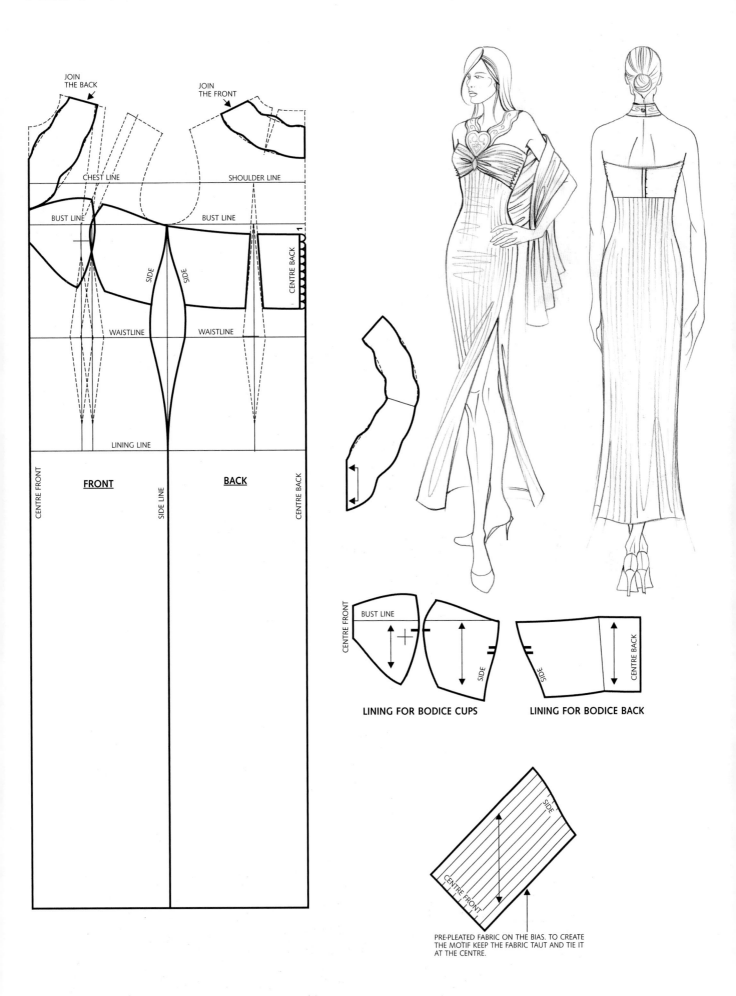

JOIN THE BACK

JOIN THE FRONT

CHEST LINE

SHOULDER LINE

BUST LINE

BUST LINE

SIDE

SIDE

CENTRE BACK

1

WAISTLINE

WAISTLINE

LINING LINE

CENTRE FRONT

FRONT

SIDE LINE

BACK

CENTRE BACK

CENTRE FRONT

BUST LINE

SIDE

SIDE

CENTRE BACK

LINING FOR BODICE CUPS

LINING FOR BODICE BACK

SIDE

CENTRE FRONT

PRE-PLEATED FABRIC ON THE BIAS. TO CREATE THE MOTIF KEEP THE FABRIC TAUT AND TIE IT AT THE CENTRE.

Dress with bell-shaped skirt

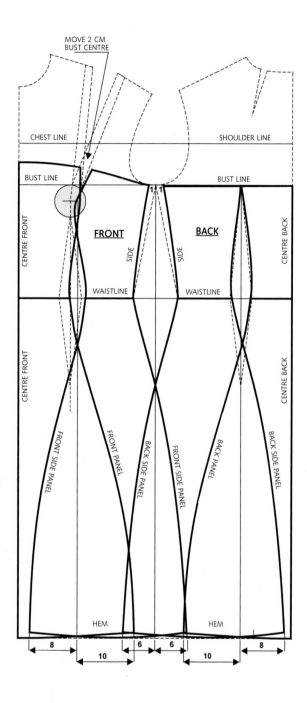

- Draw a basic pattern block for a dress with darts, with adequate ease.
- Draw the front and back neckline as desired.
- Draw the lines of the front, back, and side panels as shown in figure.
- Finish the hemline, giving it a slight curve.
- Copy all the panels separately onto another sheet of paper.

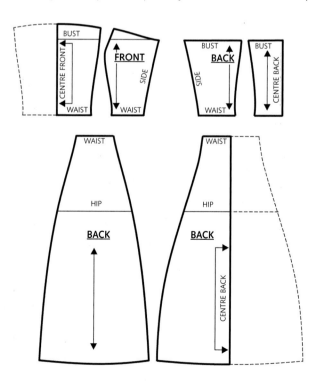

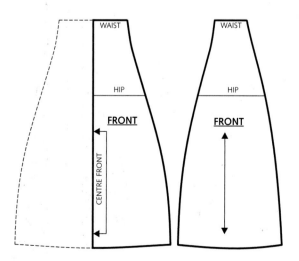

DRESS WITH POINTED DROPPED WAISTLINE

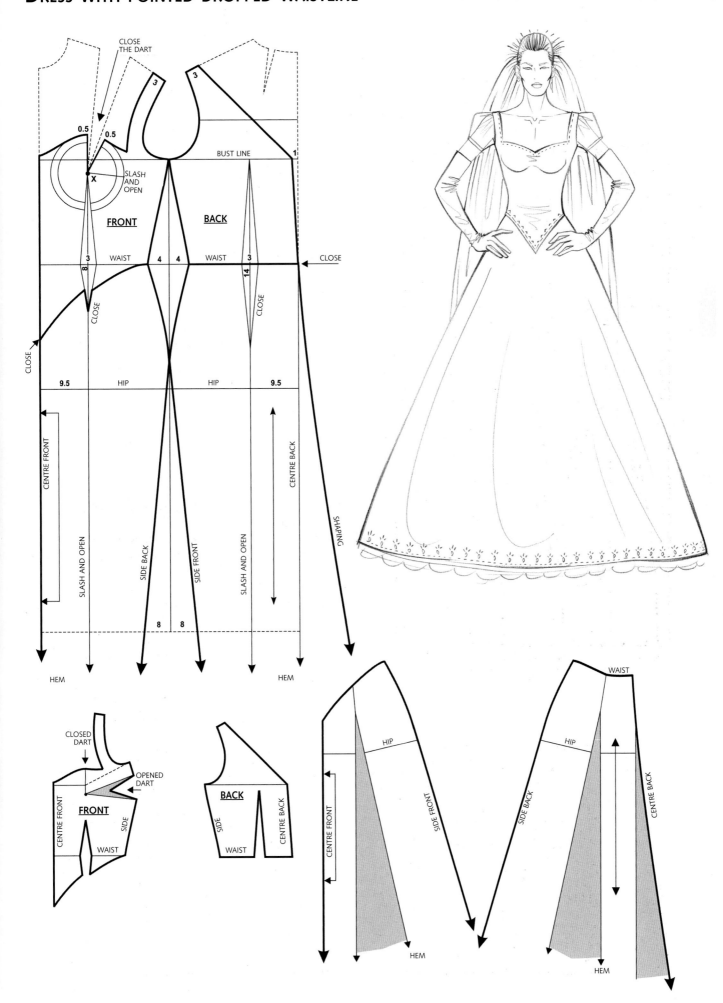

CLOSE THE DART

0.5   0.5

X   SLASH AND OPEN

FRONT   BACK

BUST LINE   1

SLASH AND OPEN

3   WAIST   4   4   WAIST   3   CLOSE

8   CLOSE   14   CLOSE

CLOSE

9.5   HIP   HIP   9.5

CENTRE FRONT   CENTRE BACK

SLASH AND OPEN   SIDE BACK   SIDE FRONT   SLASH AND OPEN   SHAPING

8   8

HEM   HEM

CLOSED DART   OPENED DART

CENTRE FRONT   FRONT   SIDE   WAIST

BACK   SIDE   WAIST   CENTRE BACK

CENTRE FRONT   HIP   SIDE FRONT   SIDE BACK   HIP   CENTRE BACK   WAIST

HEM   HEM

123

SLEEVE VARIATIONS

FITTED SHORT SLEEVE

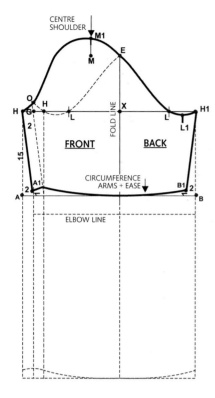

- Draw the basic fitted sleeve block with seam offset or aligned with the bodice seam.
- Draw the line A-B depending on the desired length (10-18 cm/3.94"-7.09").
- Reduce A1 and B1 depending on the desired bottom width.
- Join the bottom and the sides of the sleeve.

CAP SLEEVE

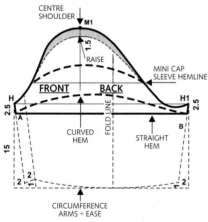

- Draw the basic fitted sleeve block with seam offset or aligned with the bodice seam.
- Raise the sleeve head by 1.5-2.5 cm/0.59"-0.98".
- Draw the bottom straight or curved at desired height.

Note: *For this sleeve the bodice shoulder must be reduced by 1.2 cm/0.47" to create greater sleeve stability.*

CUFFED SHORT SLEEVE

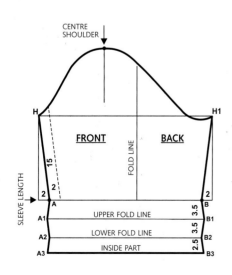

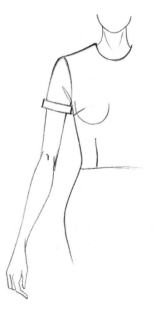

- Draw the basic fitted sleeve block with seam offset or aligned with the bodice seam.
- A1-B1 at 3.5 cm/1.38" from A-B (Upper fold line).
- A2-B2 at 3.5 cm/1.38" from A1-B1 (Lower fold line).
- A3-B3 at 2.5 cm/0.98" from A2-B2 (Inside part).

FULL SHORT SLEEVES

FULL AT THE HEM

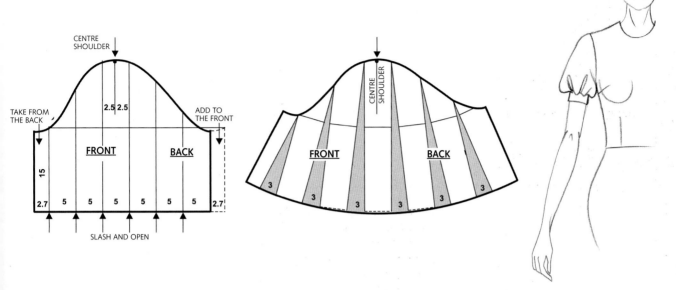

PUFFED

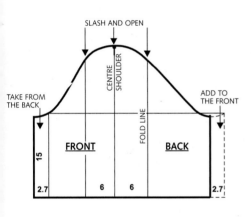
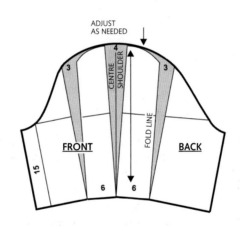

PUFFED AND FULL AT THE HEM

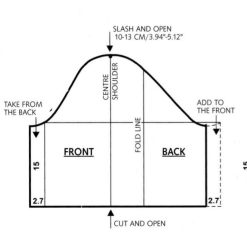
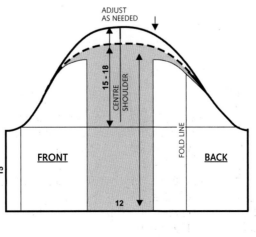

PETAL-SHAPED SHORT SLEEVE

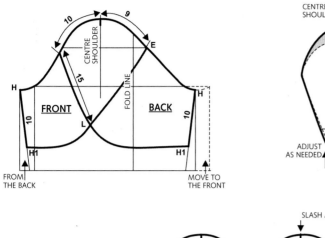

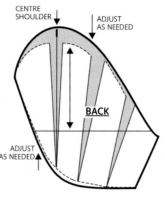

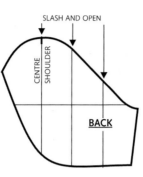

SHORT BUTTERFLY SLEEVE

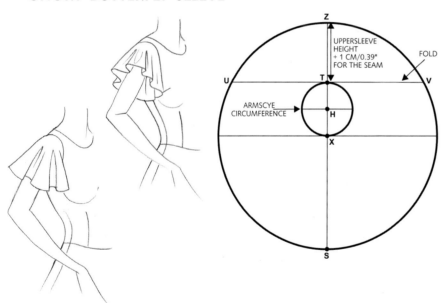

- Draw a circle with the radius X-S equal to the sleeve
  length of the longer part (in this case the lower part)
  + 1 cm/0.39" for the seam.
- Inside this circle, on the X-Z line through the centre, in the
  position desired based on the outer sleeve length, draw
  another smaller circle with a diameter equal to the armscye
  less 1 cm/0.39" for the seam.
- Cut the inner circle, leaving the seam allowance.
- Cut the outer circle, not including the margin for the hem
- Fold along the U-V line, as shown in figure because this
  sleeve has the upper part shorter.

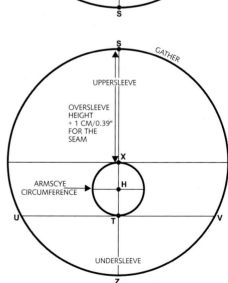

Short lantern sleeve

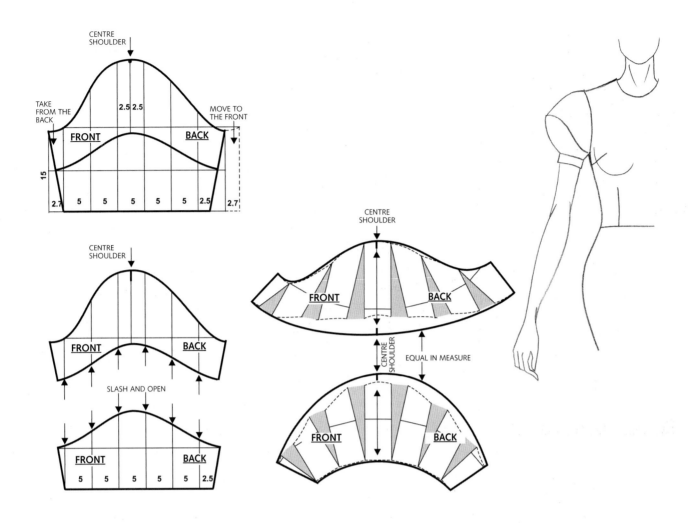

CENTRE SHOULDER

TAKE FROM THE BACK

MOVE TO THE FRONT

2.5 2.5

FRONT | BACK

15

2.7 | 5 | 5 | 5 | 5 | 5 | 2.5 | 2.7

CENTRE SHOULDER

FRONT | BACK

SLASH AND OPEN

FRONT | BACK

5 | 5 | 5 | 5 | 5 | 2.5

CENTRE SHOULDER

FRONT | BACK

CENTRE SHOULDER

EQUAL IN MEASURE

FRONT | BACK

Long lantern sleeve

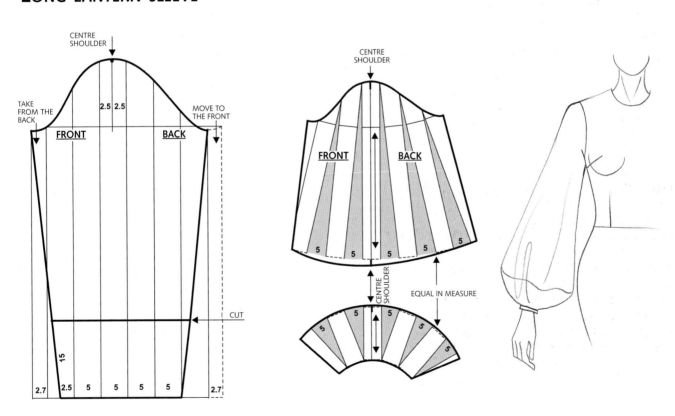

CENTRE SHOULDER

TAKE FROM THE BACK

MOVE TO THE FRONT

2.5 2.5

FRONT | BACK

CUT

15

2.7 | 2.5 | 5 | 5 | 5 | 5 | 2.7

CENTRE SHOULDER

FRONT | BACK

5 | 5 | 5 | 5

CENTRE SHOULDER

EQUAL IN MEASURE

5 | 5 | 5 | 5

FITTED SLEEVE

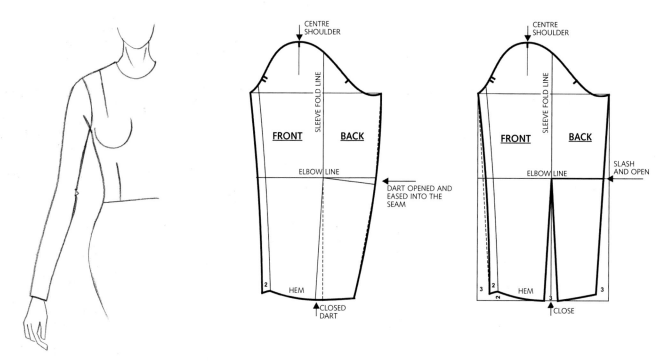

- Draw the basic long sleeve block, with seam moved forward or aligned, with adequate measurements and ease.
- Taper the end from sides and create a dart at the hemline, as desired.

- Slash along the elbow line and close the created dart, opening a dart at the elbow, which can be eased into the seam or sewn.

TWO-PIECE SLEEVE

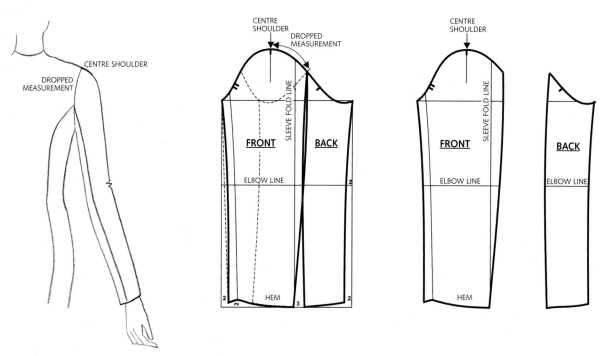

- Draw the basic long sleeve block, with adequate measurements and ease and with desired width at the hemline.
- Draw a line from the sleeve head, in the desired

position, so it coincides with the side panel seam right down to the hem.
- Separate the two pieces drawn.

WIDE AT WRIST SLEEVES

CUFFED SLEEVE

BELL SLEEVE

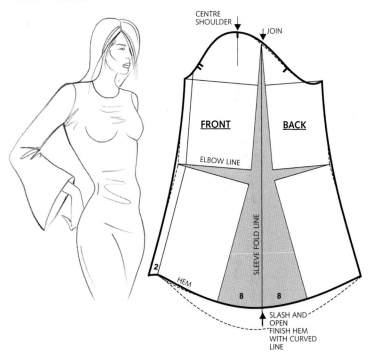

- Draw the basic fitted sleeve block, with seam moved to front or aligned with the bodice seam, with adequate measurements and ease.
- Cut along the fold line and open at the hemline as desired, based on the sleeve width.
- To get greater ease at the bottom, without compromising the

biceps zone, as in the bell sleeve, cut along the elbow line and open as shown in figure.
- Finish the hem with a curved line.
- Finish the sleeve head and check the measurements of the armscye.
- Check the measurements of the sleeve head with respect to the armscye.

ANGEL SLEEVE

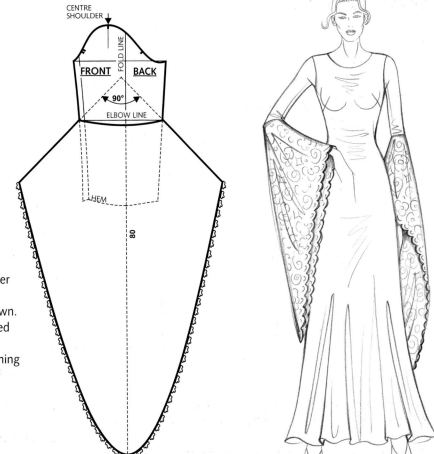

- Draw the basic fitted sleeve block and taper the end as needed.
- Discard the lower part from the elbow down.
- Extend the sleeve fold line as desired, based on the length of the sleeve opening.
- Draw the lower side of the sleeve, positioning it in square with respect to the straight of grain.
- Join the sides with the tip of the sleeve, giving a slight curve.
- Join the elbow line with a curve.

PUFFED SLEEVE

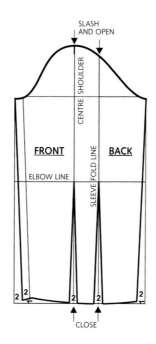

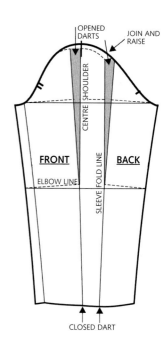

- Draw the basic fitted sleeve block aligning the seam with the bodice side and with adequate measurements and ease.
- Create two darts at sleeve bottom on the centre shoulder line and on the fold line, 2-4 cm/0.79"-1.57" wide.

- Slash along these lines and close the darts, opening them on the sleeve head.
- Finish the sleeve head raising it as desired.
- Reset the biceps and elbow lines.

PUFFED SLEEVE WITH DARTS OR GATHERS

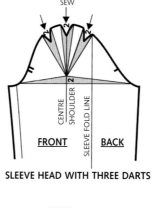

SLEEVE HEAD WITH THREE DARTS

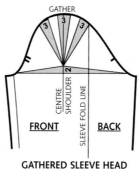

GATHERED SLEEVE HEAD

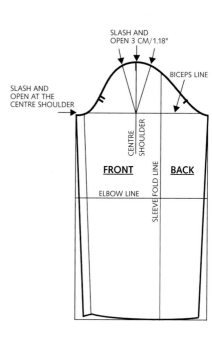

- Draw the basic fitted sleeve block aligning the seam with the bodice side and with adequate measurements and ease.
- Draw three lines from the sleeve head to the biceps line.
- Slash along these lines and along the biceps line and open

as shown in figure, or as needed.
- Finish the line of the sleeve head.
- The fullness of the sleeve head can be taken up in gathers or in three small darts, depending on the style desired.

HALF-MOON PADDED SHOULDERS

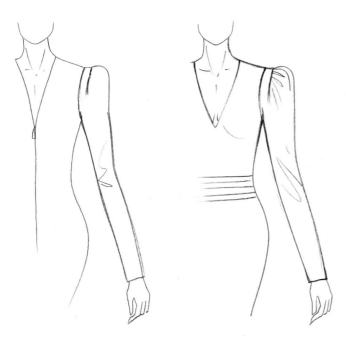

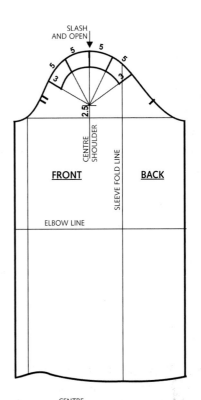

- Draw the basic sleeve block, aligning the seam with the bodice side, with adequate measurements and ease, and with the desired hem.
- Draw a 3-cm/1.18" band along the head of the sleeve and divide it in four 5-cm/1.97" sections, two sections on either side of the centre shoulder, as shown in figure.
- Slash the band and the sections and open them as shown in figure.
- Extend the centre shoulder line to the elbow line and slash it and the elbow line. Open by 3–6 cm/1.18"2.36", depending on how much gathering is desired.
- Re-draw the curve of the lower part of the sleeve head, raising it by 3-6 cm/1.18"2.36".
- Re-shape the curve and check the length of the sides of the sleeves.

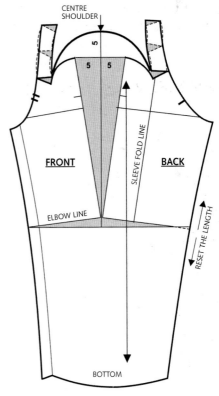

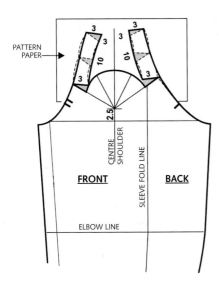

Note: *For this sleeve, the shoulder has to be reduced by 1-2 cm/0.39"-0.79", for greater stability.*

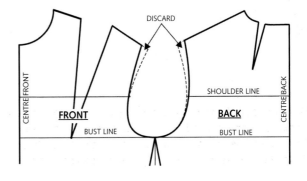

Bell Sleeves Wide at the Wrist

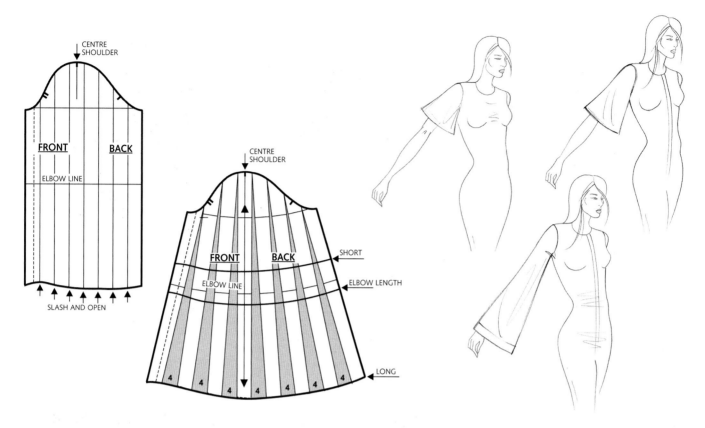

- Draw the basic sleeve block aligning the seam with the bodice side, with adequate measurements and ease, and with the desired hem.
- Draw some equidistant vertical lines parallel to the centre shoulder and the straight of grain, extending from the sleeve head to the bottom.
- Slash the pattern along these lines and open them at the bottom uniformly by 4–5 cm/1.57"-1.97". Paste the pattern thus obtained onto another sheet of pattern paper.
- Smoothly finish the lines of the sleeve head and the hem.

Puffed at the Shoulder Gathered at the Wrist

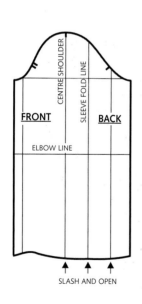 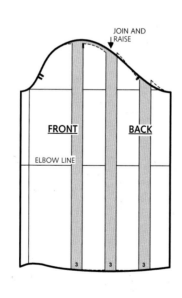 

- Draw the basic sleeve block aligning the seam with the bodice side, with adequate measurements and ease, and with the desired hem.
- Draw three or more equidistant vertical lines including the centre shoulder and the fold line.
- Slash the pattern along these lines and open them uniformly by 3–4 cm/1.18"-1.57". Paste the pattern thus obtained onto another sheet of pattern paper.
- Smoothly finish the lines of the sleeve head, raising it as desired, depending on the fullness of the gathers.

LEG-OF-MUTTON SLEEVE

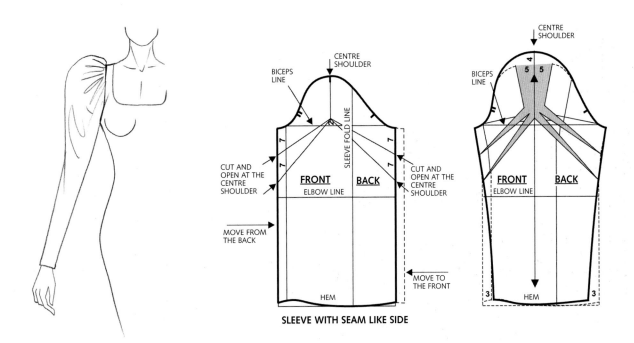

SLEEVE WITH SEAM LIKE SIDE

- Draw the basic sleeve block aligning the seam with the bodice side, with adequate measurements and ease.
- Draw four transversal lines, from the centre shoulder line, 2 cm. above the biceps line, as shown in figure.
- Slash the pattern along these lines and along the centre shoulder line, and open by 5-7 cm/1.97"-2.76", or as needed.

- Connect the lines for the sleeve head, raising it by 3–5 cm/1.18"-1.97", and reset the biceps line.
- Adjust the width of the forearm and the hem, as the style requires.
- Check the sleeve length.

FULLER LEG-OF-MUTTON SLEEVE

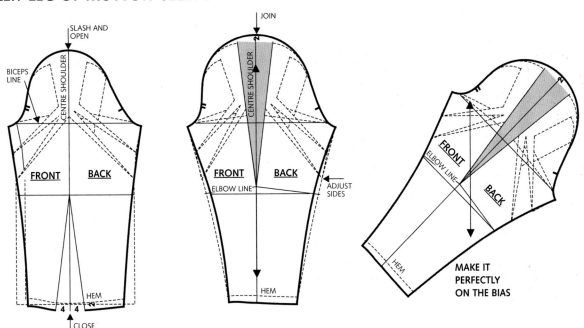

MAKE IT PERFECTLY ON THE BIAS

For fuller leg-of-mutton sleeves, the procedure is as follows:
- Draw a dart on the centre shoulder line from the hem, as wide as desired, but in any case leaving a circumference no less than the wrist circumference.
- Lengthen the sleeve by 2 cm/0.79". for ease of movement.

- Slash along the centre shoulder line and open it at the sleeve head, closing the dart at the hem.
- Finish the side lines, tapering as necessary, and those of the sleeve head, raising it by 2–3 cm/0.79"-1.18".
- Position this sleeve perfectly on the bias.

Cowl sleeve

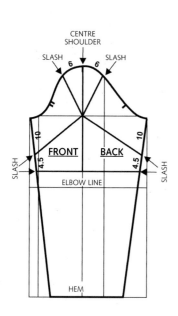

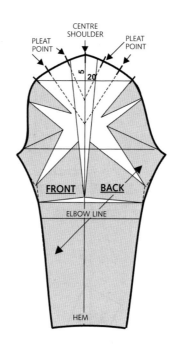

- Draw the basic fitted sleeve block, aligning the seam with the bodice side, with adequate measurements and ease.
- Draw four transversal lines, from the centre shoulder line to the biceps line, and from there to the sides, as shown in figure.
- Slash along these lines, along the centre shoulder line, and along the elbow line.
- Finish the sleeve head line, raising it by 5-7 cm/1.97"-2.76", and reset the biceps line.
- Adjust the width of the forearm and at the wrist, as the style requires.
- Check the sleeve length.

Long sleeve with central shirring

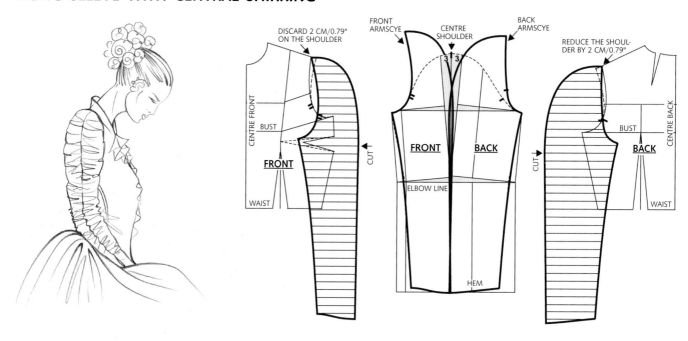

- Draw the basic fitted sleeve block, aligning the seam with the bodice side, with adequate measurements and ease.
- Slash along the centre shoulder line to the elbow and open by 3-4 cm/1.18"-1.57", for the width of the sleeve head, raising the biceps line and the elbow line.
- Adjust the hem as desired.
- Copy the armscye of the bodice block onto the sleeve head, after reducing the shoulder by 2 cm/0.79", as shown in figure.
- Draw the lines connecting the armscye and the centre shoulder.
- Separate the front and back of the sleeve and make a series of lines about 3-4 cm/1.18"-1.57" apart.
- Slash along these lines and distance them by 3-4 cm/1.18"-1.57".

Deep armscye sleeve

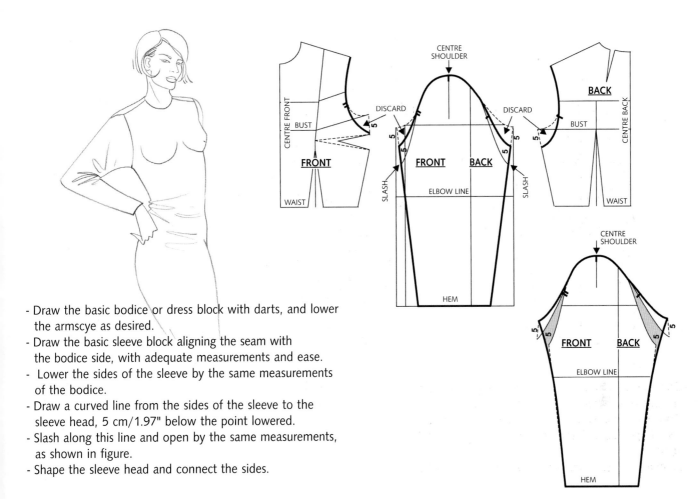

- Draw the basic bodice or dress block with darts, and lower the armscye as desired.
- Draw the basic sleeve block aligning the seam with the bodice side, with adequate measurements and ease.
- Lower the sides of the sleeve by the same measurements of the bodice.
- Draw a curved line from the sides of the sleeve to the sleeve head, 5 cm/1.97" below the point lowered.
- Slash along this line and open by the same measurements, as shown in figure.
- Shape the sleeve head and connect the sides.

Square armscye sleeve

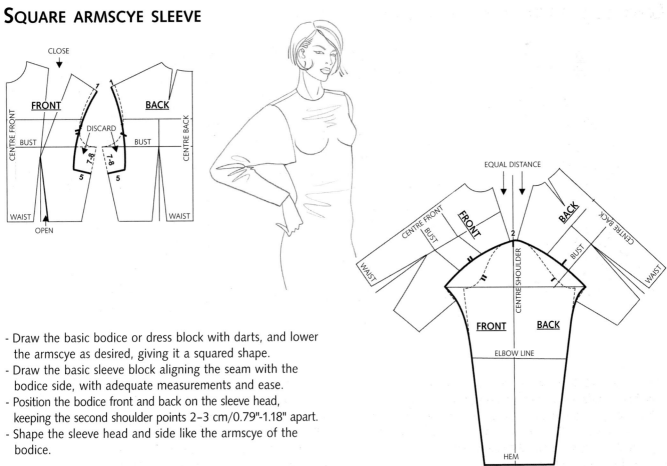

- Draw the basic bodice or dress block with darts, and lower the armscye as desired, giving it a squared shape.
- Draw the basic sleeve block aligning the seam with the bodice side, with adequate measurements and ease.
- Position the bodice front and back on the sleeve head, keeping the second shoulder points 2–3 cm/0.79"-1.18" apart.
- Shape the sleeve head and side like the armscye of the bodice.

SET-IN SLEEVE

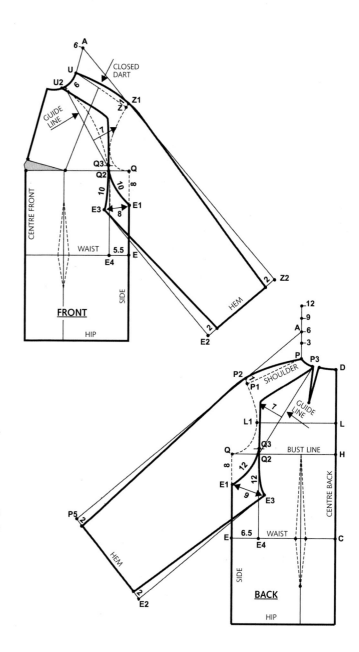

This type of sleeve is made starting from the raglan sleeve construction, changing the way it is joined to the bodice, to look like the one shown in the sketch.

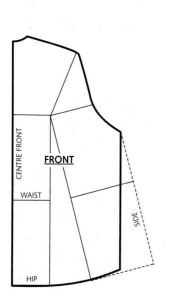

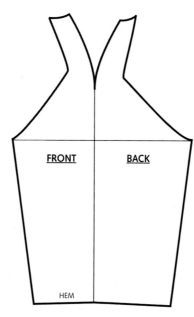

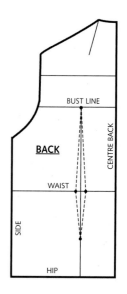

Raglan sleeve joined to the yoke

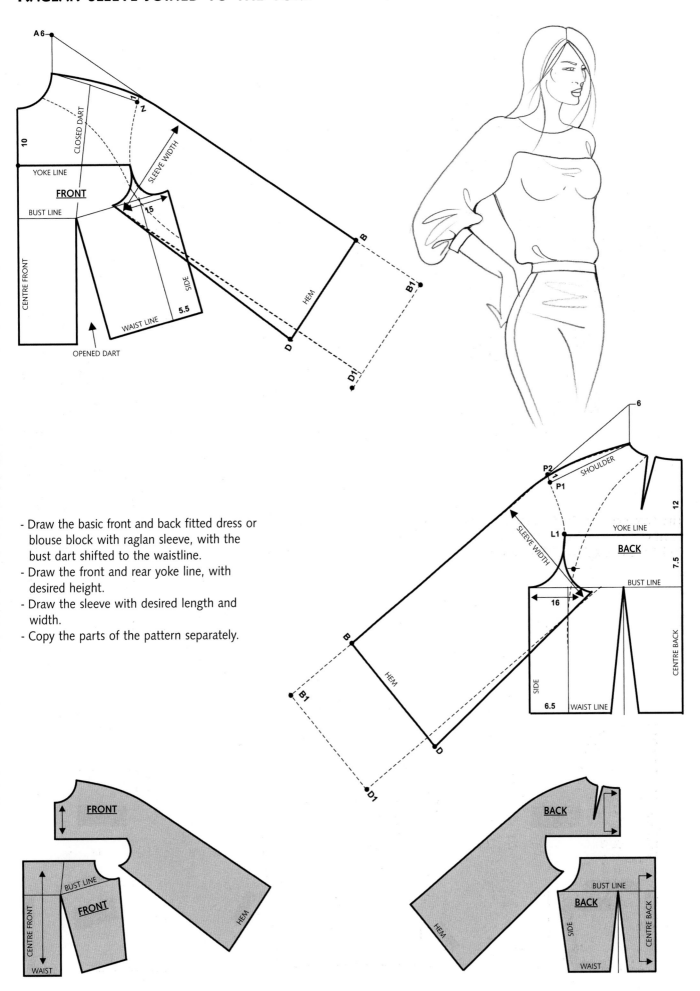

- Draw the basic front and back fitted dress or blouse block with raglan sleeve, with the bust dart shifted to the waistline.
- Draw the front and rear yoke line, with desired height.
- Draw the sleeve with desired length and width.
- Copy the parts of the pattern separately.

Raglan sleeve joined to front panel

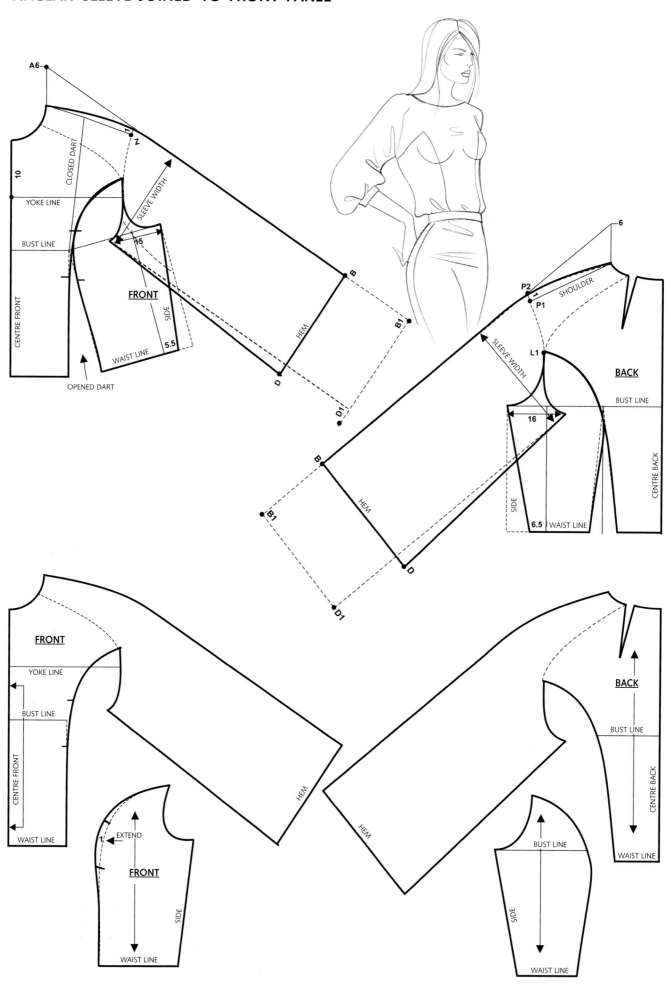

DROPPED SHOULDER

CONSTRUCTION WITH FITTED SLEEVE

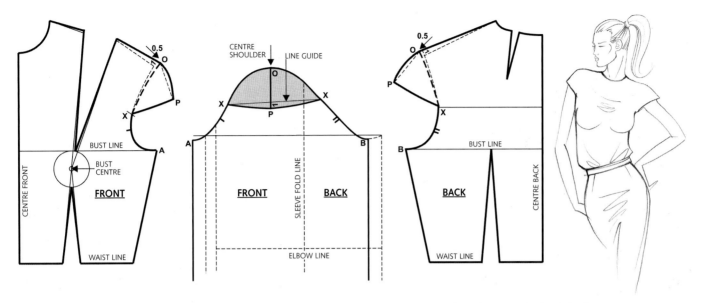

- Draw the basic bodice with or without.
- Draw the basic fitted sleeve block corresponding to the bodice, aligning the seam with the bodice side.
- Draw the point X at the same point on the front and back, midway on the armscye or in the position desired.
- Draw A–X on the front of the sleeve head, the same length as on the front bodice, and B–X on the back of the sleeve

head, the same length as on the back bodice.
- Draw the guideline joining the X points, and create the X–P–X curve, dropping 1 cm/0.39" at the centre.
- Separate the parts of the top of the sleeve, front and back, as drawn, and keep Point O 0,5 cm/0.19" away from the second shoulder point.
- Carefully draw the curve of the O–P line.

CONSTRUCTION WITH RAGLAN SLEEVE

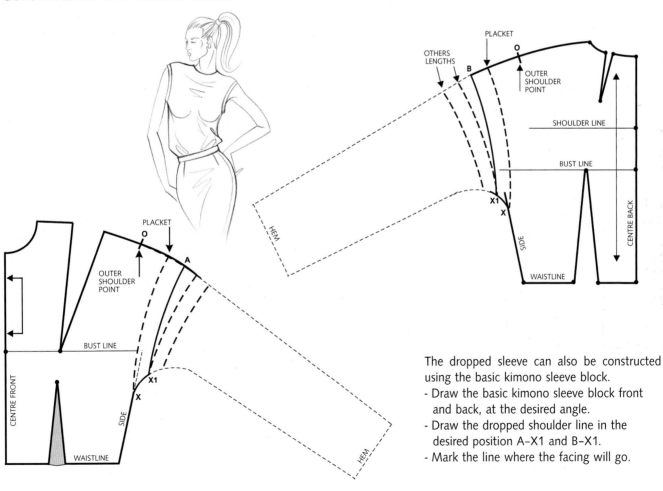

The dropped sleeve can also be constructed using the basic kimono sleeve block.
- Draw the basic kimono sleeve block front and back, at the desired angle.
- Draw the dropped shoulder line in the desired position A–X1 and B–X1.
- Mark the line where the facing will go.

141

Casual shirt sleeve

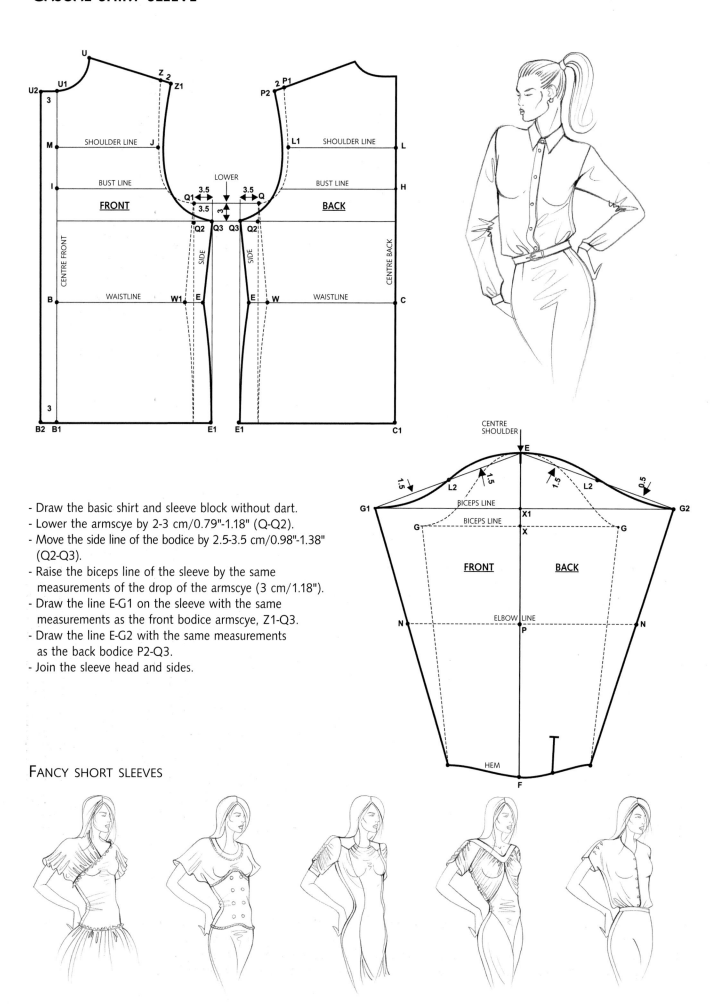

- Draw the basic shirt and sleeve block without dart.
- Lower the armscye by 2-3 cm/0.79"-1.18" (Q-Q2).
- Move the side line of the bodice by 2.5-3.5 cm/0.98"-1.38" (Q2-Q3).
- Raise the biceps line of the sleeve by the same measurements of the drop of the armscye (3 cm/1.18").
- Draw the line E-G1 on the sleeve with the same measurements as the front bodice armscye, Z1-Q3.
- Draw the line E-G2 with the same measurements as the back bodice P2-Q3.
- Join the sleeve head and sides.

Fancy short sleeves

PLEATED SLEEVES

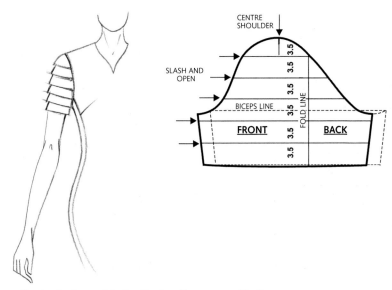

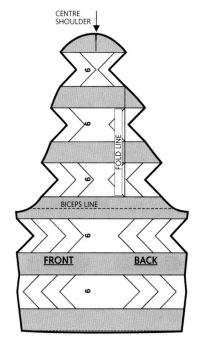

- Draw the basic sleeve block, aligning the seam with the bodice side.
- Draw the lines of the cross-folds, as needed, or following the suggestions of the sketch.
- Slash along these lines and separate the parts by twice the depth of the desired pleat (e.g. 6 cm), pasting them in parallel on another sheet of paper.
- Shape the edges as shown in figure.

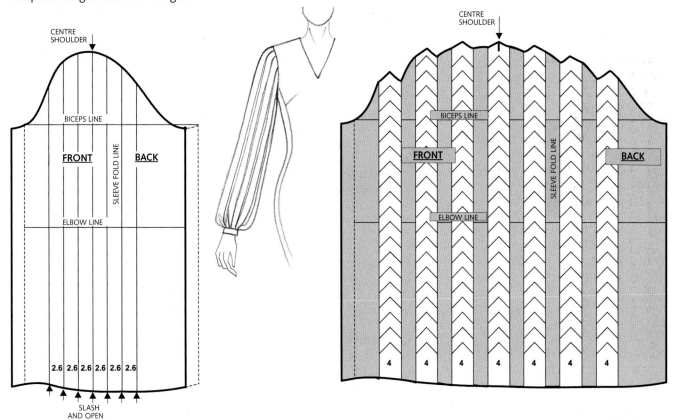

- Draw the basic sleeve block, aligning the seam with the bodice side.
- Draw the lines of the vertical folds, as needed, or following the suggestions of the sketch (from 1 to 7 pleats).

- Slash along these lines and separate the parts by twice the depth of the desired pleat (e.g. 4 cm), pasting them in parallel on another sheet of paper.
- Shape the edges as shown in figure.

FANCY SLEEVES

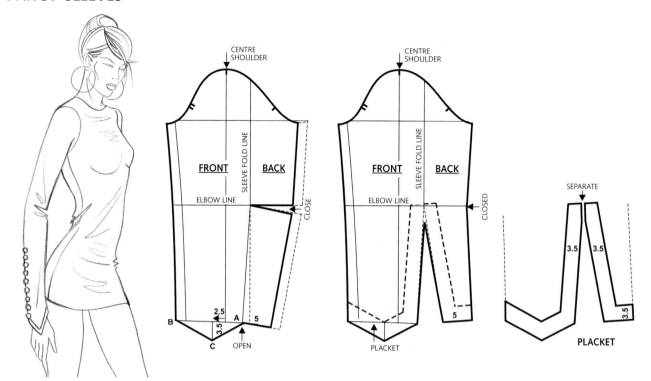

- Draw the basic fitted sleeve block, tapered towards the wrist, aligning the seam with the bodice side.
- Draw a line from the tip of the elbow dart to 5 cm/1.97" from the back seam (point A).
- About 2-2.5 cm/0.79"-0.98" from the centre shoulder line,

draw an extension of 3-3-5 cm/1.18"-1.38", and join A–B–C.
- Close the elbow dart and open one at the hemline.
- Draw the internal facing.
- Copy the facing and separate the parts.

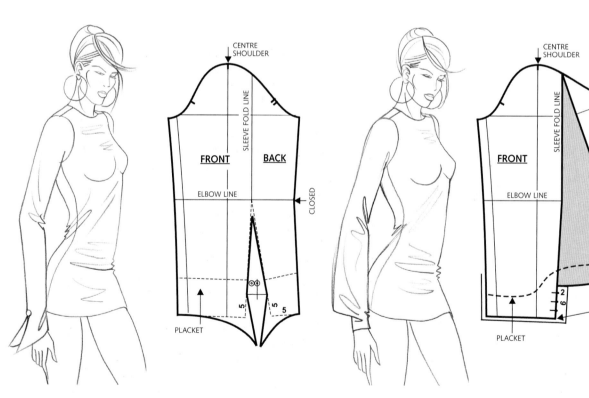

- Draw the basic fitted sleeve block, tapered towards the wrist, aligning the seam with the bodice side.
- Close the elbow dart and open one at the hemline.
- Copy the profile of the hemline, extending the sides of the dart and shaping them as in figure, or as desired.
- Draw the facing.

- Draw the basic fitted sleeve block, tapered towards the wrist, aligning the seam with the bodice side.
- Close the elbow dart and open one at the hemline.
- Widen the sleeve from top to bottom by 20-24 cm/7.87"-9.45", along the fold line.
- Draw the extensions for the fastening and the facing.

LINGERIE AND KNITWEAR

KNIT FABRICS

Knit fabrics can be made either by weft knitting, where a single strand of yarn is worked across the width of the fabric, or warp knitting, when a series of yarns are worked longitudinally in adjacent columns with respect to the fabric produced.

Weft knitting employs three principal stitches: stockinette stitch, which can be made to produce flat fabrics, also known as jersey or tubular fabric; purl stitch, and rib knit stitch.

Knit fabrics have captured a significant share of the market in the garment sector, and nearly all the stylists have a knitwear line in their collections, sportswear, casuals, and even elegant attire.

In fact, knits can be made with natural or synthetic fibres; they can be placed in collections targeted at either very high-end or very low-end markets; the knit fabric's capacity to stretch both in length and in width, and then to return to its original state, simplifies the pattern-making process with a better adaptability to the figure.

For the peculiarity of its composition, this fabric is easy to work with as it does not fray, it is comfortable to wear and it does not get rumpled.

There are various type of knit fabrics: compact and stable knits; single and light knits; structured knits; elasticized knits with two-way stretch; ribbed knits.

Compact and stable knits – This type of knit is not very elastic and should be treated like orthogonal woven fabric. This group also includes double knits characterized by longitudinal ribs on both sides. It is hard to distinguish the right side from the wrong side if there is not a decorative pattern. Raschel knits (run-resistant) use a lace-like open stitch process; they are not elastic because the longitudinal columns are blocked in some stitches of the knit. Some Raschel knits are made with thick, heavy yarns and seem like bouclé fabric or hand-knitting. Others are made with finer yarns and seem crocheted.

Single and light knits – They have small longitudinal ribs on the right side and rings that run crosswise on the back. If you pull the transversal edge of a single knit, it will curl on the right side. Single knits like jersey, tricot, and interlock are not elastic in length, but they will give when pulled crosswise.

Structured knits – These can be single or double knit. This category stands out for the structured surface, usually on the right side. Terrycloth knits and velour are knit fabrics with nap that resembles their woven counterparts; in any case, they are usually very elastic widthwise. Knits for pullovers are also classified in this category. Jacquard knits for pullovers have loose threads on the wrong side; these are the coloured yarns that are shifted from one motif to another. This process limits the crosswise elasticity. Fleece knits are pleasant to wear, on the right side they seem a single knit fabric, while on the wrong side the surface is soft and napped. They are usually rather stable and not stretchy in any direction.

Two-way stretch knits – they have a high percentage of elastic fibres. Cotton or cotton/polyester stretch knit fabrics are ideal for sportswear like bodysuits and aerobic gym suits. Elasticized nylon knits remain stretchy even when wet, and are favoured for swimwear.

Ribbed knits – This is a very stretchy kind of knit, which can be used for tops and for edging knit apparel at the wrists, the ankles, the neckline, and the waist line. A special kind is the tubular knit, which is also sold in small pieces and can be cut open along a longitudinal rib. Another kind is the ribbed knit for borders, colour-coordinated with the knit for pullovers; one edge is finished, the other must be sewn to the garment.

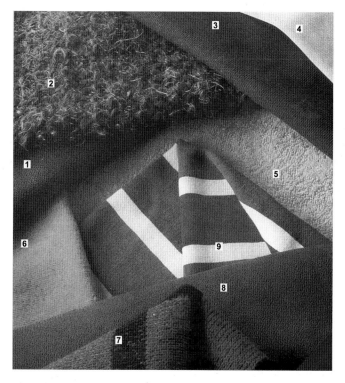

1) Double knit.
2) Raschel knit (run-resistant).
3) Jersey.
4) Tricot.
5) Terrycloth knit.
6) Velour.
7) Knit for pullovers.
8) Fleece knit.
9) Stretch knit.

THE ELASTICITY OF KNIT FABRICS

Patternmakers must be well-informed about the special qualities of knit fabrics and, in particular, about their coefficient of stretch and recovery, in order to calculate the ease to give the garment and to obtain a product suited to the requirements of comfort.

A fabric's capacity for elongation and stretch is a determinant factor for comfort, fit, stability and durability of garments.

Stretch and recovery factor

A knit fabric's stretch factor is expressed in a percentage that refers to the original length and the extension in centimetres that can be obtained under maximum tension.

The extension can range from 20% to 100% of the initial length.

A knit fabric's recovery factor is the degree and the capacity that it has to return to its original state after undergoing strong tension stress. A good knit should return easily to the original dimensions, otherwise the fabric will slacken and bags will form.

Resistance to traction with measurement of the extension and the recovery

Weft knit fabrics, for their high deformability, do not lend themselves to the execution of strip tests of traction resistance. Only warp knits with strong stability characteristics are subjected this kind of test. Cut five strips from the fabric, each precisely 50 mm/0.20" in length, in the direction of both the columns and the rows, at a certain distance from the selvages.

The strips are subject to traction on a dynamometer for fabrics so as to determine the load and stretch to breaking point. The average breaking point must not be inferior to the value established by the manufacturer, stated on the label.

For an immediate and simpler test for the patternmaker and garment maker, in the absence of precise indications, we can achieve some knowledge about a fabric's elasticity through a manual procedure of measurement, carried out as follows:

1) Fold the fabric crosswise for 8–10 cm/3.15"-3.94".
2) Insert two pins in the fold, 10 cm/3.94" apart.
3) Stretch the fabric and measure with a ruler how much longer it gets, exerting a moderate force, between the two pins.
4) The distance between the two pins after releasing the stretch can be checked to see if the fabric has become deformed.

Stretch fabrics

Fabrics made with elasticized yarns are generally classified in two main categories: high elasticity fabrics and ones with average elasticity.

Spandex-based yarns are nearly always mixed with other fibres and they are often incorporated in fabrics together with other yarns.

The primary purpose of spandex fibres is to obtain elasticity and holding power. And for this reason what type of yarn is used in the fabric and how, and in what quantity is all determined by the garment's construction, the weight of the fabric, its stretchability, and the desired holding power.

Stretchiness is the main characteristic of spandex, along with holding power, and in fact spandex fibres can stretch from 400 to 700%, that is from 4 to 7 times their length at rest, before breaking.

The most elastic spandex fibres are Glospan S-5 and Cleerspan, which show a 700% stretch capacity, while Lycra registers a stretch capacity ranging between 400 and 625%.

To obtain sufficient holding power to be the basis for such garments as: corsets and girdles, stretch ski pants, swimsuits, and other sportswear, a stretchabilty of 30–50% is recommended, with a loss of elastic recovery of no greater than 5-6%.

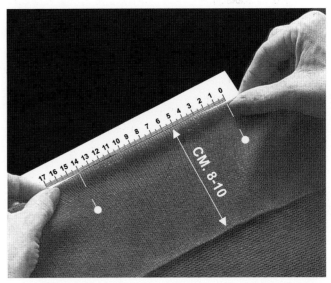

Manual test of the elasticity of a knit fabric with a stretchability of 40%. The pins are fixed 10 cm/3.94" apart with the fabric at rest.

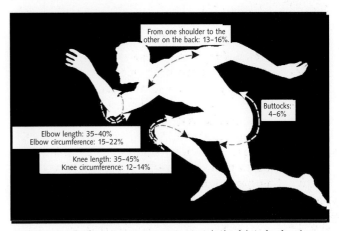

Body positions where it is necessary to stretch the fabric for freedom of movement and comfort when wearing the garment.

LINGERIE

Women's lingerie has since ancient times represented an essential part of clothing.

In 3000 B.C. the Sumerians depicted women with thongs or briefs very similar to our undergarments today.

In ancient Rome there were leather garments very similar to our present-day bras, called *mamillare* or *strophium*, the purpose of which was to hold the breasts without compressing.

In the 1500s underwear was used by the courtesans as a means of seduction; and at this time the garter emerged, used for ornamental purposes.

In 1880 the corset, already used in the preceding centuries, became an icon and a symbol of women's lingerie.

In the first decade of the 1900s the bra came to be, a light sheath wrapping around the chest to the waist or below, with sheer fabrics and lightweight, pink-coloured canvas.

In the 1920s women wore the bandeau bra, which flattened the breasts, and to hold up their stockings, there was the garter, worn at mid-thigh.

In the 1930s the most widely-used undergarment was the petticoat, and there was a transition from silk panties to cotton briefs, either white or black.

In the late thirties, with the advent of nylon, there were stockings and other undergarments, to be worn under tight skirts.

In recent decades, lingerie has undergone many changes, with innovation and creation of new garments, increasingly luxurious and sexy. We have bodysuits, matched sets, falsies, push-ups and other shapewear, and other items, light and comfortable.

With each new season, the designers present us with new and ever more seductive styles.

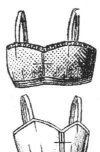

Bras from the 1920s

Briefs from the 1920s

MAIN PANTY STYLES

The line or the style of panties is defined and characterized by essentially two factors: the leg opening and the height of the sides.

The main styles:

1) *Normal panties* – moderately high cut, with elastic at the waist line.

2) *French-cut panties* – high waisted, high cut.

3) *High-waisted, wider side panels* – covers the hips and the tummy.

4) *Thong* – Similar to a very high-cut panty, but with just a narrow strip in back that leaves the bottom cheeks completely bare. It is used especially with very snug-fitting dresses and pants.

5) *Tanga* – a panty that leaves the bottom cheeks completely bare; it is very high cut and high-waisted.

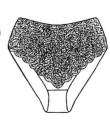

Normal panties   *French-cut panties*   *High-waisted, wider side panels*

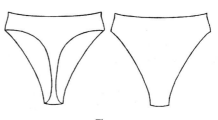

Thong   *Tanga*

FUNCTIONAL PANTIES

MAXI HIPSTERS

Maxi hipsters are high-waisted panties that cover the buttocks and the hips. They feature coverage and control of the bottom and tummy.

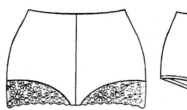 

Elegant maxi hipsters   *Sports maxi hipsters*

GIRDLE

The girdle is the progenitor of intimate apparel for shaping the figure.

It offers very strong control and binds the body from the waist to the upper part of the thighs.

Girdles differ from Maxi hipsters in that they feature more controlling power.

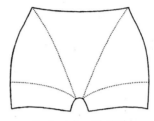 

Panty girdle with thigh coverage   *Short panty girdle*

SHAPING BRIEFS

Shaping briefs are high waisted for tummy control, and the back and sides are full for hip and bottom control. They are made with elasticized fabric or elasticized inserts.

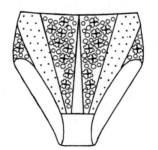 

Shaping briefs

PUSH-UP BRIEFS

This type of panties lifts and shapes the buttocks; it is high-waisted and has wide hip panels; it controls the hips and the tummy. The stretch fabric is doubled in the back where with its "V" shape, it surrounds the lower part of the buttocks, creating an upward thrust.

Push-up briefs

SUSPENDERS

Created in the early 1900s when the corset fell into disuse, suspenders or the garter belt were used to hold up stockings at thigh height.

With the emergence of pantyhose, suspenders also fell into disuse, but at the end of the 1970s, they came back into fashion for their erotic value.

Band-style suspenders   *Belt-style suspenders*

FORMS AND TYPES OF BRA

The bra is an undergarment that characterizes femininity and women's seductiveness.

This garment has ancient origins; in fact, already in some Egyptian graffiti some women wearing bras can be seen.

From the perspective of patternmaking, the bra has quite a particular structure and can be made up of as many as thirty pieces.

There are many types of bra, with different features and purposes.

After the success of Push-up bras (which make use of special angling and structuring that enhance and show off the breasts) and structured bras (with underwires and padding that determine the shape of the breast), classical, discreet models that highlight the breast volume yet have a natural look are coming back in vogue.

The latest technology has produced bras inflated with air, sculpted with gel, put together without sewing, even equipped with microchips, making every décolleté a compromise between the laws of physics and engineering applications to modify and correct the natural bustline.

Some bras are made with new materials, such as, for example, the cups that take the shape of the breast and keep it, even after washing; or those that are made of special fibres that are shaped thanks to body heat; or, again, those with cups provided with relief features that perform shiatsu-type massage; or sports bras that, thanks to the microchips and synthetic polymers, respond to changes in tension and force as the wearer swims.

   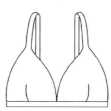 

| Without underband | With underband | Double structure bra | Triangle bra | Double shoulder strap control bra |

UNDERWIRE STYLES

| Classical | 3-piece cup | Balconette with shoulder straps | Strapless balconette | Shoulder straps crossed in back |

The padding, usually of a material similar to foam rubber, helps provide volume to those who have smaller breasts. The underwire and the padding lift the breast, highlighting the décolleté.

The fabric is given the form of the breasts, so the cups do not have seams.
The underwire guarantees effective support; it is well-matched with lightweight and snug-fitting clothes.

Sports bras are designed for exercising and working out. They have to support the breasts while permitting freedom of arm movement, and avoiding chafing or constriction during races.

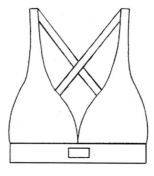

It is a comfortable bra and easy to wear. The straps may be adjustable and crossed in the back; it provides support.

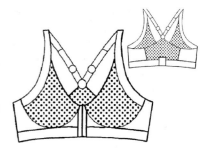

CORSETS AND BODYSUITS

BUSTIER

The bustier is the descendant of the older corset, but without its rigidity and uncomfortableness.

Today the bustier holds the figure with soft ribbing and reaches only as far as the waist, leaving the hips free; it contains the bust and shows it off, and is primarily used as an arm of seduction.

There are various styles of bustier, with different necklines and different types of bra, with or without shoulder straps.

BASQUE (GUÊPIÈRE)

The Basque, invented in 1945 in the wake of Dior's New Look, squeezes the abdomen to achieve a "wasp waist" effect.

It is a bustier that features garters, and is fastened in the back by a series of hooks. There is ribbing that models the figure, and underwires help to support the breasts.

Today it is only used for special occasions and has a unmistakably seductive purpose.

BODYSUIT

The bodysuit derives from the bustier and the corsage.

It shapes the body and supports the breasts, with gentle pressure. The bodysuit can be with or without straps; with or without sleeves; the leg opening is more or less high; the neckline more or less deep, heart-shaped, square, round, balconette-style, etc.

The uses of the bodysuit are various:

- For gymnastics or dance – based on Olympics-type costumes, with rounded neckline, shallow front and more accentuated behind; with or without sleeves.
- As a fashion complement – to be worn as external clothing, with a skirt or trousers, to complete the look; or as intimate apparel, combining in a single garment panties and bra.

There are various types of bodysuit, with various necklines, with or without straps and with various types of bra and panties:

1) Bodysuit with wireless bra.
2) Bodysuit with underwire bra.
3) Bodysuit with strapless bra.
4) Bodysuit with Push-up bra.
5) Bodysuit with contour bra.
6) Bodysuit with balconette bra.

SHAPER

The shaper is a particular type of bodysuit that, while not having ribbing that compresses, cinches the waist, supports the breasts, helps to straighten the back, and shapes the figure.

The shaper thus performs a sort of therapeutic function, thanks to new materials, and is also comfortable and functional for the aesthetics of the body.

There are various types of shaper, but the most popular are:

1) Low-cut shaper, which contains the upper thigh and, with the double layer in front, gently compresses the abdomen. The special linings under the breasts and side reinforcements can also support very full breasts

2) Average-cut shaper, with the same characteristics as above, but the elastic panel for the abdomen is more extensive.

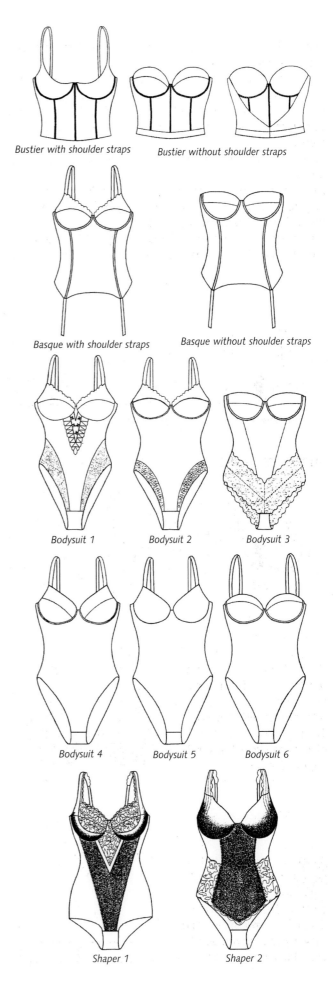

Bustier with shoulder straps   Bustier without shoulder straps

Basque with shoulder straps   Basque without shoulder straps

Bodysuit 1   Bodysuit 2   Bodysuit 3

Bodysuit 4   Bodysuit 5   Bodysuit 6

Shaper 1   Shaper 2

T-SHIRT BASIC BLOCK

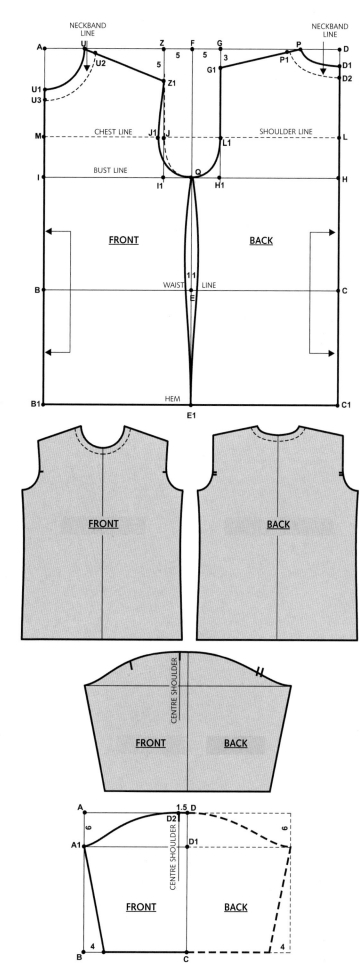

Bodice

- Draw a rectangle A-B-C-D with:
- A-B front waist measurement (e.g.: 41.5 cm/16.34").
- B-C semicircumference bust + ease 18 cm/7.09"
  (e.g.: 92 + 18 cm/7.09" = 110 : 2 = 55 cm/21.65").
- C-D1 back waist measurement (e.g.: 40 cm/15.75").
- B-E half B-C. A-F like B-E.
- Draw E-F (Side Centre).
- D1-H half C-D1.(e.g.: 40 : 2 = 20 cm/7.87").
- Draw H-I (Bust Line).
- F-G 5 cm. F-Z like F-G.
- Draw G-H1 and Z-I1. (J-J1 1 cm/0.39").
- H-L 1/3 of D1-H (e.g.: 20 : 3 cm/1.18" = 6.6 cm).
- Draw L-M parallel to H-I (Chest and shoulder lines).
- Z-Z1 5 cm/1.97". G-G1 3 cm/1.18".
- Draw the Armhole or Armscye Z1-J1-Q-L1-G1
  shaping it carefully.
- A-U 1/6 Shoulder width. (e.g.: 36.5 + 1.5 = 38 : 6 = 6.3 cm).
- Draw an arc U-U1 with the A-U measurement and the
  centre in A.
- D-P like A-U. Join P-D1.
- B-B1 extension knit as desired (18-20 cm/7.09"-7.87").
- Draw B1-C1. (Hem line).

Sleeve

- Draw a rectangle A-B-C-D with:
- A-B equal to the Sleeve length.
- B-C equal to 2 x underarm section - 2 cm/0.79".
  (e.g.: 10 cm x 2 = 20 - 2 = 18 cm).
- A-A1 6 cm/2.36".
- D-D2 1.5 cm/0.59" (Centre shoulder).
- Make a smooth run and make two copies of the sleeve.
- Check the sleeve head with the armscye.

Tank top basic block

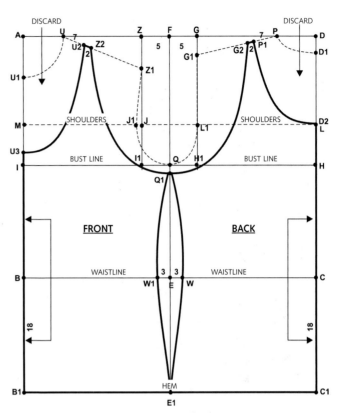

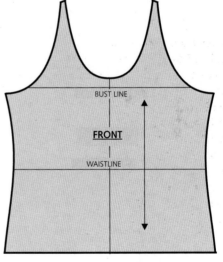

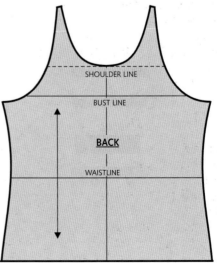

Draw the basic T-shirt block, using bust circumference + 0-4 cm/0"-1.57" ease.

Front
- U1-U3 15 cm/5.91" or as desired.
- U-U2 7 cm/2.76".
- U2-Z2 2 cm/0.79" or as desired.
- Q-Q1 2 cm/0.79".
- E-W1 3 cm/1.18" or based on the waist.

Back
- D1-D2 13 cm/5.12" or as desired.
- P-P1 like U-U2.
- P1-G2 like U2-Z2.
- E-W like E-W1.
- Join the lines as shown in the figure.

T-SHIRT WITH SHORT KIMONO SLEEVES

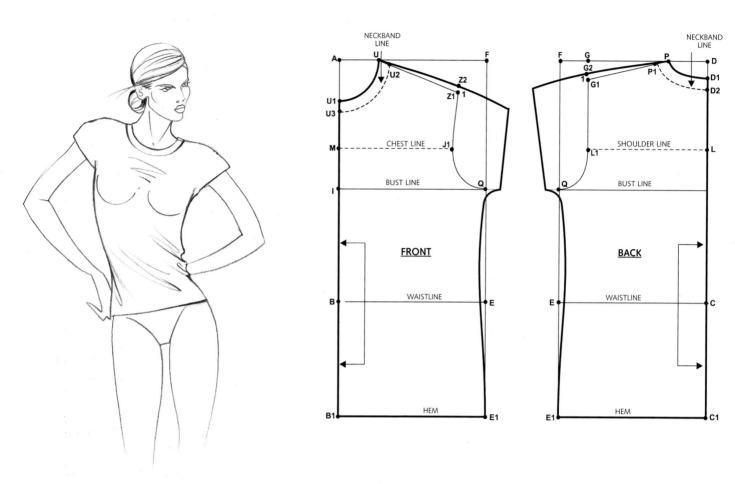

T-SHIRT WITH SHORT RAGLAN SLEEVES

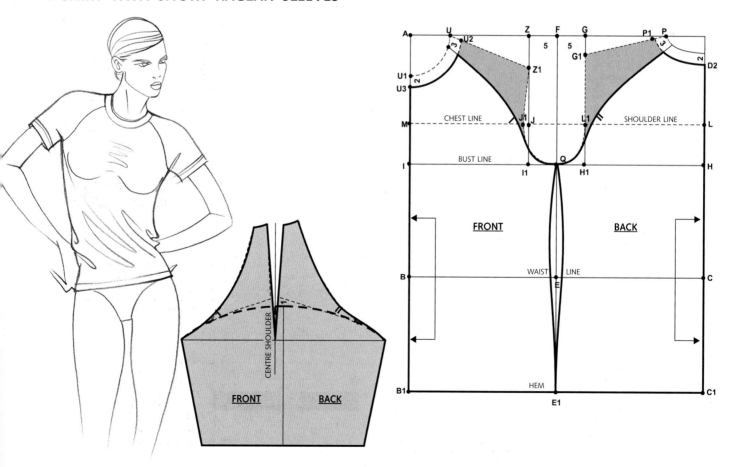

SWEATSHIRT WITH RAGLAN SLEEVES

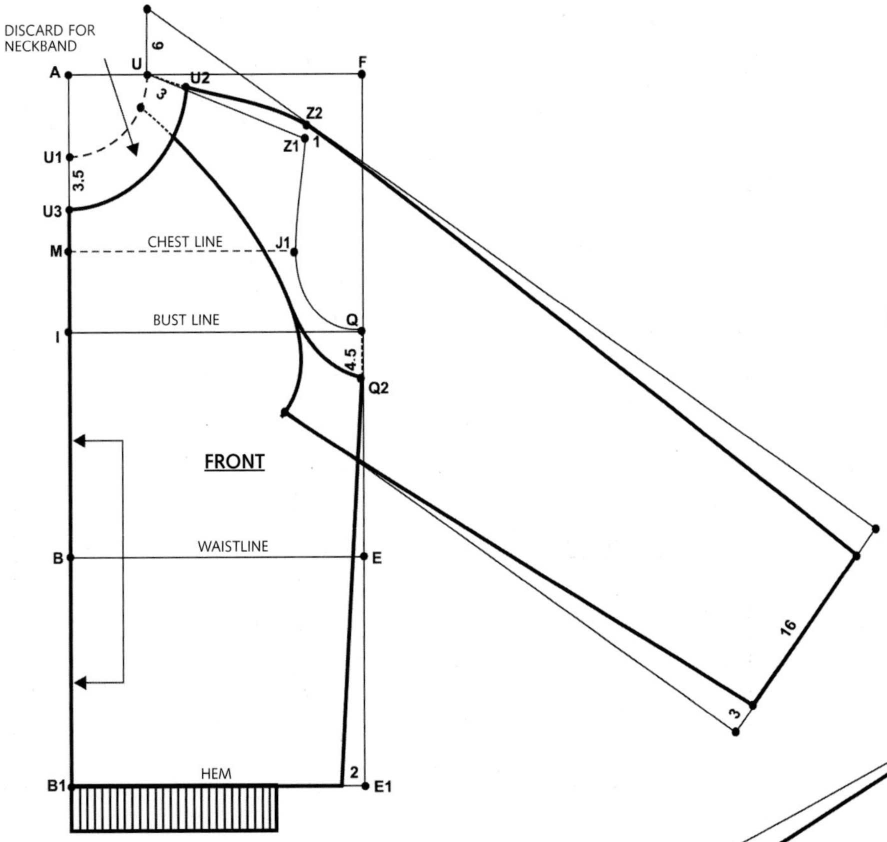

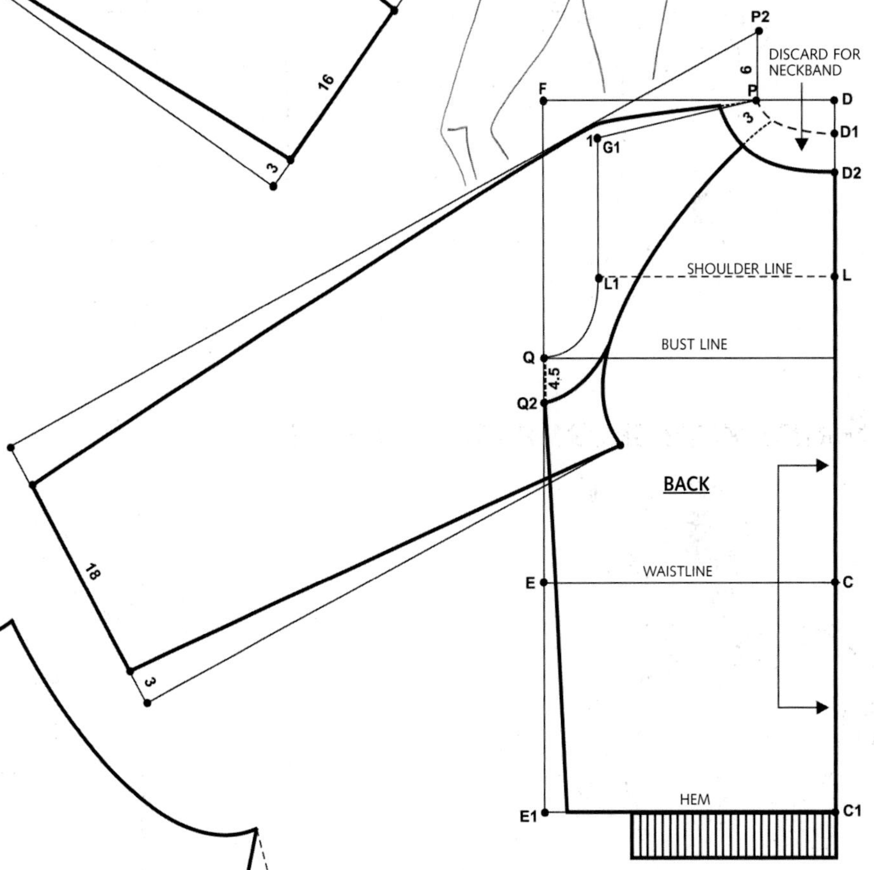

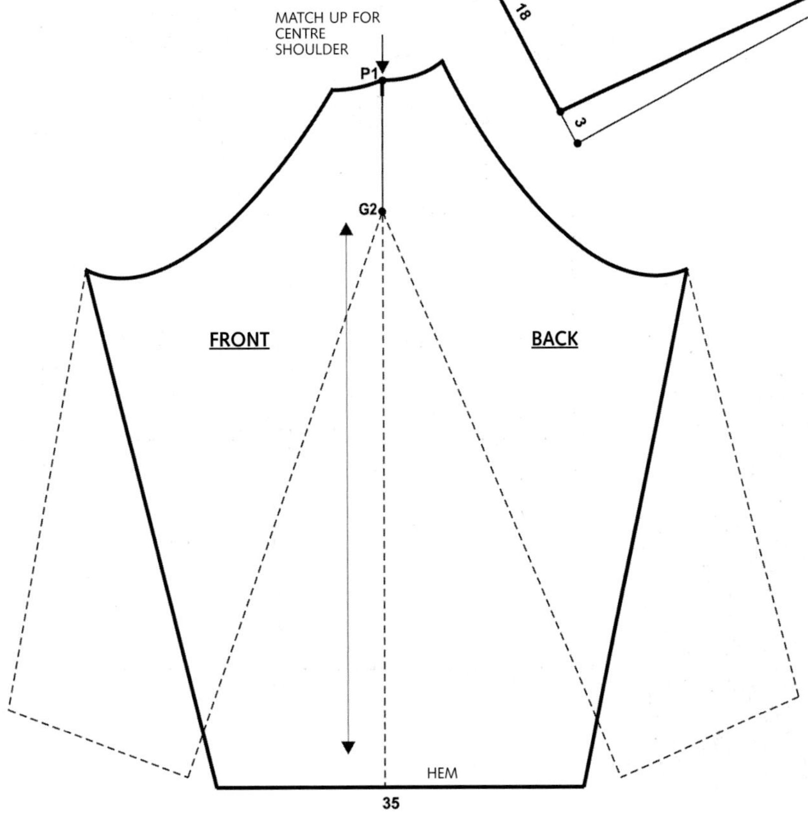

DISCARD FOR
NECKBAND

6

A   U   U2   F

3

Z2

U1   Z1   1

3.5

U3

M   CHEST LINE   J1

BUST LINE

I   Q

4.5

Q2

FRONT

B   WAISTLINE   E

16

3

B1   HEM   E1   2

P2

DISCARD FOR
NECKBAND

F   P   6   D

3

1   G1   D1

D2

L1   SHOULDER LINE   L

Q   BUST LINE

4.5

Q2

BACK

18

E   WAISTLINE   C

E1   HEM   C1

3

MATCH UP FOR
CENTRE
SHOULDER

P1

G2

FRONT   **BACK**

HEM

35

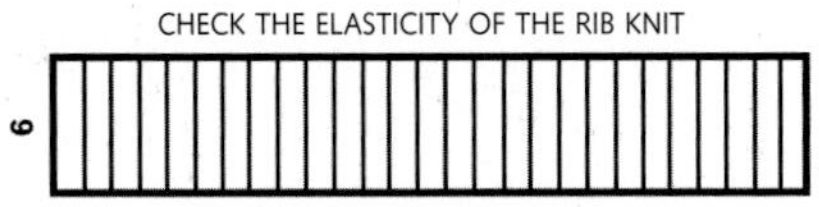

CHECK THE ELASTICITY OF THE RIB KNIT

6

RIB KNIT NECKBAND

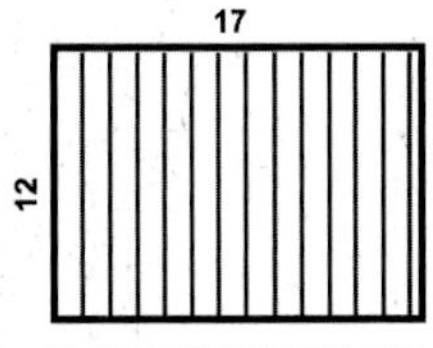

17

12

RIB KNIT WRISTBAND

KNIT JACKET

KANGAROO POCKETS

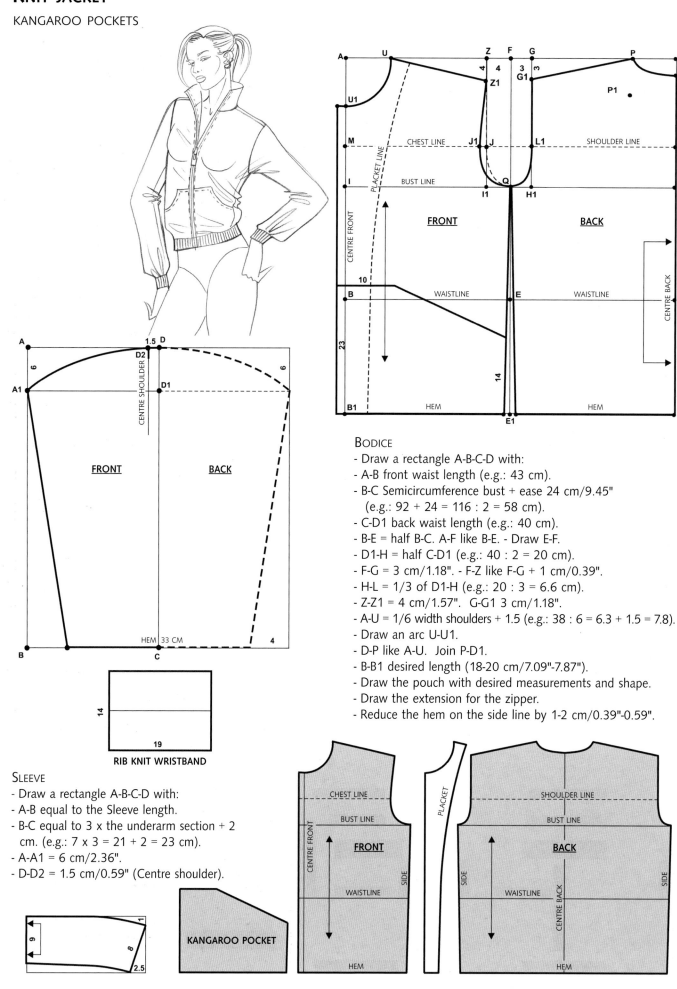

RIB KNIT WRISTBAND

KANGAROO POCKET

BODICE
- Draw a rectangle A-B-C-D with:
- A-B front waist length (e.g.: 43 cm).
- B-C Semicircumference bust + ease 24 cm/9.45"
  (e.g.: 92 + 24 = 116 : 2 = 58 cm).
- C-D1 back waist length (e.g.: 40 cm).
- B-E = half B-C. A-F like B-E. - Draw E-F.
- D1-H = half C-D1 (e.g.: 40 : 2 = 20 cm).
- F-G = 3 cm/1.18". - F-Z like F-G + 1 cm/0.39".
- H-L = 1/3 of D1-H (e.g.: 20 : 3 = 6.6 cm).
- Z-Z1 = 4 cm/1.57". G-G1 3 cm/1.18".
- A-U = 1/6 width shoulders + 1.5 (e.g.: 38 : 6 = 6.3 + 1.5 = 7.8).
- Draw an arc U-U1.
- D-P like A-U. Join P-D1.
- B-B1 desired length (18-20 cm/7.09"-7.87").
- Draw the pouch with desired measurements and shape.
- Draw the extension for the zipper.
- Reduce the hem on the side line by 1-2 cm/0.39"-0.59".

SLEEVE
- Draw a rectangle A-B-C-D with:
- A-B equal to the Sleeve length.
- B-C equal to 3 x the underarm section + 2
  cm. (e.g.: 7 x 3 = 21 + 2 = 23 cm).
- A-A1 = 6 cm/2.36".
- D-D2 = 1.5 cm/0.59" (Centre shoulder).

Wide-shoulder sweatshirt

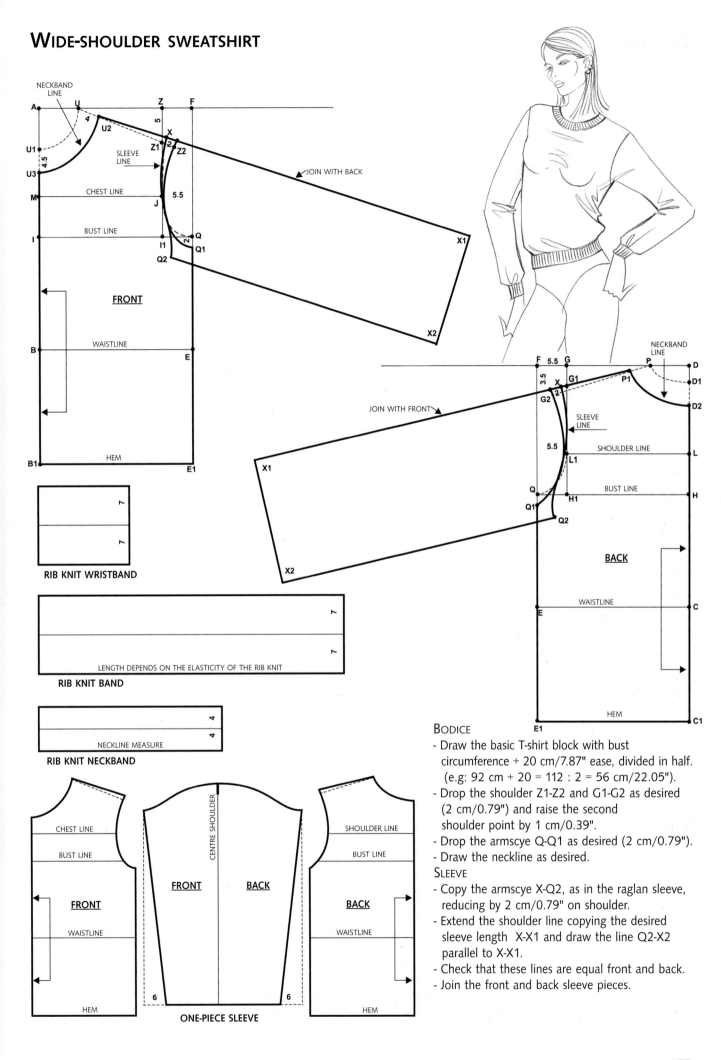

FRONT

NECKBAND LINE

A U Z F
4
U2
Z1 X Z2
5
U1
SLEEVE LINE
4.5
U3
CHEST LINE
M J
5.5
BUST LINE
I I1 Q
2 Q1
Q2
JOIN WITH BACK
X1
X2

WAISTLINE
B E
HEM
B1 E1

RIB KNIT WRISTBAND
7
7

RIB KNIT BAND
7
7
LENGTH DEPENDS ON THE ELASTICITY OF THE RIB KNIT

RIB KNIT NECKBAND
4
4
NECKLINE MEASURE

BACK

NECKBAND LINE

F 5.5 G P D
3.5
X G1 P1 D1
2
G2
D2
JOIN WITH FRONT
SLEEVE LINE
5.5
SHOULDER LINE
L1 L
Q BUST LINE
Q1 H1 H
Q2
X1
X2

WAISTLINE
E C
HEM
E1 C1

CHEST LINE
BUST LINE
FRONT
WAISTLINE
HEM

CENTRE SHOULDER
FRONT **BACK**
6 6
ONE-PIECE SLEEVE

SHOULDER LINE
BUST LINE
BACK
WAISTLINE
HEM

Bodice
- Draw the basic T-shirt block with bust circumference + 20 cm/7.87" ease, divided in half. (e.g: 92 cm + 20 = 112 : 2 = 56 cm/22.05").
- Drop the shoulder Z1-Z2 and G1-G2 as desired (2 cm/0.79") and raise the second shoulder point by 1 cm/0.39".
- Drop the armscye Q-Q1 as desired (2 cm/0.79").
- Draw the neckline as desired.

Sleeve
- Copy the armscye X-Q2, as in the raglan sleeve, reducing by 2 cm/0.79" on shoulder.
- Extend the shoulder line copying the desired sleeve length X-X1 and draw the line Q2-X2 parallel to X-X1.
- Check that these lines are equal front and back.
- Join the front and back sleeve pieces.

Cardigan sweater

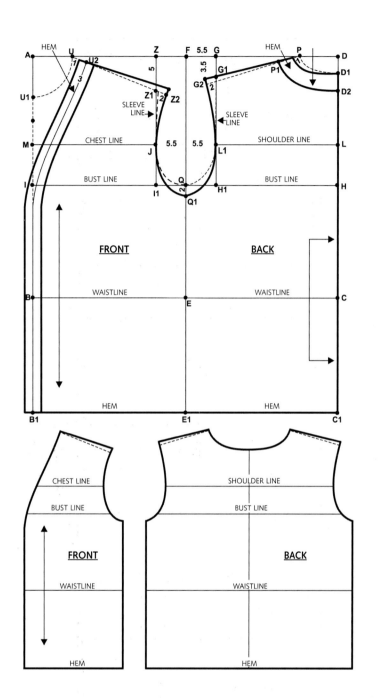

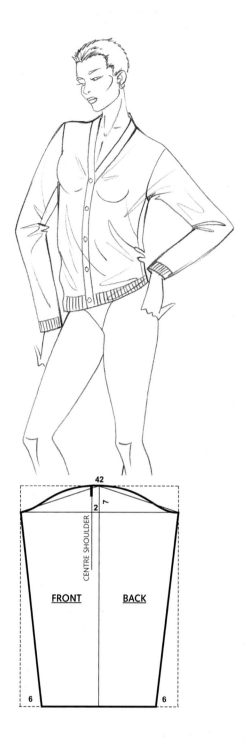

BODICE HEM BAND

SLEEVE CUFF BAND

BODICE
- Draw the basic T-shirt block with bust circumference + 20 cm/7.87", ease divided in half.
  (e.g.: 92 cm + 20 = 112 : 2 = 56 cm/22.05").
- Drop the shoulder Z1-Z2 and G1-G2 by 2 cm/0.79" and raise the second shoulder point by 1 cm/0.39".
- Drop the armscye Q-Q1 as desired (2 cm/0.79").
- Draw the neckline and the edge on front and back.
- Separate the parts.

SLEEVE
- Draw the sleeve like that of the T-shirt, with desired length.

RIB KNIT BANDS
- Make two copies of the rib knit band patterns, with lengths adjusted for the elasticity of the fabric.

UNITARD BASIC BLOCK

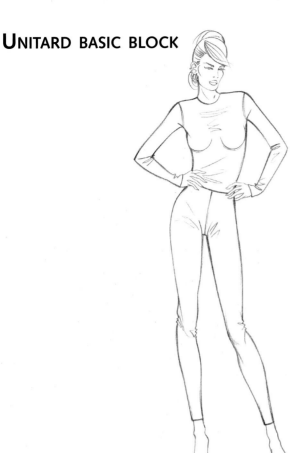

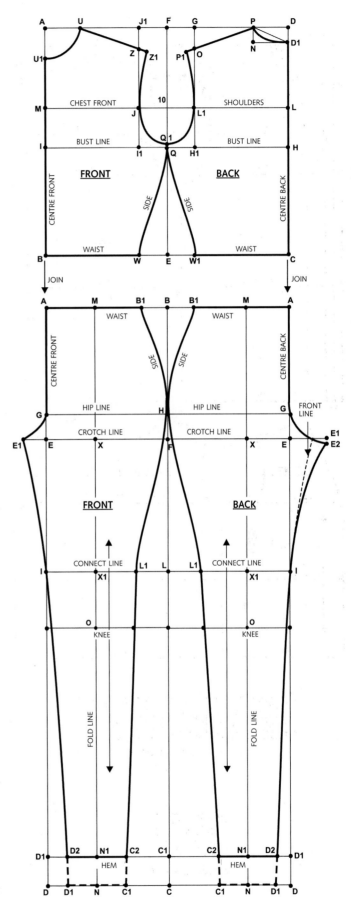

BODICE

- Draw a rectangle A-B-C-D.
- A-B = front waist length minus 1-3 cm/0.39"-1.18" based on the elasticity (e.g.: 43 - 3 = 40 cm).
- B-C = half of the bust circumference - 2 cm/0.79" (or more based on the elasticity) (e.g.: 92 - 2 = 90 : 2 = 45 cm).
- C-D1 = back waist length - 2.5 cm/0.98" (e.g.: 40 - 2.5 = 37.5 cm).
- B-E = half B-C. - A-F = like B-E. - Draw E-F.
- D1-H = half C-D1.
- Draw H-I. BUST LINE.
- D-G = half shoulders width - 1.5 cm/0.59" (e.g.: 36.5 - 1.5 = 35 : 2 = 17.5 cm).
- Draw G-H1.
- A-J1 = like D-G. - Draw J1-I1.
- H-L = 7 cm/2.76". Draw L-M (chest and shoulder line).
- G-O = 4 cm/1.57". Draw P-P1 passing through O. Shoulder's width (e.g.: 13 cm).
- J1-Z like G-O. Draw U-Z1 passing through Z. Same length as P-P1 (13 cm/5.12")
- Q-Q1 1 cm. Draw the Armscye Q1-J-Z1 and Q1-L1-P1, shaping it carefully.
- A-U = 1/3 of A-J1 + 0.5 cm/0.20" (e.g.: 7.5 : 3 = 5.8 + 0.5 = 6.3 cm).
- A-U1 like A-U minus 0.5 cm/0.20".
- D-P like A-U (6.3 cm/2.48").
- D-D1 2.5 cm/0.98". P-N like D-D1.
- B-W ¼ Waist circum. - 0.5/0.20" (e.g.: 72 cm : 4 = 18 - 0.5 = 17.5 cm).
- C-W1 like B-W.
- Draw W-Q-Q1 and W1-Q-Q1.

LEGGINGS

- Draw the basic leggings block with the same measures as the bodice.
- Join the basic bodice block with the leggings one, matching the waist line, the back centre line and the front centre line.
- Make sure the waist lines are perfectly matched.

Sleeves for unitard basic block

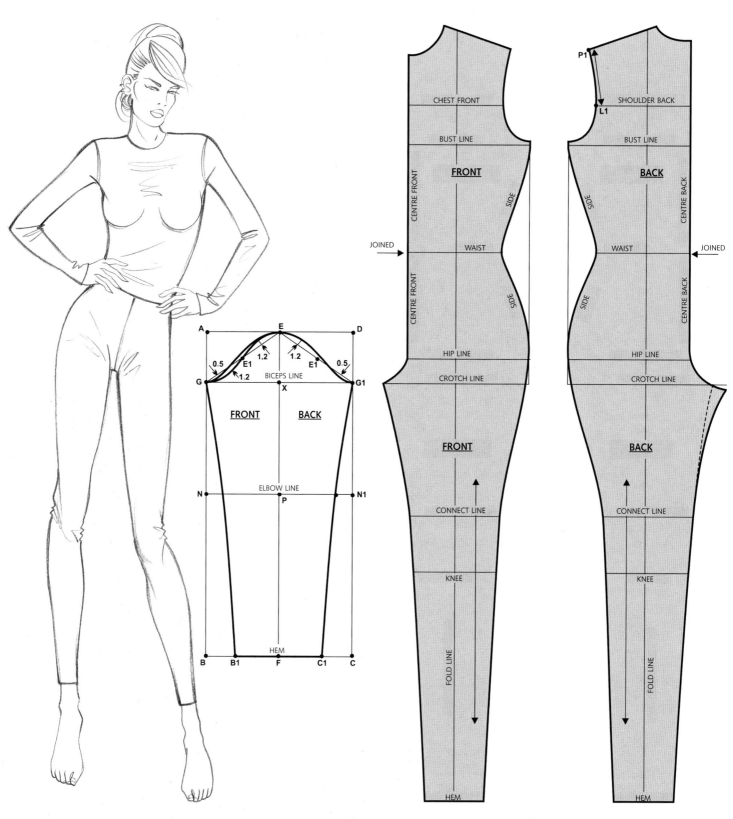

Measurements:
- Arm Circumference 29 cm/11.42".
- Ease for knit fabric.
- Arm length 58 cm/22.83".
- On the left hand side of a sheet of pattern paper, draw a rectangle A–B–E–F, with:
- A-E like bodice sector + 1/2 sector.
  (e.g.: 9.5 cm + 4.7 = 14.2 cm).

- A-B sleeve length measurement (e.g.: 58 cm/22.83").
- A-G = L1-P1 of the basic bodice back minus 1 cm/0.39"
  (e.g.: 10 - 1 = 9 cm/3.54").
- Draw G-X parallel to A-E.
- A-N = half A-B. ELBOW LINE.
- E-E1 = half G-E.
- Draw the front and back sleeve head as shown in figure.

UNITARD BASIC BLOCK

SEAMLESS SIDES

- Make the basic unitard block.
- Join the sides of the bodice front and back (Q1).
- Reduce the point B-B1 at the waist's centre front by the same measure as E-W.
- C-C1 like B-B1.

- Check Waist Circumference.
- Draw the F-N1 Side Seam.
- N1-D3 like C1-D1 on the back.
- N1-D2 like C1-D1 on the front.
- Check the total hem based on desired measurement.

BASIC BLOCK FOR AEROBICS FULL BODYSUIT

SEAMLESS FRONT AND SIDES

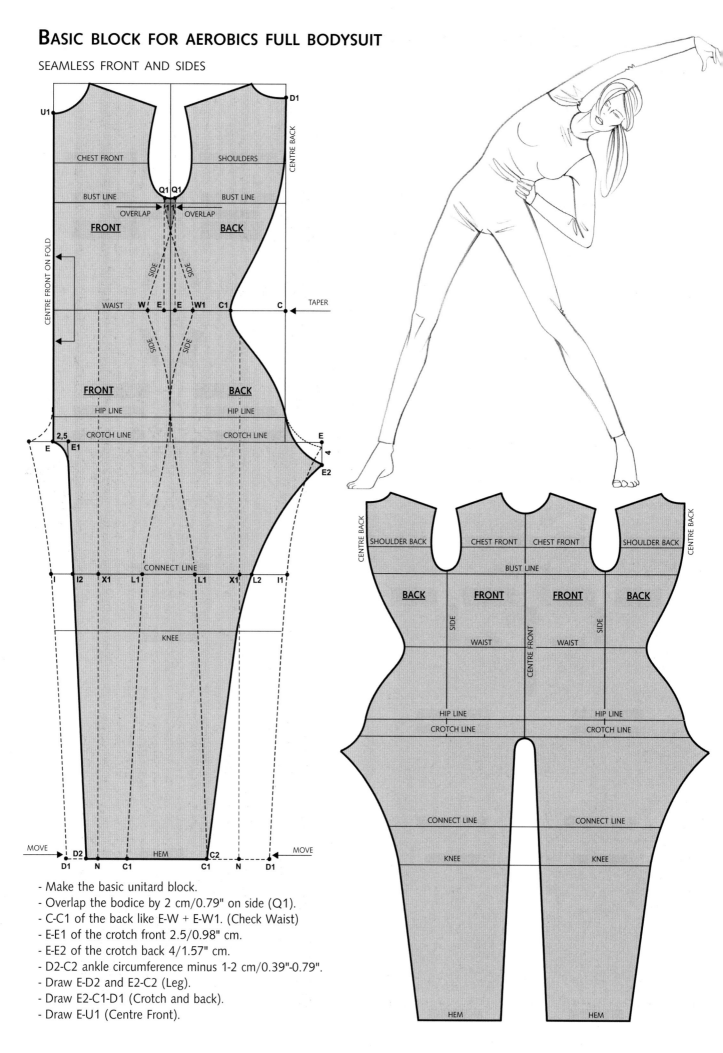

- Make the basic unitard block.
- Overlap the bodice by 2 cm/0.79" on side (Q1).
- C-C1 of the back like E-W + E-W1. (Check Waist)
- E-E1 of the crotch front 2.5/0.98" cm.
- E-E2 of the crotch back 4/1.57" cm.
- D2-C2 ankle circumference minus 1-2 cm/0.39"-0.79".
- Draw E-D2 and E2-C2 (Leg).
- Draw E2-C1-D1 (Crotch and back).
- Draw E-U1 (Centre Front).

BASIC BLOCK FOR BODYSUIT WITH DARTS

OR SWIMSUIT

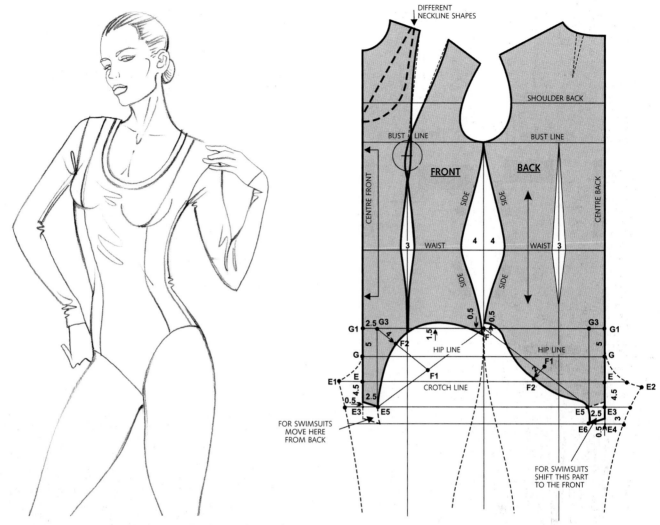

- Make the basic block for full bodysuit (bodice and pants) with darts, with ease from 0–10 cm/from 0"-3.94", based on the elasticity of the fabric.
- At the hip level, make the following modifications:
- G–G1 = 5 cm/1.97".
- Draw a line parallel to the hip line.
- E–E3 = 4.5 cm/1.77".
- Draw a line parallel to the crotch line.
- E3–E5 = 2.5 cm/0.98". Draw E5–G3.
- E3–E4 on back = 3 cm/1.18".
- E4–E6 on back, like E3–E5 (2.5 cm/0.98").
- Draw the diagonal E5–F.
- Mark point F1 midway between E5 and F.
- G3–F2 on front = 4 cm/0.78".
- F1–F2 on back = 2 cm/0.79".
- Draw the leg opening in front, E5–F2–F as shown in figure.
- Draw the leg opening in back, E6–F2–F as shown in figure.
- Raise point E3 in front and E6 in back by 0.5 cm/0.20" and connect the points.

Note: *The seam in the lower part of the bodysuit crotch is usually brought forward, for convenience in fastening.*
In the swimsuit it is moved toward the centre or the back, for a better look and greater comfort.

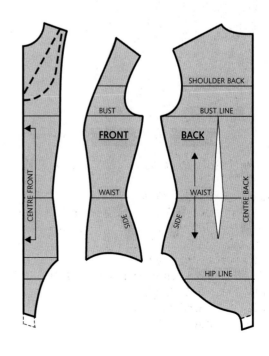

BASIC BLOCK FOR BODYSUIT WITHOUT DARTS

WITH FITTED SLEEVES

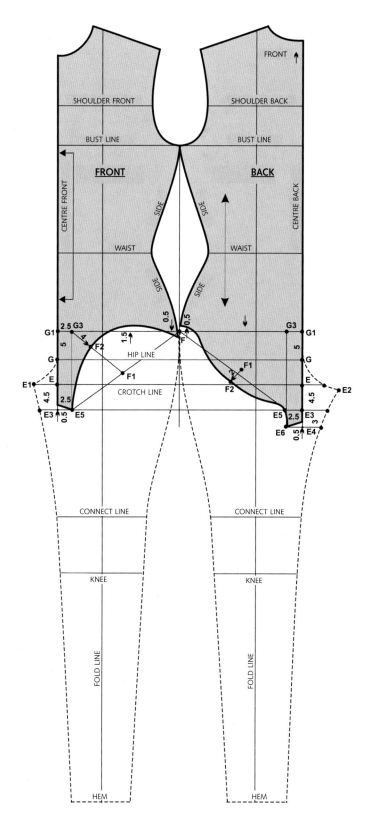

- Make the unitard basic block without darts and with ease suited to the type of knit fabric.
- At the hip level, make the following modifications:
- G–G1 = 5 cm/1.97".
- Draw a line parallel to the hip line.
- E–E3 = 4.5 cm/1.77".
- Draw a line parallel to the crotch line.
- E3–E5 = 2.5 cm/0.98". Draw E5–G3.
- E3–E4 on back = 3 cm/1.18".
- E4–E6 on back, like E3–E5 (2.5 cm/0.98").
- Draw the diagonal E5–F.
- Mark point F1 midway between E5 and F.
- G3–F2 on front = 4 cm/1,57".
- F1–F2 on back = 2 cm/0.79".
- Draw the leg opening in front, E5–F2–F as shown in figure.
- Draw the leg opening in back, E6–F2–F as shown in figure.
- Raise point E3 in front and E6 in back by 0.5 cm/0.20" and connect the points.

Basic tank suit block

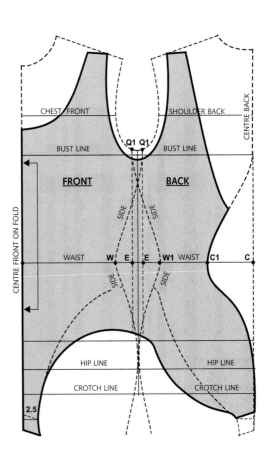

- Make the basic block for dartless bodysuit with ease suited to the elasticity of the knit fabric.
- Overlap the bodice by 2 cm/0.79" on side (point Q1).
- C–C1 on the back like E–W–+E–W1 (waist curves).
- Join centre back and the leg opening.
- Make the neckline and the armscye as ample as desired or according to the sketch.
- Position the pattern with the centre front on the fold, or make two copies of the pattern.

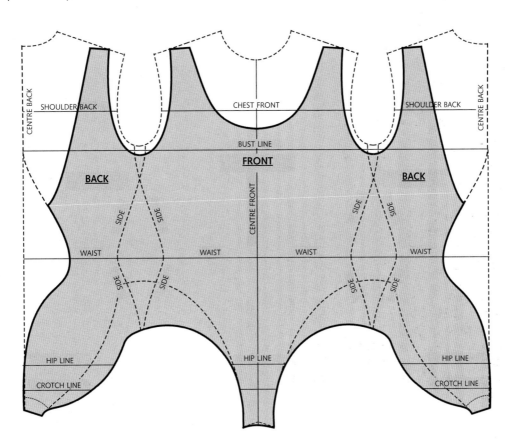

Two-piece knit gym set

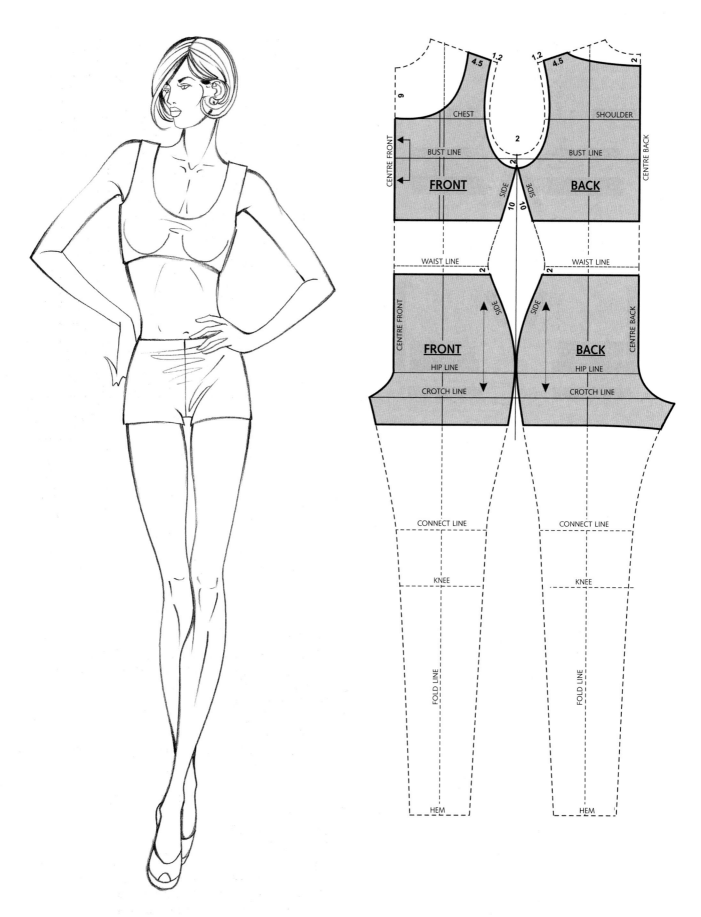

- Make the unitard basic block.
- Draw the bodice and tight-fitting culottes as shown in figure.

RAGLAN-SLEEVE BODYSUIT

HIGHER-CUT LEGS

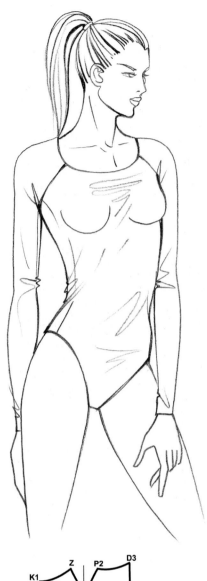

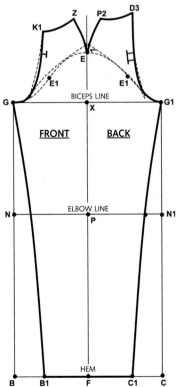

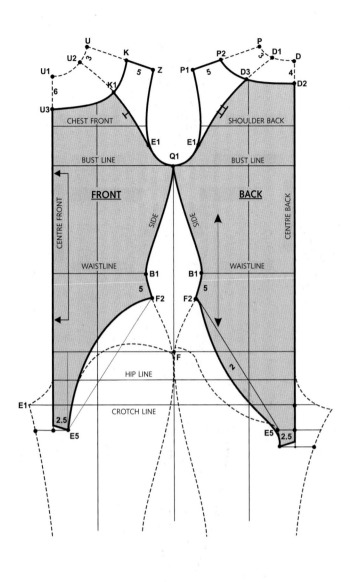

BODYSUIT
- Make the basic block for bodysuit with fitted sleeve.
- B1–F2 = 5 cm/1.97", or based on desired leg opening.
- Draw E5–F2 as shown in figure.
- U–U2 = 3 cm/1.18".
- D1–P like U–U2.
- Q1–E1 = 5 cm/1.97".
- Draw Q1–E1–U2 in front, and Q1–E1–D1 in back.
- U1–U3 = 6 cm/2.36".
- K–Z = 5 cm/1.97".
- Draw U3–K based on the desired neckline.
- P1–P2 like K–Z.
- D–D2 = 4 cm/1.57".
- Draw D2-P2.

SLEEVE
- Make the fitted sleeve of the unitard.
- G-E1 and G1-E1 like Q1-E1 of the bodice.
- Copy the part of the front bodice E1-K1-K-Z, position it in front of the sleeve and connect as shown in figure.
- Repete the process with the back E1-D3-P2-P1.

167

Swimsuit with 2-piece bra

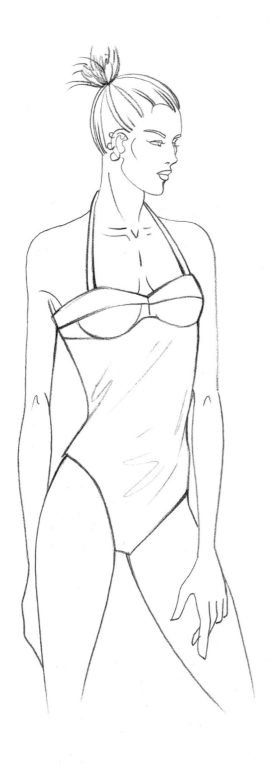

- Make the basic tank suit block or the basic bodysuit block with darts, allowing ease from 0–10 cm/from 0" to -3.94", depending on the elasticity of the fabric used.
- At the bust level, draw the form of the bra with a transversal slash, as shown in figure.
- Join this with the curve of the back décolleté, with desired shape and width.

TANKSUIT WITH RUCHING

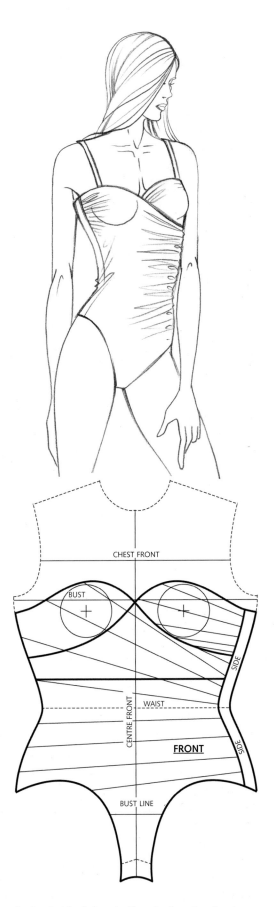

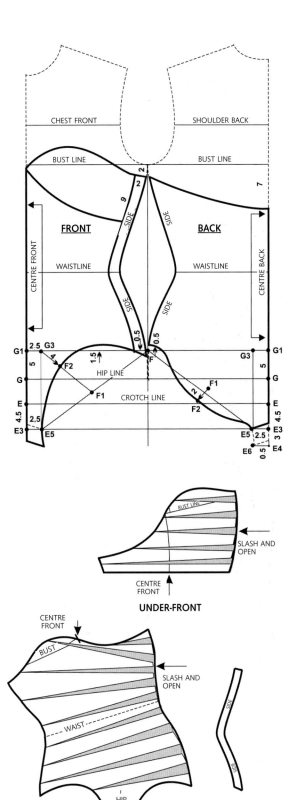

FRONT

BACK

CHEST FRONT

SHOULDER BACK

BUST LINE

BUST LINE

CENTRE FRONT

CENTRE BACK

WAISTLINE

WAISTLINE

HIP LINE

CROTCH LINE

UNDER-FRONT

CENTRE FRONT

SLASH AND OPEN

BUST LINE

OVER-FRONT

CENTRE FRONT

BUST

WAIST

HIP

SLASH AND OPEN

SIDE STRIP

SIDE

FRONT

CHEST FRONT

BUST

CENTRE FRONT

WAIST

SIDE

BUST LINE

- Make the basic block for dartless tank suit, allowing ease suiting the fabric.
- Draw the shape of the cuts based on the sketch as shown in figure.

- Copy the under-front and the over-front and draw lines across them as needed; slash and open to create the desired shirring.
- Copy the pattern without shirring for the lining.

BASIC BLOCK FOR PANTIES

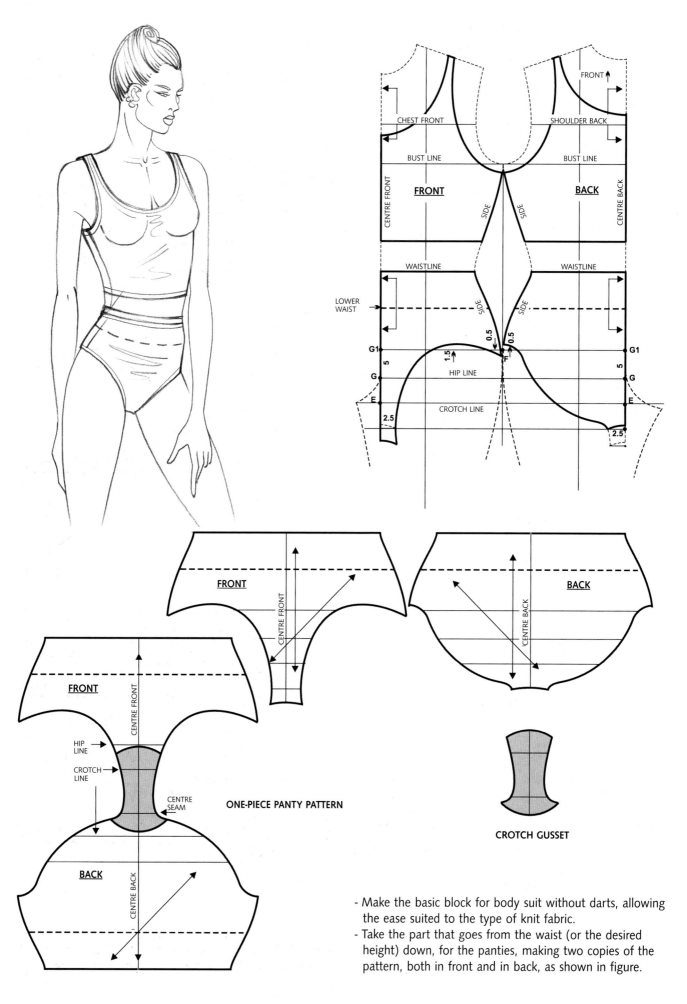

CHEST FRONT   **SHOULDER BACK**

FRONT↑

BUST LINE   BUST LINE

FRONT   **BACK**

CENTRE FRONT   CENTRE BACK

SIDE   SIDE

WAISTLINE   WAISTLINE

LOWER WAIST

SIDE   SIDE

0.5   0.5

G1   F   G1

5   1.5   5

G   HIP LINE   G

E   CROTCH LINE   E

2.5   2.5

FRONT   CENTRE FRONT

BACK   CENTRE BACK

FRONT   CENTRE FRONT

HIP LINE

CROTCH LINE

CENTRE SEAM

ONE-PIECE PANTY PATTERN

BACK   CENTRE BACK

CROTCH GUSSET

- Make the basic block for body suit without darts, allowing the ease suited to the type of knit fabric.
- Take the part that goes from the waist (or the desired height) down, for the panties, making two copies of the pattern, both in front and in back, as shown in figure.

BASIC BRA BLOCK

VERTICAL DARTS

- Draw the basic bodice block with darts, allowing zero or less ease, depending on the type of fabric.
- Mark the centre of the bust with point X.
- Draw a circle with X as its centre, allowing a radius of 6-7 cm/2.36"-2.76" (depending on the fabric and on the breast size).
- Draw the height of the centre front, the centre back, and the sides (keeping about 2 cm/0.79" under the armscye).
- Create a 1 cm/0.39" dart on the centre front, for better breast support.
- Widen the dart under the breast by 2 cm/0.79", and over it by 1 cm/0.39".
- Reduce the side seam by 0.5 cm/0.20" and that of the centre back by 2-2.5 cm.
- Neatly join all the lines as shown in figure.

HORIZONTAL SEAM

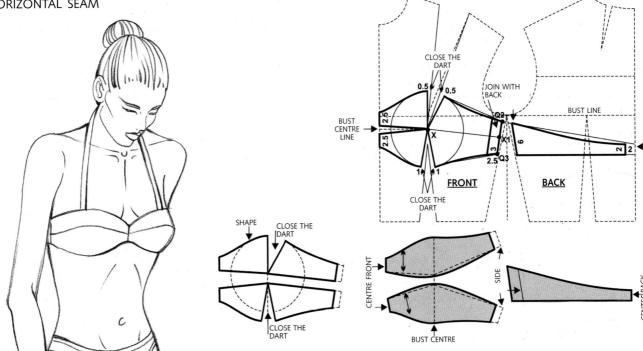

- Draw the basic block like the previous one.
- Draw the line X-X1 in the middle of Q2-Q3.
- Close the darts both above and below and neatly join the lines after dividing the two halves.
- To shift the side seam forward, remove 2.5-3 cm/0.98"-1.18" from the front side and add it to the back side seam.

BASIC BLOCK FOR BRAS

TRIANGLE BRA GATHERED AT BOTTOM

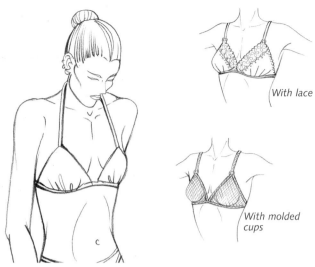

With lace

With molded cups

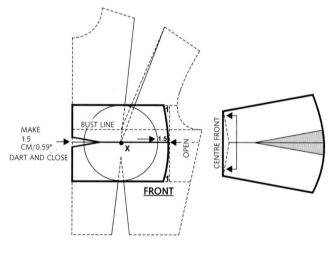

CLOSE THE DART

BUST CENTRE LINE

FRONT

OPEN THE DART

GATHER

- Close the shoulder dart, opening the waist dart.
- Draw the line U-X.
- Draw the bust circle based on the cup size and shape as shown in figure.

GATHERED IN THE CENTRE FRONT AND AT THE SIDES

This bra is a simple rectangle drawn around the circle of the bra cup, as shown in figure.
- Make a dart on the centre front and close it, opening another on the side, to create greater fullness on the side and less in the centre front.

MAKE 1.5 CM/0.59" DART AND CLOSE

BUST LINE

OPEN

FRONT

CENTRE FRONT

WITH LININGS

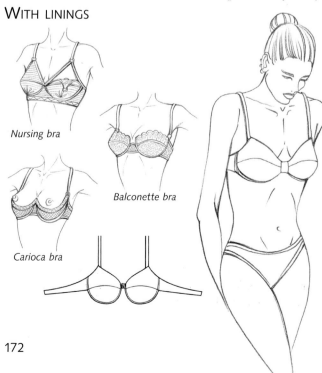

Nursing bra

Balconette bra

Carioca bra

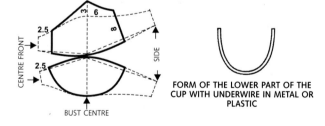

CENTRE FRONT

2.5

2.5

SIDE

BUST CENTRE

FORM OF THE LOWER PART OF THE CUP WITH UNDERWIRE IN METAL OR PLASTIC

- Make the basic block with horizontal seam.
- Shape the upper part as desired.
- Create the channelling for the underwire in the lower part of the cup.
- For Balconette bras, only the lower part is reinforced, while on the upper part there is just a band of lace.
- The Carioca is similar to the Balconette, but with nothing on the upper part.
- In the nursing bra, there has to be an opening on the upper part with a fastener such as buttons or the like.

FANCY BIKINI BOTTOMS

LOW-CUT BIKINI

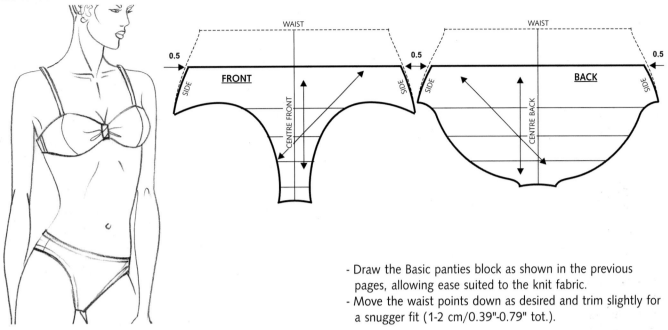

- Draw the Basic panties block as shown in the previous pages, allowing ease suited to the knit fabric.
- Move the waist points down as desired and trim slightly for a snugger fit (1-2 cm/0.39"-0.79" tot.).

CHEVRON BIKINI BOTTOM

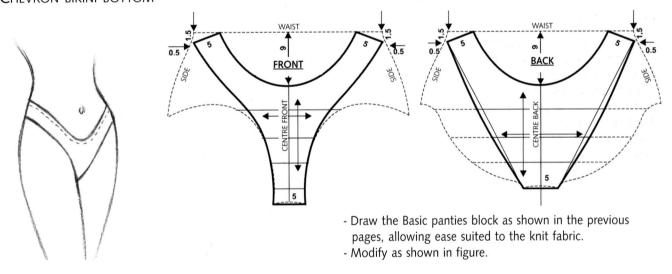

- Draw the Basic panties block as shown in the previous pages, allowing ease suited to the knit fabric.
- Modify as shown in figure.

CHEVRON BIKINI WITH RUCHING IN FRONT

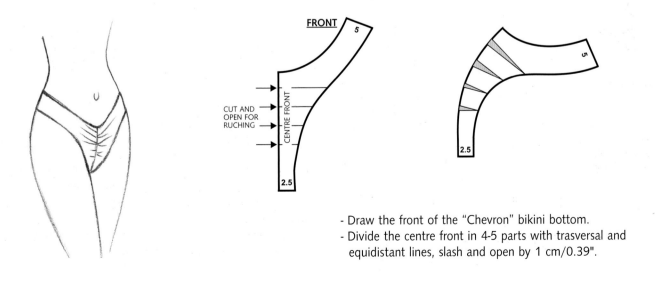

- Draw the front of the "Chevron" bikini bottom.
- Divide the centre front in 4-5 parts with trasversal and equidistant lines, slash and open by 1 cm/0.39".

Two-piece lycra swimsuit

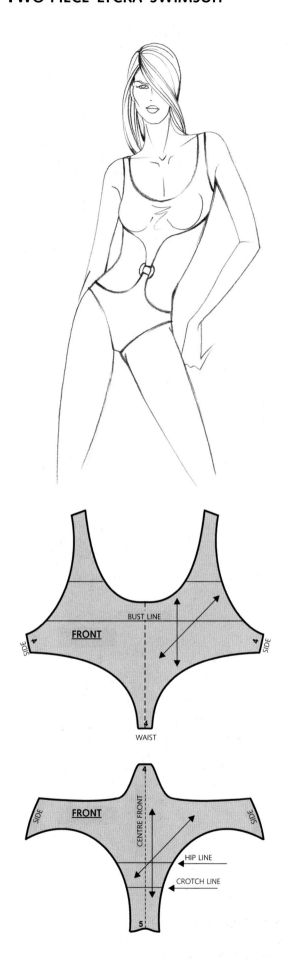

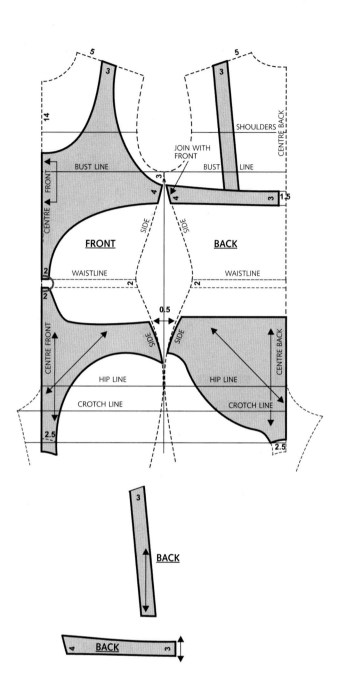

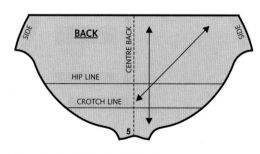

- Make the basic tanksuit block.
- Draw the bodice and the snug-fitting bottoms as shown in figure.

APPLICATION OF MOLDED CUPS

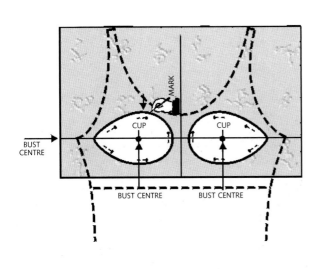

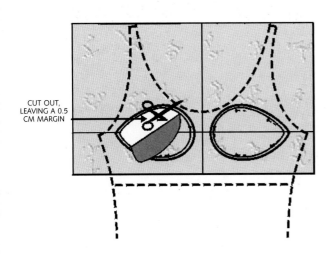

UNLINED CUP   LINED CUP

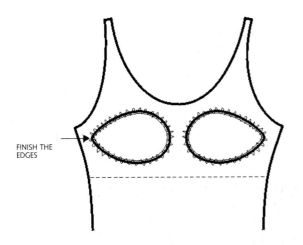

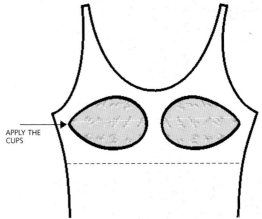

- Position the two cups on the pattern.
- Trace the outline of the cups.
- Cut out the outline drawn, leaving a margin of 0.5 cm/0.20" for finishing the edges.

- Carefully finish the border.
- Line the cups with the same fabric as the top.
- Apply the cups to the swimsuit.

French knickers

French knickers, culottes, are rather roomy women's underwear in the form of shorts, usually made of silk, but sometimes of cotton or synthetic fibres.

Culottes are often embellished with lace or embroidery.

Already in the 1700s in France ladies were wearing culottes, and they were snug-fitting pants that joined with silk stockings, these too quite snug, over the knee.

This style became outmoded with the advent of the *sans culottes*, the most ardent revolutionaries who dressed in contrast with the hated aristocrats.

Nowadays culottes are used both as lingerie and as a short pyjama, to be worn with a camisole made of the same fabric.

BASIC FRENCH KNICKER BLOCK WITH LACY INSERTS

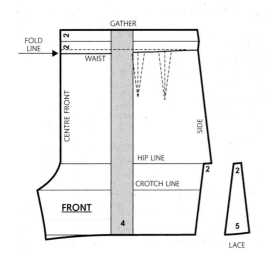

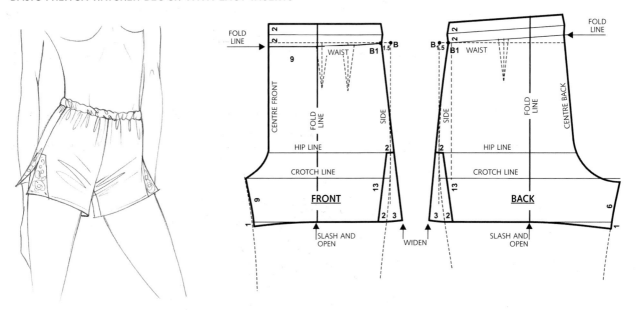

- Make the basic trousers block with darts, adjusting for the desired length.
- Eliminate the darts and discard into the sides 1-1.5 cm/0.39"-0.59".
- At the bottom hem of the front and back, at 1 cm/0.39".
- Widen the bottom hem by 3-4 cm/1.18"-1.57" on the front and back side seams.
- Make the extension for the elastic waistband, as desired.
- Slash along the fold line in the front and back, and open it

3-5 cm/1.18"-1.97" for fullness.
- Neatly join the lines at the waist as well as at the hem.
- If a lace insert is planned, mark the area in question, in this case on the side, showing the measurements desired and separate it in parts.

Culottes can even be made without a seam on the sides. In this case, join the front and back on the side seam.

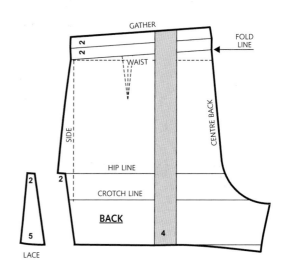

TULIP-SHAPED FRENCH KNICKERS

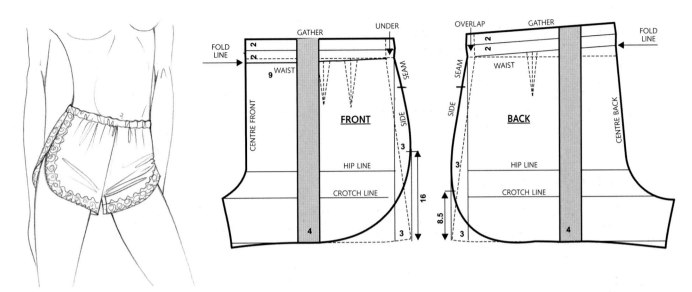

- Draw the basic French knickers block with the desired length.
- Extend the front and back side lines by 3-4 cm/1.18"-1.57" for overlap.

- Draw the rounded outline of the sides on both the front and the back.
- Make the curve of the back lower than that of the front, as shown in figure.

FRENCH KNICKERS WITH YOKE

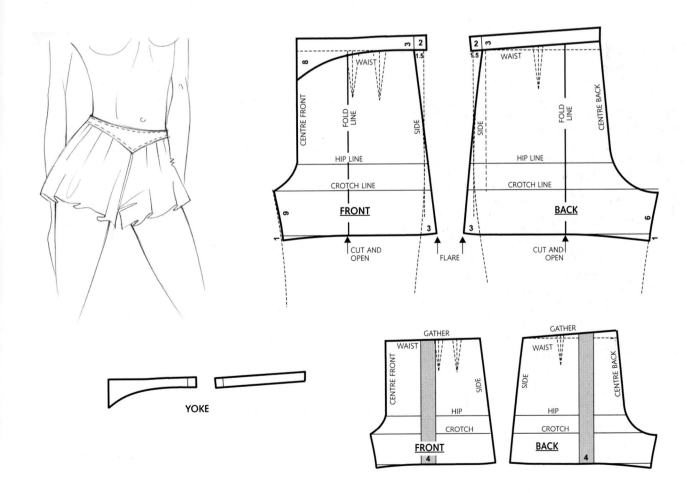

YOKE

MATERNITY BRIEFS

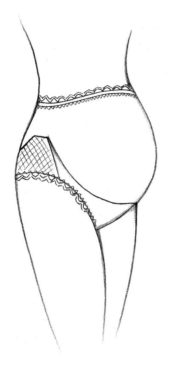

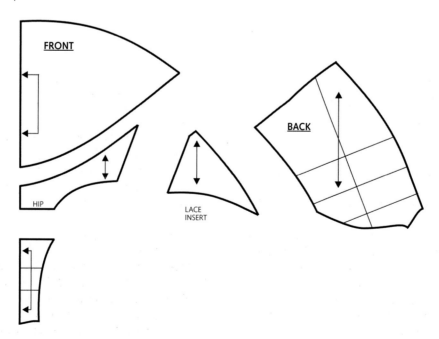

- Draw the basic panties block.
- Join the front and back on the side, overlapping them by 1 cm/0.39", as shown in figure.
- Move a part of the bottom of the back to the front.
- Join the leg opening as illustrated in figure, or according to the style.
- Extend the centre front by 8-9 cm/3.15"-3.54".
- Draw the lines for the cuts and the lace inserts as shown in figure, or according to the style.
- Copy all the pattern pieces.

Slips

1

2

3

4

The slip is the first lingerie garment to be worn next to the skin, and is usually made of silk, nylon or other lightweight fabrics, and trimmed with lace or various forms of embroidery. Form-fitting at the top, it flares slightly toward the hem, and is generally supported by two slender straps.

In antiquity, the slip was a garment worn by the Germans in direct contact with the skin.

In the Middle Ages it was a women's skirt to be worn underneath the actual gown; and in 1600s and 1700s it was quite extensively worn: ladies wore no less than two or even three of them under their dresses, in addition to the Farthingale, or guardinfante, all to make their clothing very full, as was the fashion.

In our own times, it resurfaced in the 1920s with a new name: slip, worn over the bra and garter belt: but in the post-War period, it disappeared once again.

At the start of the 1950s, it was replaced by the slip in rigid fabric. It fell into disuse with the miniskirt fashion, but again reappeared at the close of the 1970s with the practical function of keeping clothing away from the skin.

Since the close of the 1980s, it has acquired the exclusive valence of female seduction.

Today it comes in various styles and lengths, with elasticized fabrics, or with the bra built into it, as snug-fitting as a leotard, but loose around the legs.

BASIC STYLES OF SLIP

1) Classical, knee-length slip with side split which enables freedom of movement.

2) Knee-length slip with seam under the breast, enhancing the silhouette and offering delicate breast support.

3) Slip in fabric or elasticized lace, with everyday bra, and just barely long enough to cover the bottom.

4) Slip in elasticized fabric or lace, with strapless evening bra, suited to strapless dresses, with a length that just barely covers the bottom.

SLIP WITH ROUNDED NECKLINE

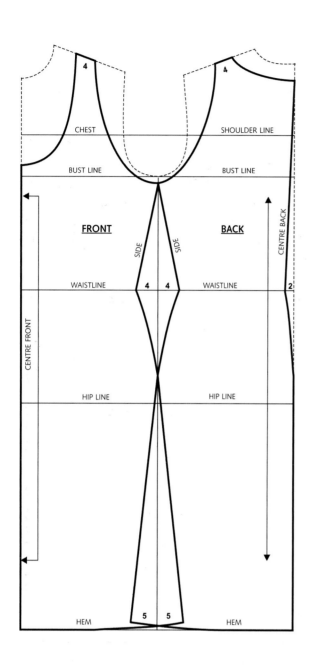

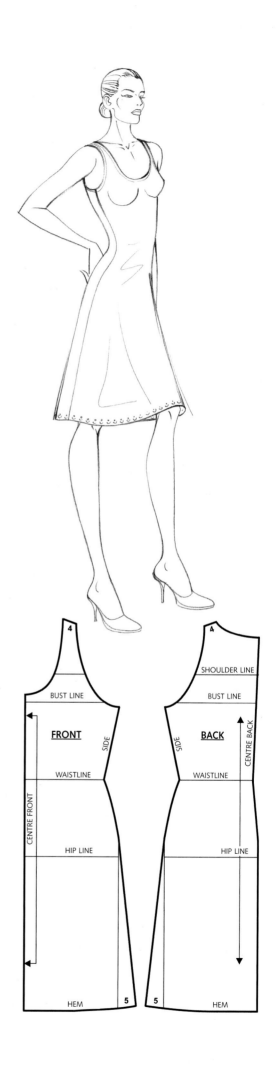

CHEST

SHOULDER LINE

BUST LINE

BUST LINE

FRONT

BACK

SIDE

SIDE

CENTRE BACK

CENTRE FRONT

WAISTLINE

WAISTLINE

HIP LINE

HIP LINE

HEM

HEM

- Draw the basic dress without darts in the size desired and
  with adequate ease.
- Make the front and back round neckline to the depth
  desired and determine the width of the shoulder straps.
- Taper the sides depending on the waist circumference and
  the ease desired.
- Flare the hem line as needed.
- Copy the front and back onto another sheet of paper.

SLIP WITH LACE DETAILS

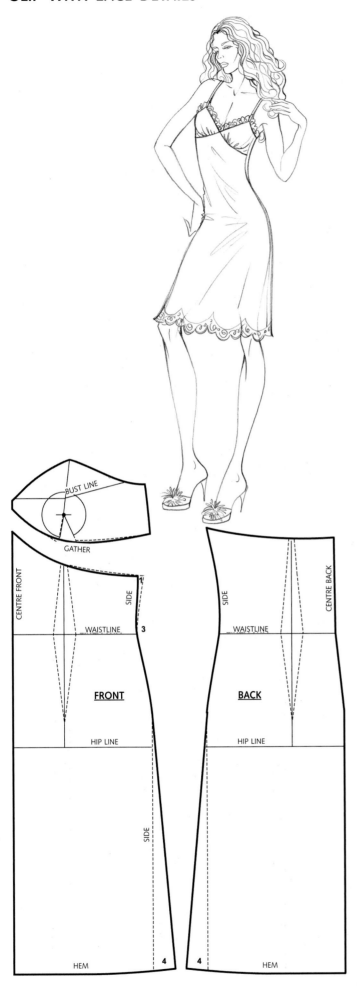

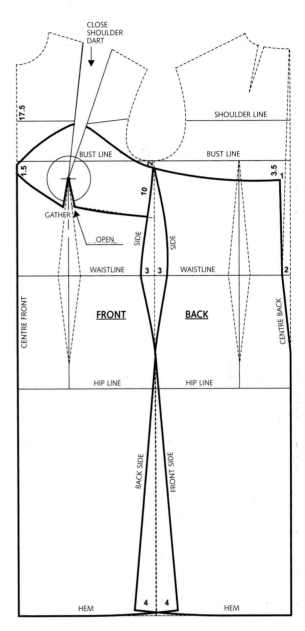

- Draw the basic dress block with darts and adequate ease.
- Draw the seam lines and the neckline.
- Widen the front waist dart by 1 cm/0.39" only in the seam position, for fullness.
- Close the bust dart and absorb it in the one under the bust.
- Taper the centre back by 2 cm/0.39"at the waist.
- Flare the skirt at the hem and along the side seams, taking in the waist line by 3-4 cm/1.18"-1.57".
- Copy the pieces, tidying up the outlines.

BABYDOLL NIGHTGOWN WITH BUTTERFLY SLEEVES

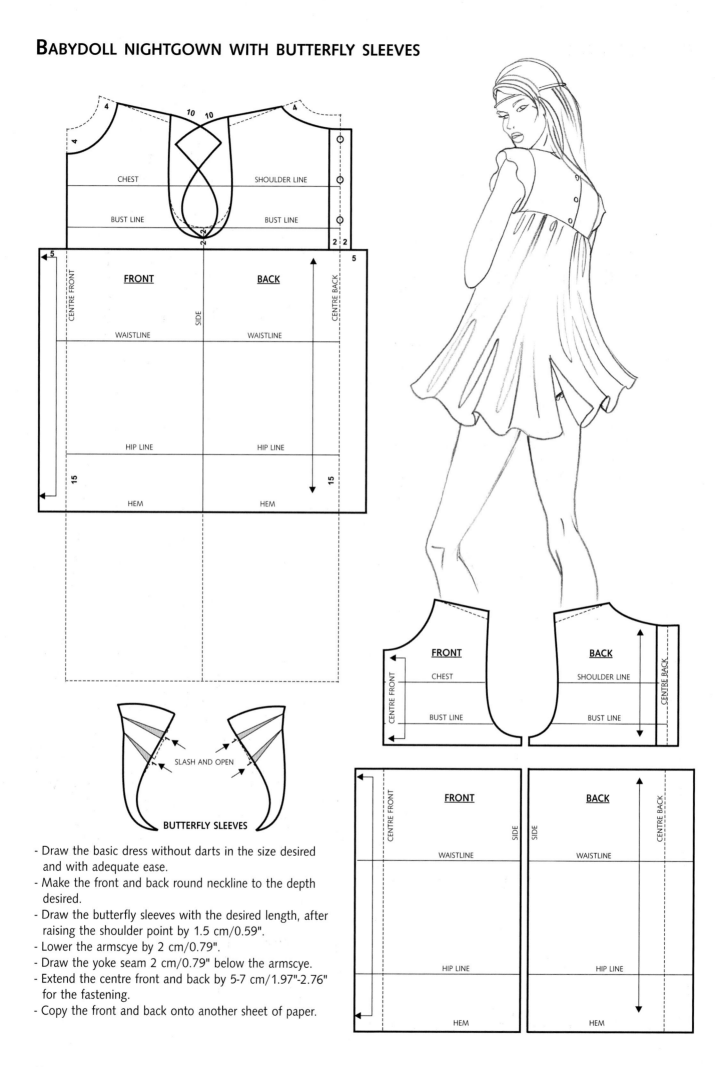

- Draw the basic dress without darts in the size desired and with adequate ease.
- Make the front and back round neckline to the depth desired.
- Draw the butterfly sleeves with the desired length, after raising the shoulder point by 1.5 cm/0.59".
- Lower the armscye by 2 cm/0.79".
- Draw the yoke seam 2 cm/0.79" below the armscye.
- Extend the centre front and back by 5-7 cm/1.97"-2.76" for the fastening.
- Copy the front and back onto another sheet of paper.

V-NECK NIGHTGOWN

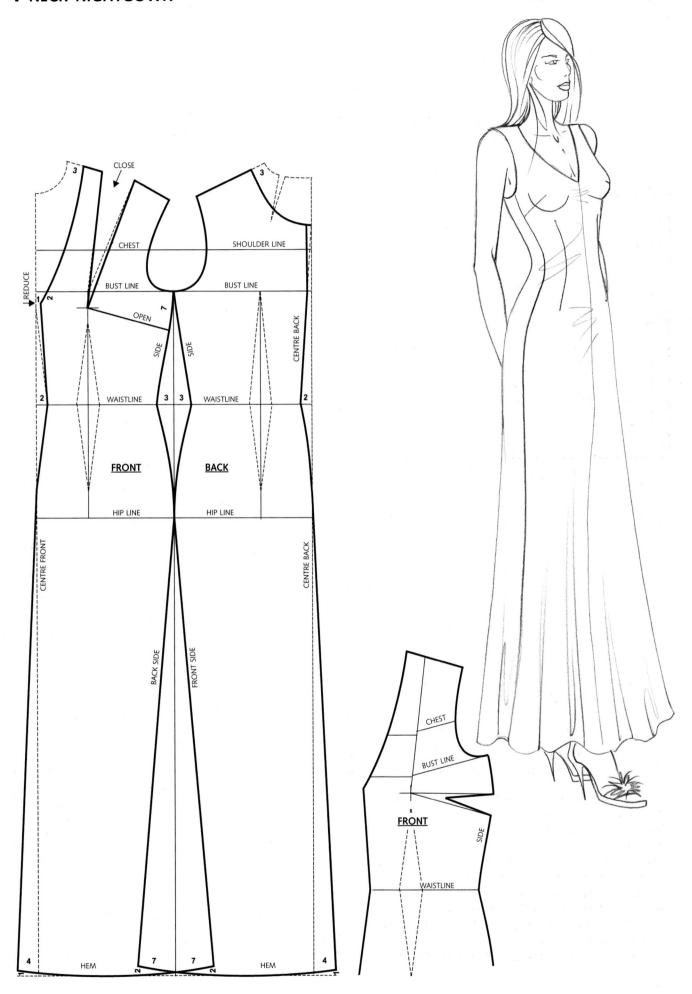

CLOSE

CHEST

SHOULDER LINE

BUST LINE

BUST LINE

REDUCE

OPEN

SIDE

SIDE

CENTRE BACK

WAISTLINE

WAISTLINE

FRONT

BACK

HIP LINE

HIP LINE

CENTRE FRONT

CENTRE BACK

BACK SIDE

FRONT SIDE

HEM

HEM

CHEST

BUST LINE

FRONT

SIDE

WAISTLINE

NIGHTGOWN WITH ROUND YOKE

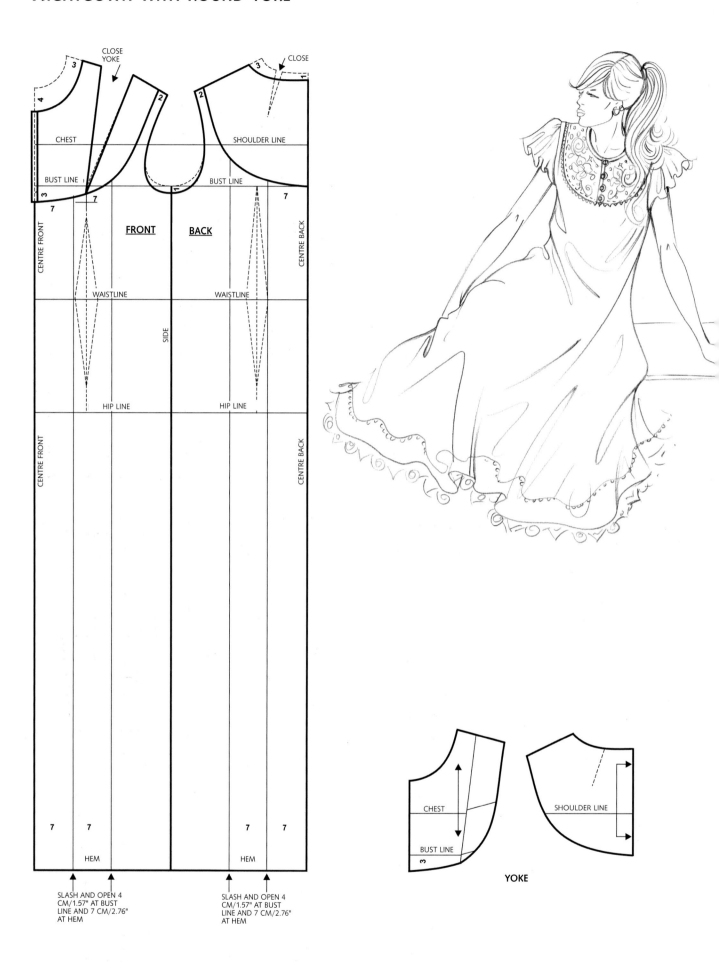

CLOSE
YOKE

CLOSE

3

4

3

2

2

3

1

CHEST

SHOULDER LINE

BUST LINE

BUST LINE

3

7

7

7

CENTRE FRONT

FRONT

BACK

CENTRE BACK

WAISTLINE

WAISTLINE

SIDE

HIP LINE

HIP LINE

CENTRE FRONT

CENTRE BACK

7

7

7

7

HEM

HEM

SLASH AND OPEN 4
CM/1.57" AT BUST
LINE AND 7 CM/2.76"
AT HEM

SLASH AND OPEN 4
CM/1.57" AT BUST
LINE AND 7 CM/2.76"
AT HEM

CHEST

SHOULDER LINE

BUST LINE

3

YOKE

BUTTON-DOWN PYJAMA

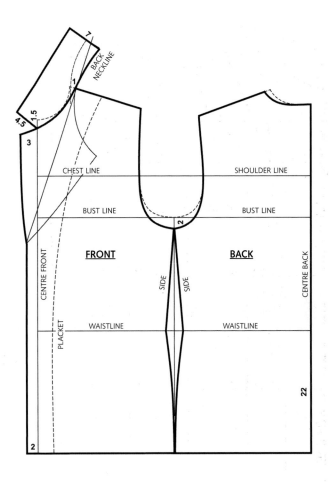

TOP
- Draw the basic shirt block without darts and with adequate ease.
- Apply the desired length (22 cm/8.66") from the waist to the hem.
- Make the extension for the button placket and for the lapels.
- Draw the collar.
- Draw the placket.

BOTTOMS
- Draw the basic trousers with darts and with adequate ease.
- Join the front and back, keeping them 2-3 cm/0.79"-1.18" apart for ease, as shown in figure.

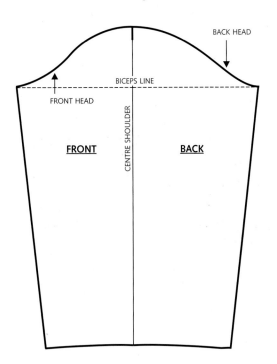

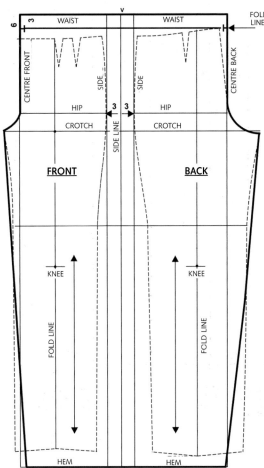

Pyjama with asymmetrical top

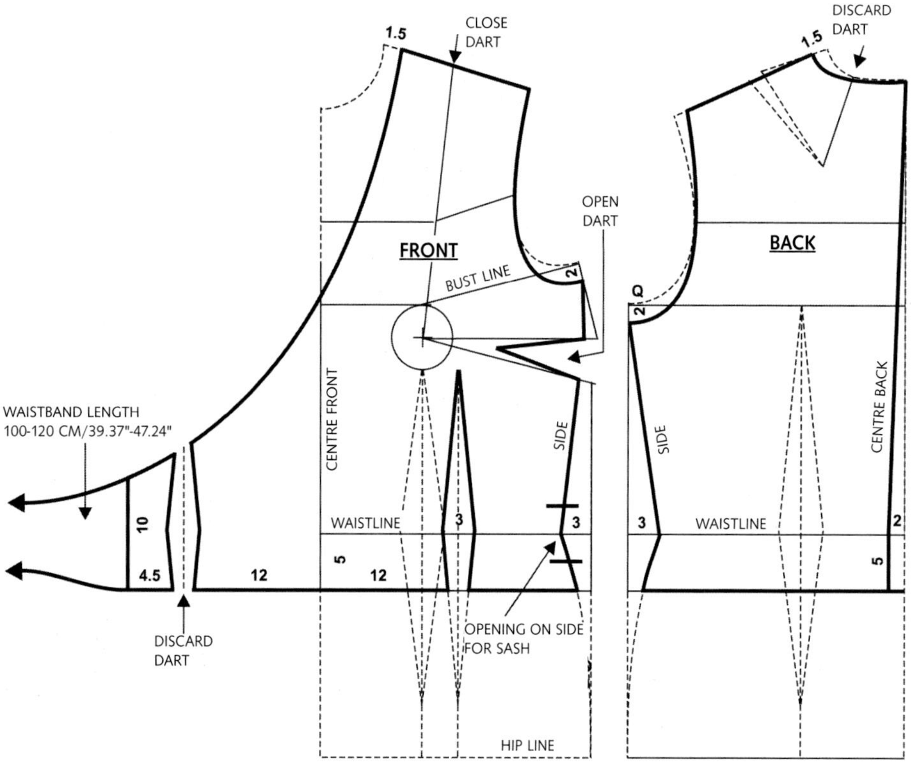

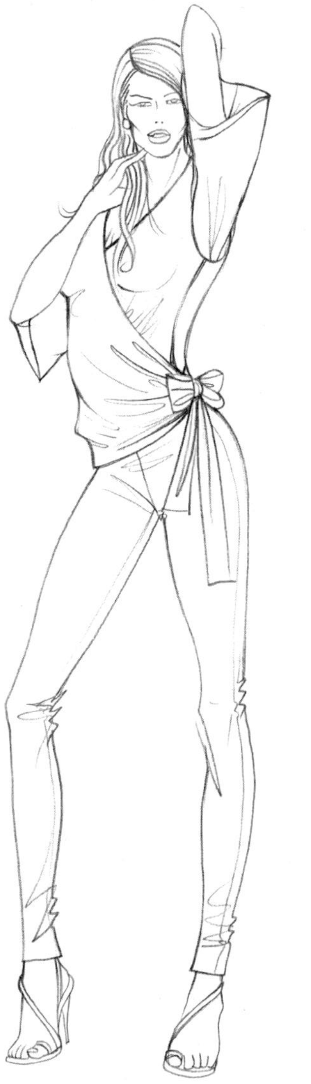

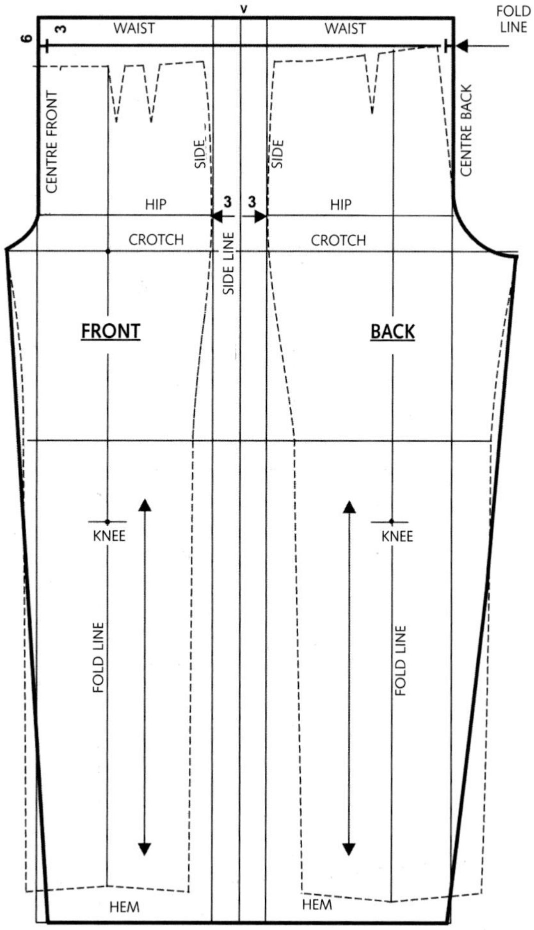

FRONT

BACK

WIDE SLEEVE

PYJAMA OR TRACKSUIT BOTTOMS

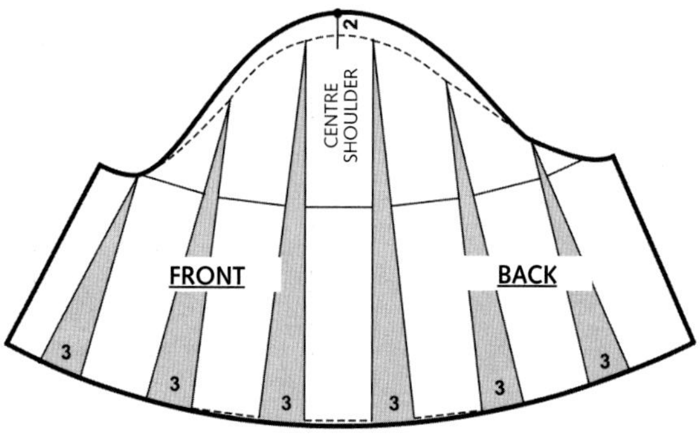

Top

- Draw the basic bodice block with darts.
- Lower the armscye by 2 cm/0.79".
- Make the desired length.
- Move the shoulder dart to side.
- Make the front neckline and the extension for the overlap.
- Make the back neckline.
- Move the waist dart in front toward the side and reduce it as desired.
- Taper the waist line depending on the fullness desired.
- Discard the back neckline dart.
- Taper the waist line by 2 cm/0.79" at the centre back.
- Draw the waistband with the desired length starting from the front extension.

SHAWL COLLAR BATHROBE

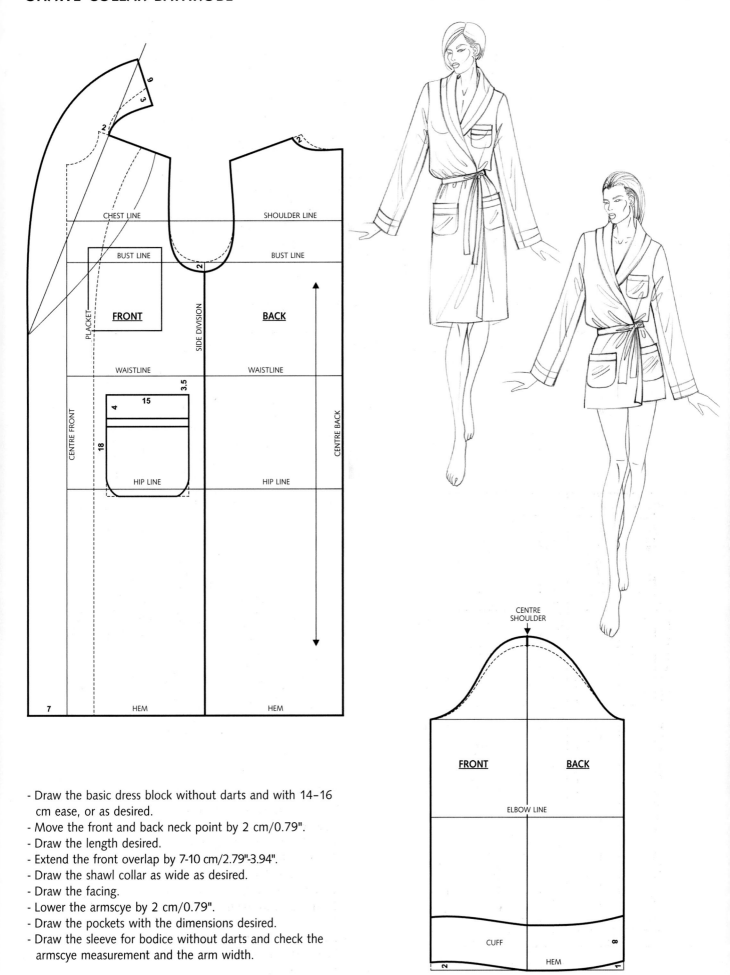

- Draw the basic dress block without darts and with 14–16 cm ease, or as desired.
- Move the front and back neck point by 2 cm/0.79".
- Draw the length desired.
- Extend the front overlap by 7-10 cm/2.79"-3.94".
- Draw the shawl collar as wide as desired.
- Draw the facing.
- Lower the armscye by 2 cm/0.79".
- Draw the pockets with the dimensions desired.
- Draw the sleeve for bodice without darts and check the armscye measurement and the arm width.

Hooded bathrobe

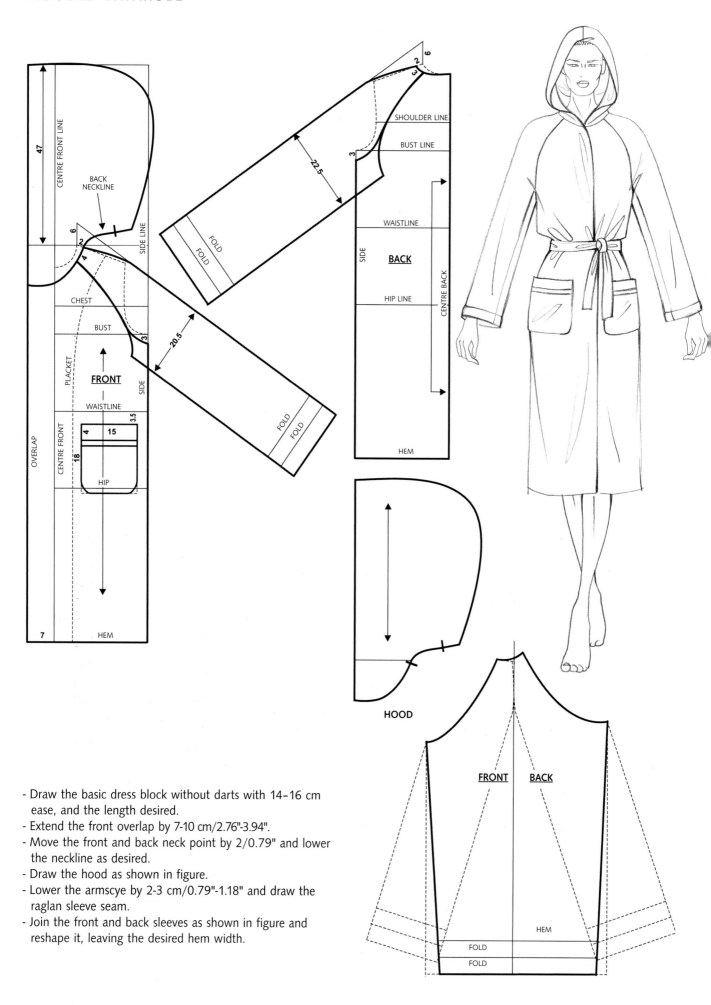

- Draw the basic dress block without darts with 14–16 cm ease, and the length desired.
- Extend the front overlap by 7-10 cm/2.76"-3.94".
- Move the front and back neck point by 2/0.79" and lower the neckline as desired.
- Draw the hood as shown in figure.
- Lower the armscye by 2-3 cm/0.79"-1.18" and draw the raglan sleeve seam.
- Join the front and back sleeves as shown in figure and reshape it, leaving the desired hem width.

MENSWEAR – WAISTCOATS AND JACKETS

WAISTCOATS AND JACKETS

WAISTCOATS

The waistcoat is a fitted bodice, without sleeves and with a buttoned front, to be worn under a jacket, typical male attire. In vogue from the 1600s on, it was a transformation of the brocade, satin or damask doublet, somewhat longer, with or without sleeves, with pockets and a V-shaped neckline from which the shirt's lace jabot poked out. In 1800 it grew simpler, becoming single-breasted with a shawl collar, generally in a light-coloured cloth or a variegated fabric. Still today the waistcoat is used with the tuxedo and the morning suit, in starched white piquet, with shawl collar.

The waistcoat can be single-breasted, double-breasted, or crossed; it can have a shawl collar or be collarless, with a V-shaped or round neckline.

The fabric is usually the same as the rest of the suit; in back there can be an adjustable belt; there are two pockets in the front and a button closure.

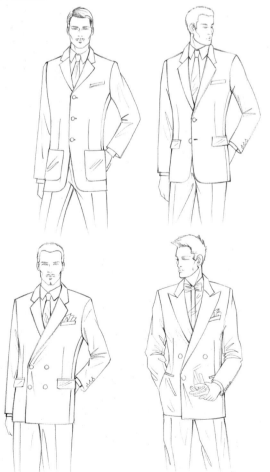

JACKETS

The jacket is the top part of the man's suit.

The precursor of the jacket goes back to the time of the Romans, who wore a tight-fitting doublet called a *synthesis* or *vestis cenatoria*, imported from the Orient.

In the Middle Ages the jackets were made for the first time by sewing together various kinds of fabric, using a needle and thread.

The only men's jacket we have from this period is conserved at the museum of Lyon.

In France in the 1300s, there was the jacque, a type of jacket made of humble materials, for the poorest people.

In the 1600s, young men wore the frock, similar to today's dress coat.

In the 1800s, the jacket took the form of a frock-coat, or it had a straight cut right down to the hips, like the present-day style, and it was worn by men of class and elegance.

At the start of the 1900s, the breast pocket began to appear on the lefthand side and, with time, the jacket's line was gradually modified, according to the changing fashions.

The classical men's jacket can be single- or double-breasted.

The single-breasted version can have three buttons with the lapel break point just below the breast, or two buttons with the lapel break point at the waist or at hip height.

The double-breasted jacket can have four or six buttons.

The shape of the upper part of the lapel, for both single- and double-breasted jackets, is very varied: notch, peak, shawl, etc. The pocket styles can be: patch, welt, or flap, etc.

The length of the jacket varies according to the dictates of fashion and depending on the occasion for which it is to be worn.

In the back, jackets can have: a central vent, two side vents, a pleat, or nothing.

The fabric used for the jackets varies depending on the season and fashion. In summer, it can be linen, cotton, summer-weight wool, etc.; in winter woolen gabardine, ottoman, tweed, vicuna, etc.

TUXEDO

The tuxedo is evening wear, or for formal occasions, usually made of wool and silk blends of cloth.

It is made of a single- or double-breasted jacket, often black, but sometimes white, navy blue, burgundy, or purple, usually with the lapels of various shapes, in a contrasting fabric, such as satin.

The trousers are black with a silk stripe on the outside of the legs. In England, they are called "Dinner jackets", while in much of Europe they are known as "Smoking", reference to the jacket's early similarity to Victorian smoking jackets.

SPENCER

This is a typical men's or women's long-sleeved jacket that extends to waist length.

In the 1800s it had a military character with showy frog-fastenings, and it took the name of Hussar or Hungarian-style Spencer jacket.

The Spencer can be single- or double-breasted, with various styles of collar, and lapels in a contrasting satin fabric, as in the tuxedo.

MORNING DRESS

Morning dress is formal attire, with a black jacket and long, wide tails, sweeping from the front to the back, and grey and black striped trousers.

The suit is usually made complete by a light-coloured waistcoat, either pearl grey or white.

The morning dress was the rage in the early 1900s.

SAFARI JACKET

This is a cotton or linen jacket with ample patch pockets on the hips and at the breasts, with pleats and epaulettes, once widely used in the colonial African territories.

Today, it is a jacket used especially in the summer, by both men and the fairer sex.

FLIGHT JACKET

An article of clothing for both men and women, the length does not exceed roughly 65–70 cm.

They are generally a sports type of attire with broad shoulders and a comfortable fit, set-in sleeves, raglan or kimono, and often with imaginative motifs and styles.

They have very large pockets, with original motifs.

The placket can be either single- or double breasted, and closed by buttons or a zipper.

There are a full range of fabrics for winter jackets including gabardines, various weights of cloth, fleece, hound's tooth patterns, plaids, and for the younger styles, lined denims, etc.

For spring/summer versions, there are brushed cottons, prints, jeans, etc.

INDUSTRIAL CHART OF MEN'S MEASUREMENTS

SIZE CHART WITHOUT COMFORT ALLOWANCES IN CM

Measurements of circumference						
SIZES	44	46	48	50	52	54
Chest circumference	88	92	96	100	104	108
Waist circumference	80	84	88	92	96	100
Hip circumference	89	92	96	100	105	110
Back shoulders width	42	43	44	45	46	47
Width sector*	10	10.5	11	11.5	12	12.5
Neck circumference	40	41	42	43	44	45
Measurements of length						
STATURE	170	172	175	176	178	180
Waist length	45.2	46.3	47	47.7	48.4	49.1
Armscye depth	18	18.2	18.5	18.9	19.3	19.7
Elbow length	29	30	31	32	33	34
Sleeve length	60	61	62	63	64	65
Hip height	19.2	19.6	20	20.4	20.8	21.2
Seat depth	23.2	23.6	24	24.4	24.8	25.2
Knee height	58	59	60	61	62	63
Outer leg length	104	106	108	110	112	114

Control measurements

COMFORT ALLOWANCES BASED ON THE TYPE OF APPAREL IN CM

CLOTHING TYPES	Shirt and waistcoat	Fitted jacket	Loose jacket Fitted over-coat	Winter jacket	Raincoat Cagoule	Lined windbreaker
Chest circumference	14/18	18/24	22/26	26/30	28/34	30/36
Hips circumference	14/16	16/20	20/24	26/30	28/34	30/36
Back shoulders width	1/1.5	1.5/2	2/2.5	2.5/3.5	3.5/4	4/5
Front and back waist length	1	1/1.5	1.5/3	2/3	2/3	2.5/3.5

MEASUREMENTS FOR THE JACKET

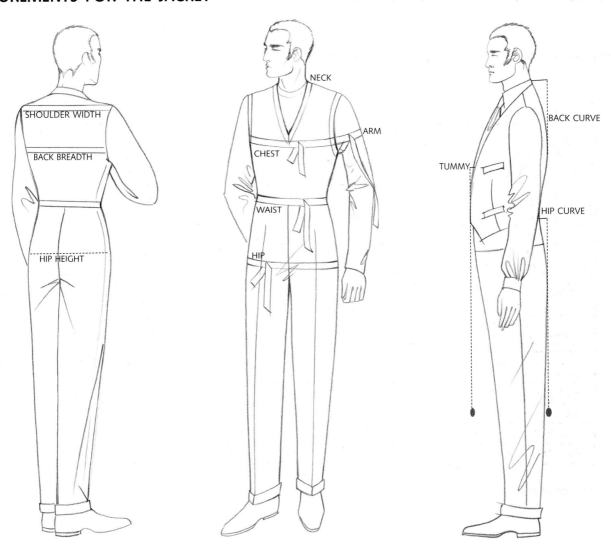

SHOULDER WIDTH
This is measured at shoulder level from one tip to the other, holding the tape horizontally.

BACK BREADTH
This is measured at armpit level, from the start of one arm to the other, taking care not to enter in the hollow.

HIP HEIGHT
This is measured from the waistline to the fullest point of the hips, keeping the tape snug against the figure all along the side.

BACK CURVE
This is an important measurement, and easy to discover. Hold a ruler vertically at the centre of the back and measure the distance from the neck to the ruler.

HIP CURVE
Hold a ruler to the centre of the hip in the back, at the fullest point, and measure the distance from the waistline to the ruler.

TUMMY
To take this measurement, have the subject's position at ease, but not too relaxed, so as not to err in excess.
Place a ruler on the fullest part of the abdomen and holding it perfectly vertically, measure the distance between it and the hip line.
Measurements of a man with average build, 175 cm height, Size 48.

The measurements that we describe are approximate and are used for the construction of the basic block.
Each manufacturer or individual may have different measurements, but the procedure for construction does not change.

- UNDERARM LEVEL . . . . 23.7 cm
- BACK WAIST HEIGHT 47   cm
- FRONT WAIST HEIGHT 50   cm
- HIP HEIGHT 21   cm
- SHOULDER DROP . . . . 4.8   cm
- SLEEVE LENGTH 60   cm
- ELBOW HEIGHT 29   cm
- CHEST GIRTH 96   cm
- WAIST CIRCUMF. 88   cm
- HIP CIRCUMF 96   cm
- NECK CIRCUMF. 42   cm
- ARM CIRCUMF. . . . . 30.1 cm
- SHOULDER WIDTH 44   cm
- BACK CURVE . . . . 4.8   cm
- TUMMY 2   cm

These measurements are expressed without the addition of ease, which, for the jacket, is:
- 20-24 cm for chest and hip circumference.
- 2 cm for shoulder width.
- 1 cm for back and front length.

MEN'S JACKET – BASIC BLOCK

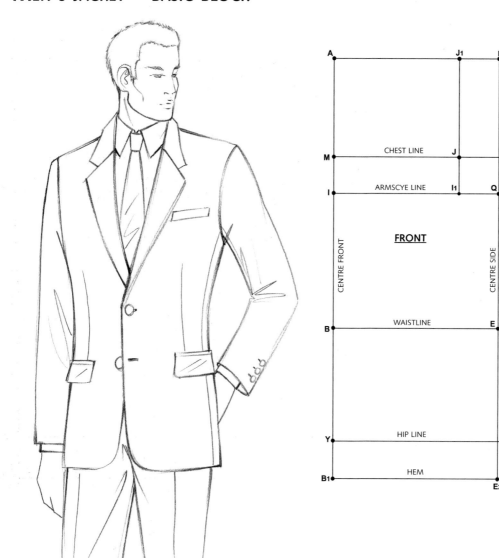

SIZE 48

Measurements: (without ease)
- Chest Circumference   96 cm/37.80"
- Waist Circumference   88 cm/34.65"
- Hip Circumference   96 cm/37.80"
- Neck Circumference   42 cm/16.54"
- Waist length   47 cm/18.50"
- Shoulder width   44 cm/17.32"

- Draw a right angle A-B-C, with:
- A-B Waist length + jacket ease.
  (e.g.: 47 + 1 = 48 cm).
- B-C Half circumference of the chest + ease.
  (e.g.: 96 + 24 = 120 : 2 = 60 cm).
- C-D like A-B.
- D-C1 jacket length (e.g.: 75 cm).
- Join D-C1 and write CENTRE BACK.
- B-B1 like C-C1.
- Join A-B1 and write CENTRE FRONT.
- B1-C1 like B-C.
- Join B1-C1 and write HEM LINE.
- B-E half B-C.
- B1-E2 like B-E.
- A-F like B-E.
- Join F-E2 and write CENTRE SIDE.

- D-H half D-C + 0.5/0.20" (e.g.: 48 : 2 = 24 + 0.5 = 24.5 cm).
- H-I parallel to B-C. Write ARMSCYE LINE.
- E2-E3 6 cm/2.36".
- Q-Q2 like E2-E3.
- Join Q2-E3 and write MOVED SIDE.
- B-Y and C-X Side height (e.g.: 20 cm).
- Draw Y-X and write HIP LINE.
- D-G half shoulders width + ease.
  (e.g.: 44 + 2 = 46 : 2 = 23 cm).
- H-L 1/4 of D-H (e.g.: 24.5 : 4 = 6.1 cm).
- Draw L-M write SHOULDER LINE and CHEST LINE.
- H-H1 like D-G (e.g.: 23 cm).
- Draw G-H1.
- I-I1 like D-G - 0.5 on the back (e.g.: 23 - 0.5 = 22.5 cm).
- Draw I1-J1 parallel G-H1.

Back

- H-H3 16 cm/6.30".
- H-H2 0.6 cm/0.24".
- Make up the right angle H3-H2-D1.
- Draw H2-D1 like H-D with curved line.
- G-O 4 cm/1.57".
- D1-N = 1/3 of D-G + 1 (e.g.: 23 : 3 = 7.6 + 1 = 8.6 cm).
- N-P = 2.3 cm/0.91". Draw D1-P in shape.
- P-P1 = Shoulder Length + 1 (e.g.: 16 + 1 = 17 cm).
- Draw P-P1 in shape, passing through O.
- Q2-Q3 = 2.5 cm/0.98".
- Draw the Armhole P1-L1-Q3, shaping it carefully.
- E1-W = 3 cm/1.18".
- C-C3 = 1.2-1.7 cm/0.47"-0.67".
- C1-C2 as C-C3.
- Draw the line of the centre back D1-L-H-C3-C2.
- E3-E4 = 2 cm/0.79".
- Draw the side line Q3-W-E4.

Front

- A-U = half of A-J1 minus 0.5 cm/0.20"
  (e.g.: 22.5 - 0.5 = 22 : 2 = 11 cm).
- A-U1 = 8 cm/3.15".
- U-U2 = 2 cm/0.79".
- Draw the break line to the desired height
  (e.g.: 8 cm from the waist).
- I-S1 = 12 cm/4.72". I-I2 16 cm/6.30".
- I1-I3 = 4.5 cm. B-B3 as I-I2.
- B-B5 as I-I1. (e.g.: 22.5 cm).
- Draw the waist dart.
- J1-V = 4 cm/1.57".
- U-Z like P-P1 of the back minus 1 (e.g.: 17 - 1 = 16 cm).
- Draw U-Z, passing through V.
- Q-Q1 = 2 cm/0.79".
- Q2-Q4 = 3 cm/1.18".
- Draw the Armhole Z-J-Q1-Q4, shaping it carefully.
- E1-W1 = 3 cm/1.18".
- Draw the side line Q4-W1-E5.
- E3-E5 = 2 cm/0.79".
- U1-U3 = 3-3.5 cm/1.18"-1.38". Draw the outline of the
  lapel.

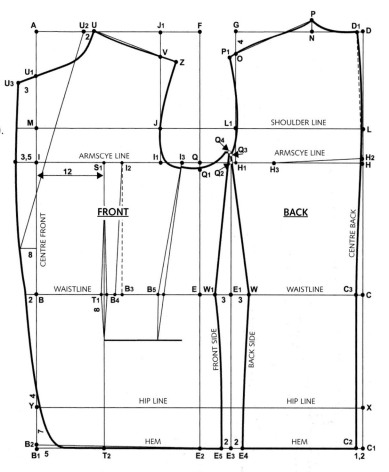

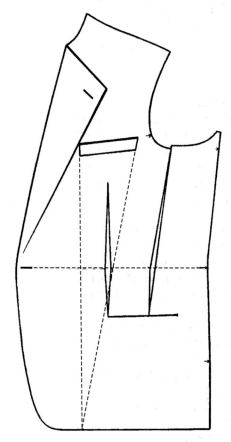

Note: *The waist darts and the side tapering are set in relation to the dif-*
ference desired between hips and waist, which is proportionally distributed
on the waist dart line and the side seam, along with the creation of a small
1.5 cm dart with tips on the armhole and the pocket line.

SEAM ALLOWANCES FOR THE JACKET

MARKERS FOR THE IRON WORK

STRETCH

SHRINK

Seam allowances
Seam allowances are parallel to the seams.
The back shoulder seam allowance is optional and requires that we should in any case sew 0.6 cm below the marked line.

Iron work
"Iron work" is an essential part of jacket making if you want to achieve a perfect line and freshness of style.
The iron is used to correct the shoulder line from the shoulder point to the humerus; any looseness must be gathered up; the fit of the neckline must be determined; flatten and adjust the darts; give the correct shape to the side panel and the armscye.

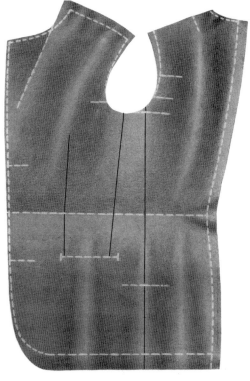

JACKET COLLAR

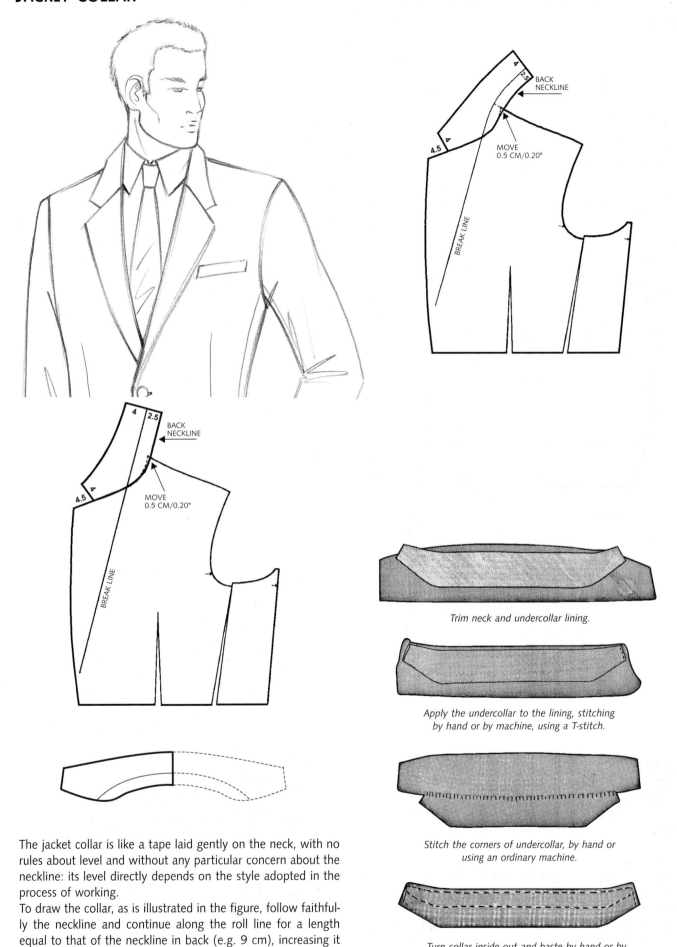

The jacket collar is like a tape laid gently on the neck, with no rules about level and without any particular concern about the neckline: its level directly depends on the style adopted in the process of working.

To draw the collar, as is illustrated in the figure, follow faithfully the neckline and continue along the roll line for a length equal to that of the neckline in back (e.g. 9 cm), increasing it by as much as the absorption calls for (0.5 cm) and moving away from the shoulder point by 0.5 cm.

Trim neck and undercollar lining.

Apply the undercollar to the lining, stitching by hand or by machine, using a T-stitch.

Stitch the corners of undercollar, by hand or using an ordinary machine.

Turn collar inside out and baste by hand or by machine using chain stitch; finish the lining and iron to smooth out the collar.

Men's jacket basic sleeve block

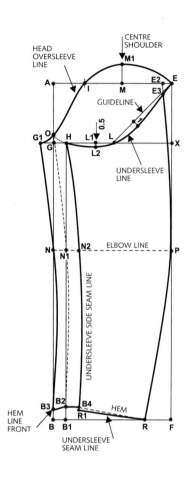

Measure: - Arm circumference 29 cm/11.42".
            - Arm Length 62 cm/24.41".

On the left hand side of a sheet of pattern paper,
draw a rectangle A–B–E–F, with:
- A-E like Section of Jacket basic block + 1/2 sector + 1
  cm/0.39". (e.g.: 14.5 + 7.25 = 21.75 + 1 = 22.75 cm).
- A-B sleeve length (e.g.: 62 cm).
- A-G = L1-P1-1 of the basic bodice back.
  (In this case: 12 - 1 = 11 cm/4.33").
- Draw G-X parallel to A-E.
- A-N = half A-B (e.g.: 62 : 2 = 31). ELBOW LINE.
- A-M = ½ AE + 1. (e.g.: 22.75 : 2 = 11.4 + 1 = 12.4 cm).
  CENTRE SHOULDER.
- M-M1 = 1/3 A-G. (e.g.: 11 : 3 = 3.6 cm).
- A-I = 1/4 A-E. (e.g.: 22.75 : 4 = 5.7 cm).

- G-H = 2.5 cm/0.98".
- Draw H-B1 parallel to A-B.
- X-L = half G-X. (e.g.: 22.75 : 2 = 11.37 cm).
- Draw the guideline E-L.
- L-L1 = half H-L.
- L1-L2 = 0.5 cm/0.20".
- G-O = 1.5 cm/0.59".
- G-G1 = 2.5 cm/0.98".
- E-E2 = 1.5 cm/0.59".
- Draw accordingly the front head E-M1-I-O-G1.
- Draw accordingly the back head E-L-L2-H-O.
- B1-B2 = 2 cm/0.59".
- B3-B2 and N-N1 2.5 cm/0.98".
- B2-R = 1/2 sleeve hem width (e.g.: 16-17).
- B2-B4 like B2-B3.
- B4-R1 = 0.5 cm/0.20".
- Finish with a curved line. R-E3 and R1-H Undersleeve.

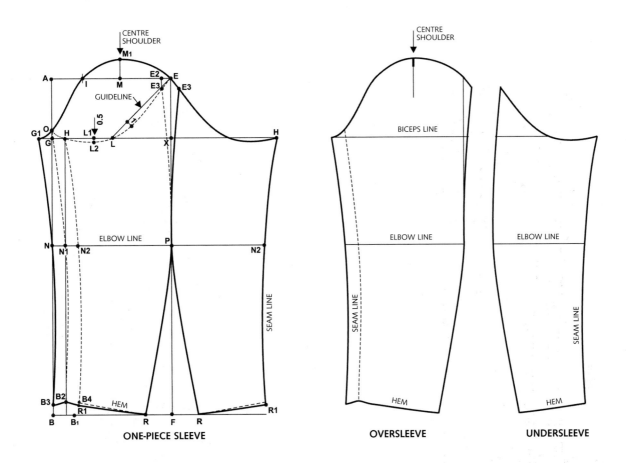

ONE-PIECE SLEEVE   OVERSLEEVE   UNDERSLEEVE

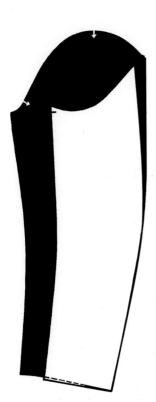

Open sleeve
Copy the undersleeve E3-P-R-R1-H-L2-L-E3, and position it on the E-F fold line on the front part and smoothly joint the sleeve head line.
Check the total length of the sleeve head, which must be superior to that of the armscye, by a variable amount, depending on the type of fabric.

Assembly of the sleeve
In assembling the sleeve, first of all, the parts on the elbow seam have to be basted; then take up the undersleeve with a rotary effect to bring it even at the hem; then the oversleeve is re-attached.
The finished sleeve will appear as the image shown here to the right.

Note: To have the correct balance of the sleeve, the shoulder centre must be adjusted, and it can be shifted to the back by a few millimetres, depending on the configuration and the posture of the subject.

Hammer dart

The hammer dart is movable, and is usually applied to the front panels of jackets for stout subjects.

The hammer dart is a powerful tool, and its primary purpose is to channel into a seam in the pocket the opening in the centre front, which in turn was there to softly drape the widest point of the belly.

In addition to this advantage, the hammer dart lends greater stability, which provides an overall solution to the problem of balance for the double breasted jacket front and a very obvious advantage in terms of reducing the work put into making the jacket.

Execution of the hammer dart

Single-breasted jacket

- Make a slash on the centre front, below the waist line, up to the waist dart, and another from tip to tip of the two waist darts, along the pocket line.
- Make another slash from the tip of the waist dart to the corner of the hem on the centre front, in the first version, or straight down to the hem in the second version.
- Rotate the slashed parts, opening the centre front as needed, overlapping the part on the bottom; opening along the pocket line, and overlapping the slash toward the side dart, as shown in figure.

Double-breasted jacket

- Follow the same procedure as for the single-breasted jacket, keeping in mind that the hammer dart slash is made starting from the centre front, leaving intact the line for the buttoned overlap, as in the single-breasted jacket.
- Smoothly trace over the outlines and double check the measurements when it is done.

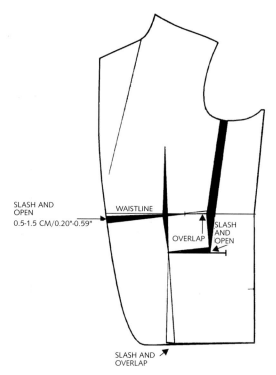

2 HAMMER DART FOR SINGLE - BREASTED JACKET

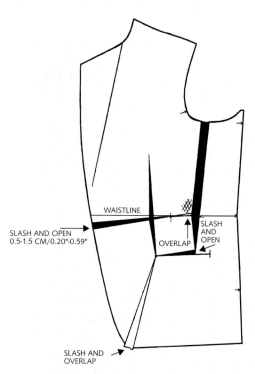

1 HAMMER DART FOR SINGLE-BREASTED JACKET

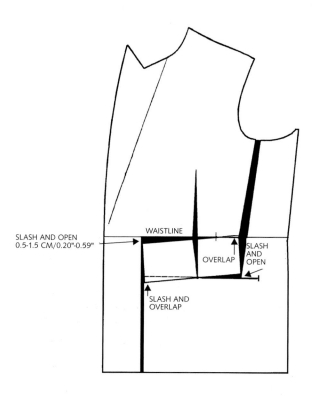

HAMMER DART FOR DOUBLE-BREASTED JACKET

THREE-BUTTON SINGLE-BREASTED JACKET

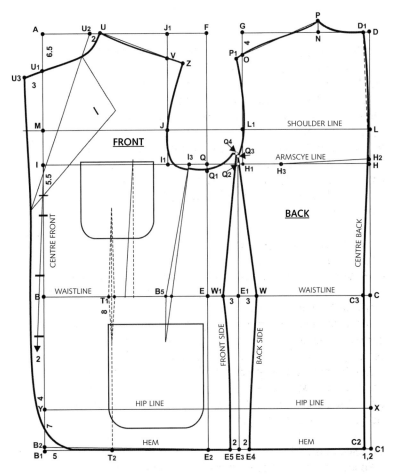

- Draw the jacket basic block with the desired measurements and adequate ease.
- Make the lapel break point 5-5.5 cm below the underarm level.
- A-U1= 6.5 cm.
- Draw the overlap line and lapels according to new measures.
- Draw the pockets as shown.

Note: *For this jacket front it is good practice to specify with accuracy the extent of the belly, in order not to find oneself at grips with a sloppy overlap.*
Furthermore, it is important to take great care in the pattern layout on the fabric, the selvedge of which should be perfectly parallel to the edge of the pattern, for the waistline to the underarm level, especially with striped fabrics.

Note: *For Glen plaids, this single-breasted pattern is recommended, but to permit the exact match of the pattern at the salient points of the jacket, the torso has to be rather elongated, to play up the void at the waist and to support the side pieces with more force, converging the length on armscye.*
The style is obtained by closing the regular dart and creating a "hammer dart".
The central dart should be eliminated so as not to spoil the pattern of the fabric.
The back should be less rounded and the sides should be made with a straight line.

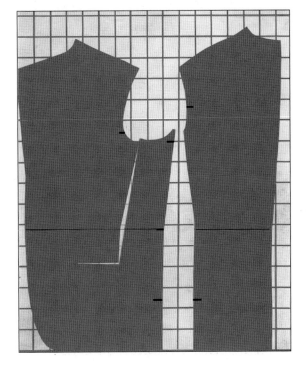

LOOSE-FITTING JACKET WITH YOKE

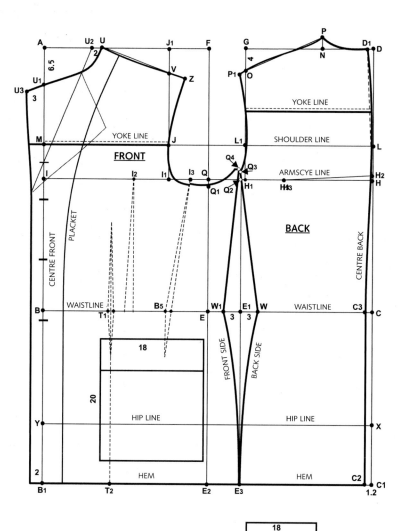

- Draw the basic jacket block with the necessary measurements and ease.
- Eliminate the darts and reduce the waist tapering to give the loose fit desired.
- Draw the breakpoint in the right place.
- Draw the front and rear yoke line at the desired height.
- Draw the pocket.
- Draw the facing.
- Copy all the parts of the pattern.

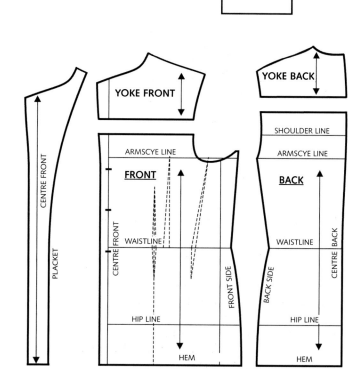

SAFARI JACKET

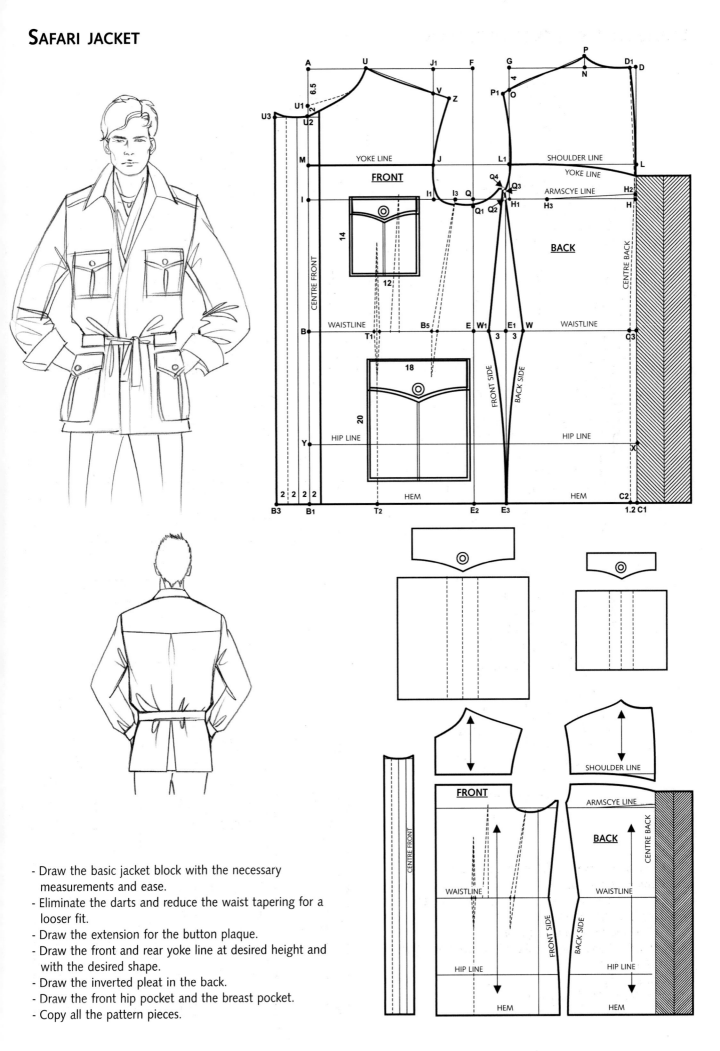

- Draw the basic jacket block with the necessary measurements and ease.
- Eliminate the darts and reduce the waist tapering for a looser fit.
- Draw the extension for the button plaque.
- Draw the front and rear yoke line at desired height and with the desired shape.
- Draw the inverted pleat in the back.
- Draw the front hip pocket and the breast pocket.
- Copy all the pattern pieces.

BASIC BLOCK DOUBLE-BREASTED JACKET

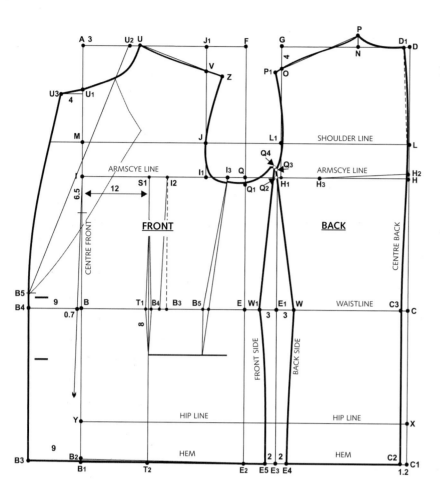

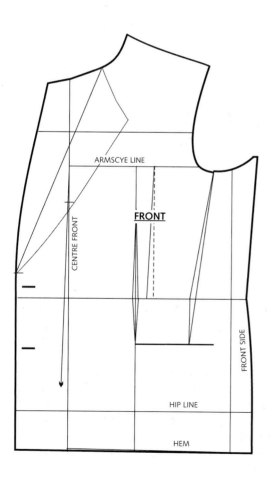

- Draw the basic jacket block with the necessary measurements and ease and desired length.
- Extend the overlap of the centre front B1-B3 and B-B4 by 9 cm/3.54".
- U1-U3 = 4 cm/1.57".
- B4-B5 = 2-3 cm/0.79"-1.18".
- Join B3-B5-U3 as shown in figure.
- Connect U2 to B5 for the breakline.

DOUBLE-BREASTED JACKET WITH PEAKED LAPELS

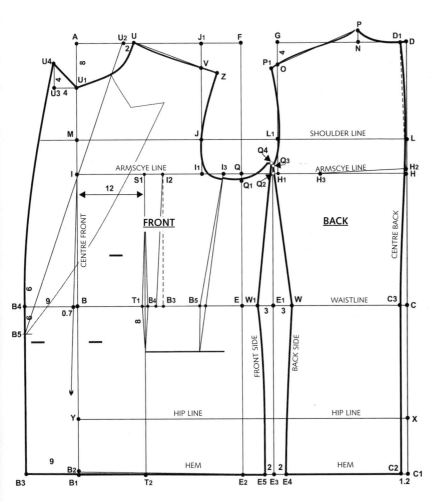

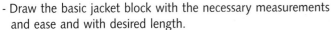

- Draw the basic jacket block with the necessary measurements and ease and with desired length.
- Extend the overlap of the centre front B1-B3 and B-B4 = 9 cm/3.54".
- U1-U3 = 4 cm/1.57" and U3-U4 = 4-5 cm/1.57"-1.97".
- Join B3-B5-U3 as shown in figure.
- Draw the roll line from U2 to B5; B5 is about 6 cm/2.36" below the waist line (or according to the style).

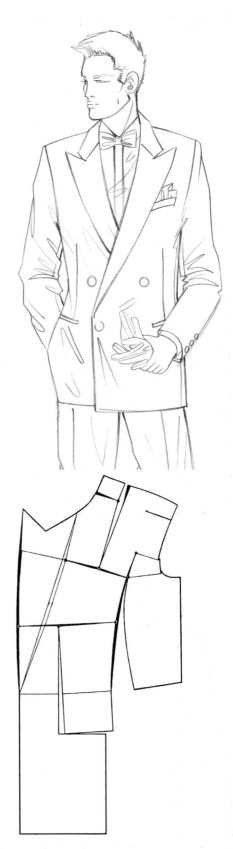

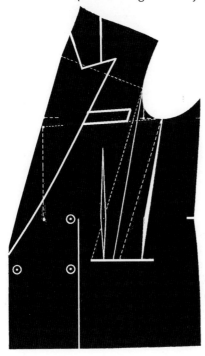

The double-breasted jacket is a form that is influenced by the fullest part of the belly, in a decisive way.

In this case, the "hammer dart" can be used on a standard jacket block.

The pattern shown above is suitable for subjects with a slight belly. In the upper area and at the sides, it is identical to the single-breasted jacket, and moreover, it has a hammer dart, created by lengthening the dart by 0.5 cm/0.20" and suppression in the pocket.

It is not an easy pattern, but it does solve certain problems.

SINGLE-BREASTED TUXEDO JACKETS WITH PEAKED LAPELS

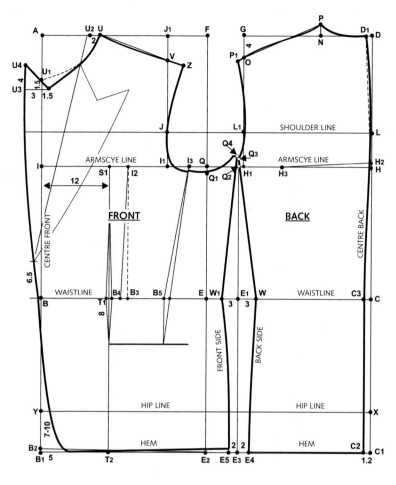

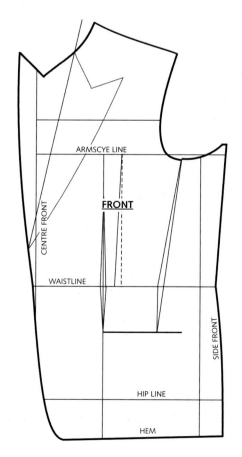

The tuxedo jacket is a special jacket, but as far as the pattern is concerned, it is not very different from the everyday version. If the pattern presents particular devices, it is solely owing to the fact that it requires great stability at the neckline.

The tuxedo is usually made with a sturdy fabric.

For this type of garment, peaked or shawl lapels are almost always called for.

To make this style, follow the lines illustrated clearly in figure.

Tuxedo with shawl collar

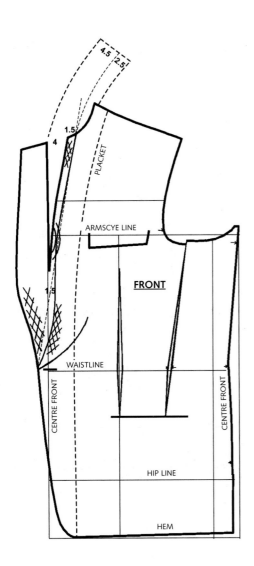

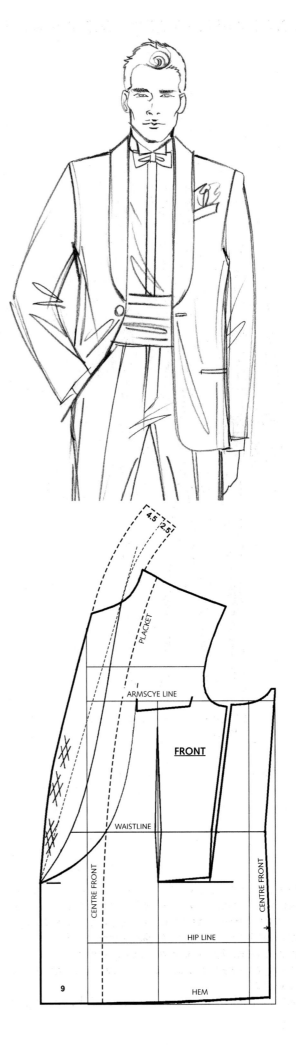

Single-breasted tuxedo

To make this shawl neckline, it is necessary first of all to give a graceful style to the roll line, establishing an accentuated break at waist level (at the point where it narrows).

Parallel to the roll line, make the back part of the dart (at distance of 1.5 cm/0.59").

Depth of the dart = 4 cm/1.57".

The side is a straight line and suitably adjusted in light of the inward curve to be made on the back.

This jacket's shawl lapel requires iron work shrinking at the points indicated in figure.

Double-breasted tuxedo

This style differs from the one above in the lapel length and the fuller curve.

It is made using the Tuxedo basic block, obviously altered for the double-breasted overlap.

Morning dress

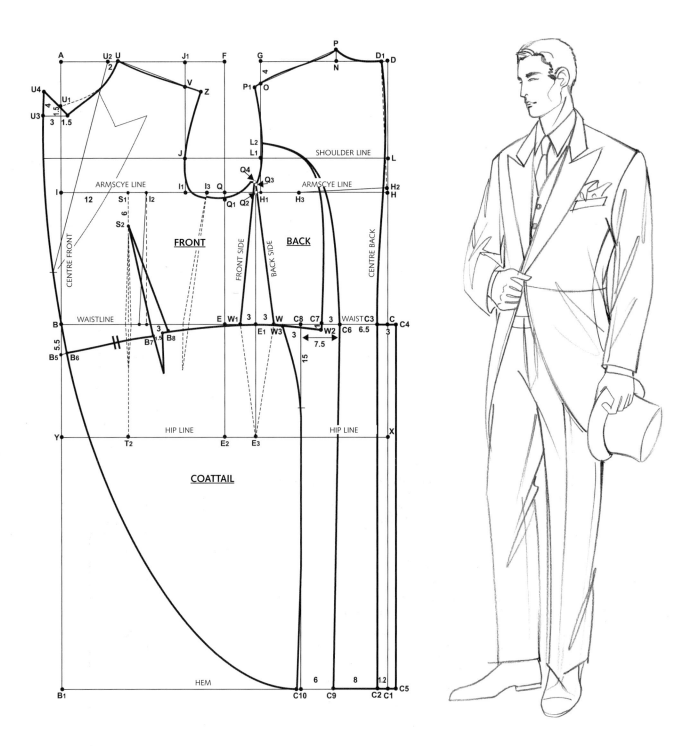

The morning dress (or swallow-tail coat) is very formal attire, appropriate for very special occasions or important ceremonies. The long coattails of the black jacket are cut in such a way that, starting from the single button, they curve downwards around the back in a swallow-tail shape.

The jacket is worn over uncuffed trousers of the same fabric (vicuña) with pale stripes, a pearl grey waistcoat and a silver, pearl grey, black, or white silk tie.

For the morning dress pattern, use the regular basic jacket block, with the necessary measurements and ease, and peaked lapels.

- Draw the basic block for a jacket with peaked lapels.
- Extend the centre back C-C1 as desired (e.g. 60-65 cm from the waist point).
- Draw the hem line C1-B1.
- B-B5 = 5.5 cm/1.97". Draw B5-E1-C7 with a curved line.
- C1-C9 of back = 10 cm/3.94".
- Draw the line of the side panel L2-C6-C9.
- Draw the side panel L2-W2-W-Q3.
- Draw the "swallow tail" in back C2-C3-C4-C5.
- Draw the dart on the front B7-S2-B8.
- Draw the lines of the coattail B6-C10 - W2-C10 - B6-W2.
- Make a small dart at the top of the coattail, 1-1.5 cm/0.39" 0.59"at point B7.

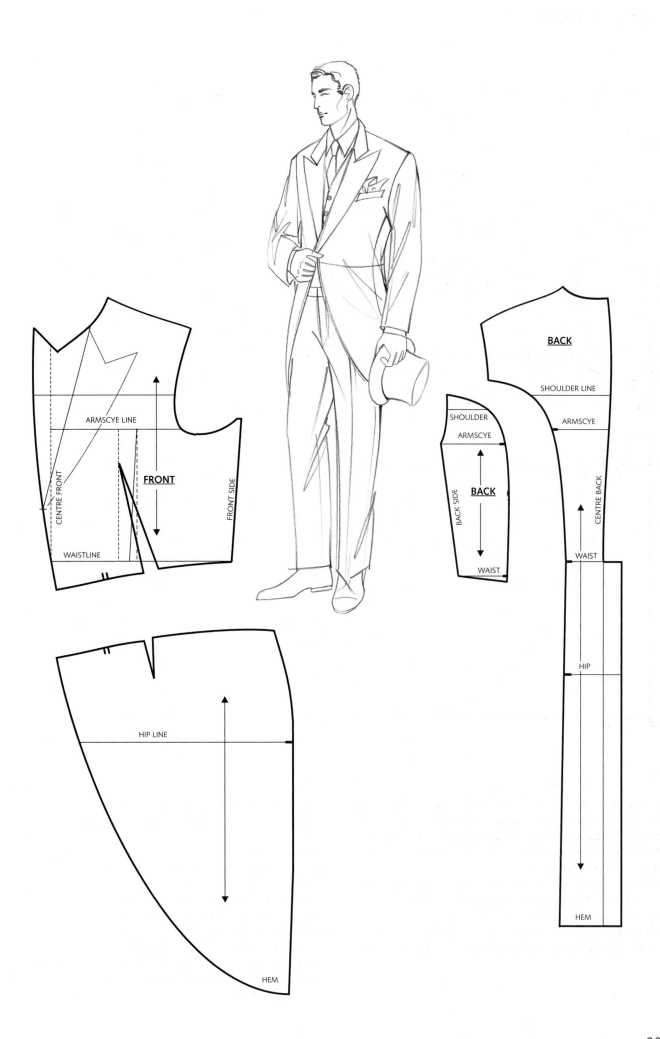

ARMSCYE LINE

CENTRE FRONT

FRONT

FRONT SIDE

WAISTLINE

HIP LINE

HEM

SHOULDER

ARMSCYE

BACK SIDE

BACK

WAIST

BACK

SHOULDER LINE

ARMSCYE

CENTRE BACK

WAIST

HIP

HEM

FULL EVENING DRESS

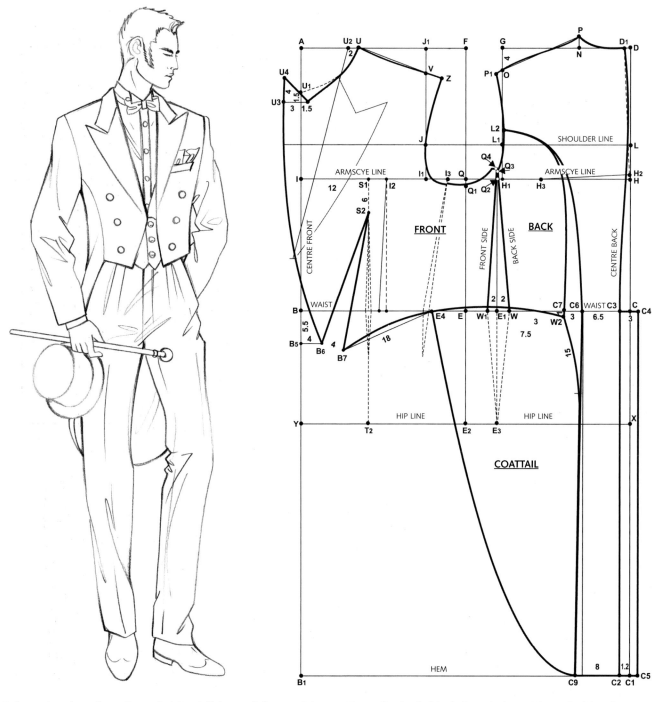

Full evening dress (or tails, or "white tie") is a suit for special ceremonies or extraordinary occasions. At its peak in the nineteenth century, it is characterized by a jacket that is short in front and long in the back, with two long and narrow tails.

The lapels are peaked and lined with a silk facing, grosgrain or herringbone.

The trousers are the same colour as the jacket, usually black, with shiny stripes of braiding down the sides; the waistcoat is white piqué; the shirt is white with a stiff, detachable white-wing collar and a plain starched bib; the bowtie is matching white.

For the tails pattern, as for the morning dress, use the regular basic jacket block, with the necessary measurements and ease, and peaked lapels.

The full evening dress coattails are narrower than those of the morning dress.

- Draw the basic block for a jacket with peaked lapels.
- Extend the centre back C-C1 as desired (e.g. 60-65 cm from the waist point).
- Draw the hem line C1-B1.
- B-B5 = 5.5 cm/1.97".
- B5-B6 = 4 cm/1.57".
- Draw the dart on the front B6-S2-B7.
- C3-C6 = 6.5 cm/2.48".
- C7-E4 = 25 cm/9.84".
- E4-B7 = 18 cm/7.09".
- Draw B7-E4-W2 with a curved line.
- 21-C9 of back = 8 cm/3.15".
- Draw the line of the side panel L2-C6-C9.
- Draw the side panel L2-W2-W-Q3.

SPENCER JACKET

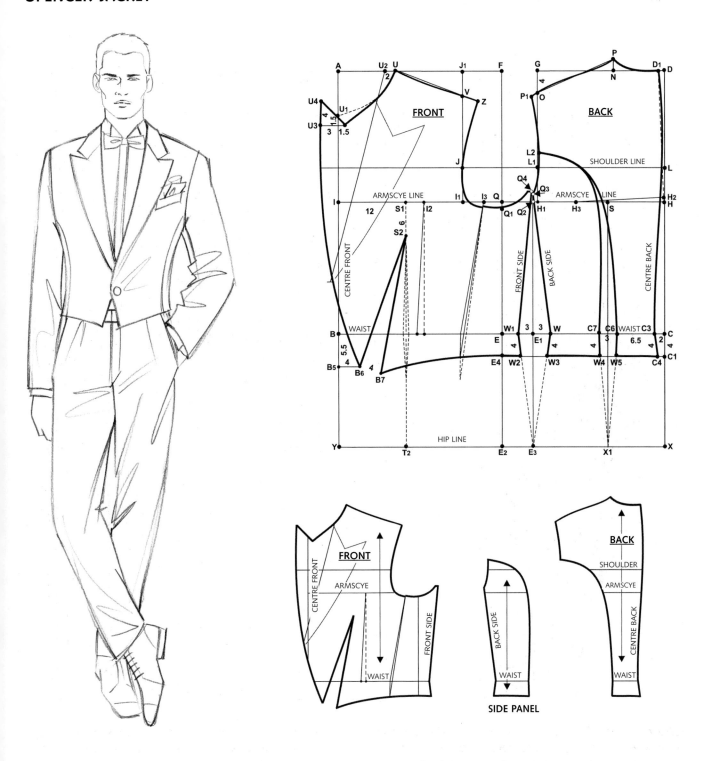

The Spencer is a short jacket that recalls the upper part of full evening dress, and is therefore quite elegant.

It was a typical element of both men's and women's wear in the nineteenth century, and today is mainly worn by young people, perhaps as a non-traditional style for wedding attire.

This jacket extends 4-5 cm/1.57"-1.97" below the waist and is tight-fitting.

It should be worn with trousers in a contrasting classic colour: black, white, cream, or other.

For making the pattern to the Spencer, it is necessary to refer to the evening dress jacket, since the lines are essentially the same in the upper part.

- Draw the basic block for a jacket with peaked lapels.

- Extend the centre back C-C1 of 3.5-5 cm/1.38"-1.97".
- E-E4 as C-C1. Draw C1-E4.
- B-B5 4.5-5.5 cm/1.77"-2.17" and B5-B6 4 cm/1.57".
- Draw the dart on front B6-S2-B7.
- B6-S2 equal to B7-S2.
- C-C3 2 cm/0.79". Draw the line of the centre back.
- H-S 10.5 cm/4.13". Draw S-X1.
- Calculate the width of the darts and the side tapering.
- Draw the lines of the side panel L2-C6-W5 - L2-C7-W4
- Draw the line of the side back Q3-W-W3.
- Draw the line of the side front Q4-W1-W2.
- Draw a curved line B7-E4-W2.
- Join W3-W4 - W5-C4.

Basic block for men's waistcoat

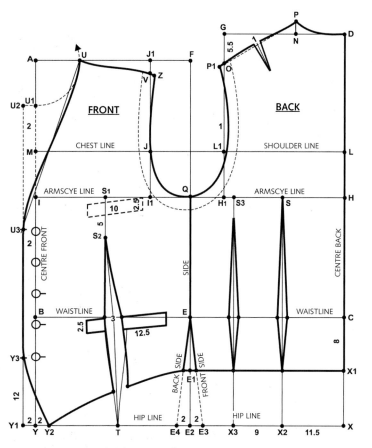

Measurement: (without ease)
- Chest girth   96 cm/37.80"
- Waist circumference   88 cm/34.65"
- Hip circumference   96 cm/37.80"
- Neck circumference   42 cm/16.54"
- Front waist length   47 cm/18.50"
- Back waist length   47 cm/18.50"
- Shoulder width   44 cm/17.32"

- Draw a right angle ABC, with:
- A-B = Front waist length - 1 cm/0.39".
  (e.g.: 47 - 1 = 46 cm).
- B-C Semicircumference bust + ease.
  (e.g.: 96 + 8 = 104 : 2 = 52 cm).
- C-D = Back waist length + 1/0.39". (e.g.: 47 + 4 = 51 cm).
- B-Y and C-X 18-20 cm/7.09"-7.87".
- Draw Y-X. HIP LINE.
- Join A-Y. CENTRE FRONT.
- Join D-X. CENTRE BACK.
- B-E = half B-C.
- A-F = half B-E.
- Y-E2 like B-E
- Join F-E2. SIDE LINE.
- D-H = half C-D + 4. (e.g.: 51 : 2 = 25.5 + 4 = 29.5 cm).
- H-I parallel to B-C. ARMSCYE LINE.
- D-G = half shoulders width + ease
  (e.g.: 44 + 1 = 45 : 2 = 22.5 cm).
  H-L 1/4 D-H + 1. (e.g.: 29.5 : 4 = 7.3 + 1 = 8.3 cm).
- Draw L-M and write SHOULDER LINE and BUST LINE.
- H-H1 like D-G (e.g.: 22.5 cm). Draw G-H1.
- I-I1 like D-G -1 of back (e.g.: 22.5 - 1 = 21.5 cm).
- Draw I1-J1 parallel G-H1.

Back
- G-O = 5.5 cm/1.97".
- D-N = 1/3 of D-G + 1 (e.g.: 22.5 : 3 = 7.5 + 1 = 8.5 cm).
- N-P = 2.5 cm/0.98". Draw D-P in shape.
- P-P1 Shoulder length. (e.g.: 16 cm).
- Draw P-P1 in shape, passing through O.
- Draw the Armhole P1-Q shaping it carefully.
- Create a dart 1 cm/0.39" wide at the shoulder centre.
- C-X1 8 cm/3.15". Draw X1-E1 parallel X-E2.
- E2-E4 2 cm/0.79". Draw E-E4. SIDE BACK.
- H-S and X-X2 11.5 cm/4.53".
- S-S3 and X2-X3 9 cm/3.54".
- Draw two waist darts as required.
Front
- A-U 1/3 of A-J1 + 1. (e.g.: 21.5 : 3 = 7.16 + 1 = 8.16 cm).
- A-U1 like A-U.
- U-U2 2 cm/0.79".
- Y-Y1 2 cm/0.79". Draw Y1-U2 OVERLAP.
- Y-Y2 2 cm/0.79".
- Y1-Y3 12 cm/4.72".
- U2-U3 18-20 cm/7.09"-7.87". Draw the line U-U3.
- I-S1 and Y2-T 13 cm. Draw S1-T.
- S1-S2 5 cm/5.12".
- Create a bust dart by 3-3.5 cm/1.18"-1.38" wide.
- J1-V 2.5 cm /0.98".
- U-Z like P-P1 of back minus 2 (e.g.: 16 - 2 = 14 cm).
- Draw U-Z in shape, passing through V.
- Draw the Armhole Z-J-Q shaping it carefully.
- E2-E3 2. Draw E-E3. SIDE FRONT.

DEEP V-NECK WAISTCOAT

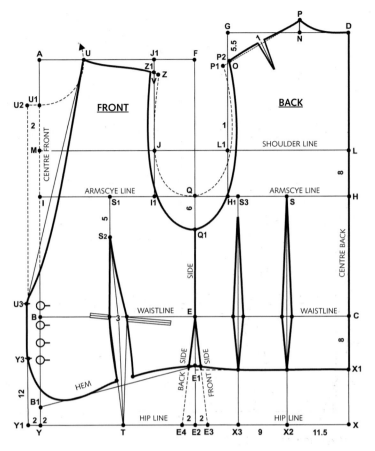

- Draw the waistcoat base.
- U2-U3 35 cm/13.78". Draw U-U3 and shape as shown in the figure.
- B-B1 = 15-16 cm/5.91"-6.30". Draw B1-E1.
- Connect the points with a curved line at the hem.
- Z-Z1 and P1-P2 1-2 cm /0.39"-0.79".
- Q-Q1 = 6 cm/2.36".
- Connect the points to draw the armscye.

SINGLE-BREASTED WAISTCOAT WITH SHAWL COLLAR

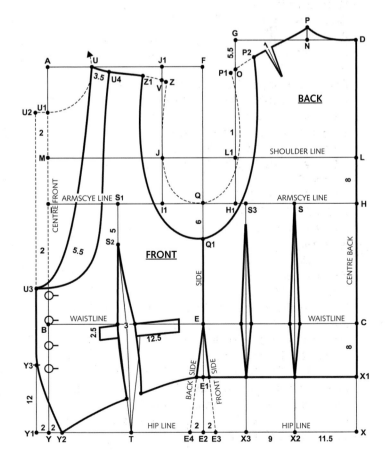

- Draw the waistcoat base.
- U2-U3 = 30 cm/11.81". Draw U-U3 shaping carefully.
- U-U4 = 3.5-4 cm/1.38"-1.57". Draw U4-U3 shaping carefully.
- Z-Z1 and P1-P2 3-4 cm/1.18"-1.57".
- Q-Q1 = 6 cm/2.36".
- Connect the points to draw the armscye.

DOUBLE-BREASTED WAISTCOAT

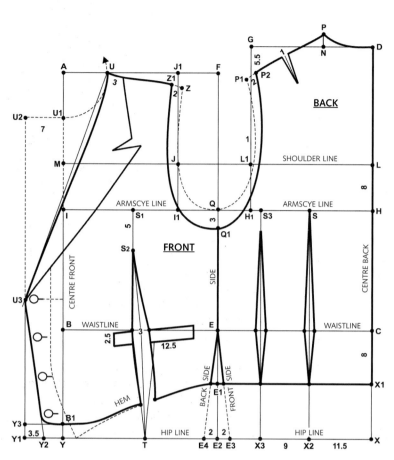

- Draw the waistcoat base.
- U1-U2 and Y-Y1 =
  6.5-7 cm/2.56"-2.76".
- U2-U3 32 cm/12.60".
- Draw U-U3 and shape as in figure.
- Y1-Y2 = 3-3.5 cm/1.18"-1.38".
- Draw Y2-U3.
- B-B1 = 16-17 cm/6.30"-6.69". - Draw B1-E1.
- Connect the points with a curved line at the hem.
- Z-Z1 and P1-P2 = 1-2 cm/0.39"-0.79".
- Q-Q1 = 3-3.5 cm/1.18"-1.38".
- Connect the points to draw the armscye.

CROSS-FRONT WAISTCOAT

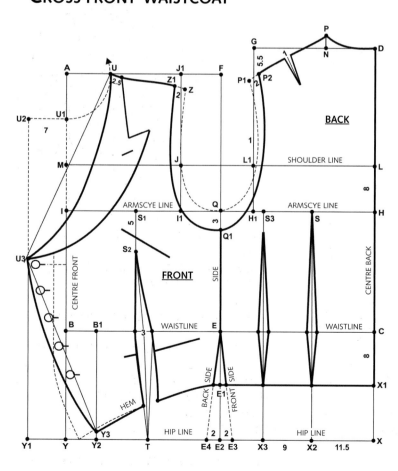

- Draw the waistcoat base.
- U1-U2 and Y-Y1 =
  6.5-7 cm/2.56"-2.76".
- U2-U3 = 25 cm/9.84".
- Draw U-U3 and shape like in figure.
- B-B1 = 5-5.5 cm/1.97"-2.17".
- Draw B1-Y2. Y2-Y3 = 1.5 cm/0.59".
- Draw Y3-U3 shaping carefully.
- Connect the points with a curved line at the hem.
- Z-Z1 and P1-P2 = 1-2 cm/0.39"-0.79".
- Q-Q1 = 3-3.5 cm/1.18"-1.38".
- Connect the points to draw the armscye

Low waistcoat

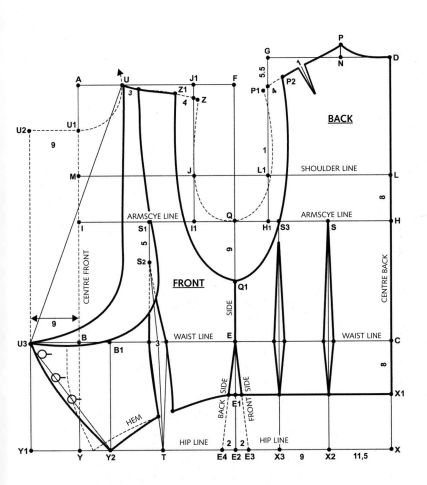

- Draw the waistcoat base.
- U1-U2 and Y-Y1
  8-9 cm/3.15"-3.54".
- U3 at the waist line.
- Draw U-U3 and shape the shawl collar as
  shown in figure
- B-B1 = 5-5.5 cm/1.97"-2.17".
- Draw B1-Y2.
- Draw Y2-U3 shaping carefully.
- Connect the points with a curved line at the hem.
- Z-Z1 and P1-P2 3-4 cm/1.18"-1.57".
- Q-Q1 = 9-9.5 cm/3.54"-3.74".
- Connect the points to draw the armscye.

Backless waistcoat

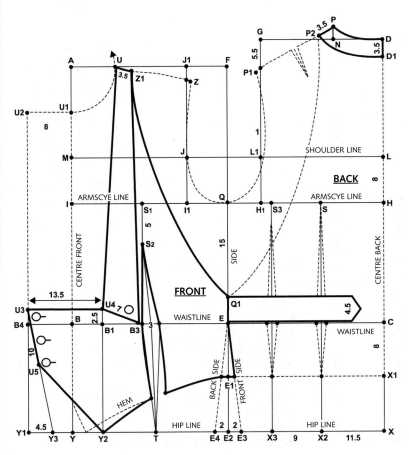

- Draw the waistcoat base.
- U1-U2 and Y-Y1
  7-8 cm/2.76"-3.15".
- Draw U2-Y1.
- U3 by 2-2.5/0.79"-3.54" from the waistline.
- B-B1 = 5-5.5/1.97"-2.17".
- Draw B1-Y2.
- U3-U4 = 13-13.5 cm/5.12"-5.31" and Y1Y3
  4-4.5 cm/1.57"-1.77".
- Draw Y3-U3. - B4-U5 10-10.5 cm/3.94"-4.13".
- Draw U3-U5-Y2.
- Connect with curved line the bottom.
- U-Z1 and P-P2 3.5-4 cm/1.38"-1.57".
- Q-Q1 = 14-15 cm/5.51"-5.91".
- Connect the points to draw the armscye.

Note: *The back is made up of just the collar and the belt tab.*

215

Seam allowances for the waistcoat

Markings for the iron work

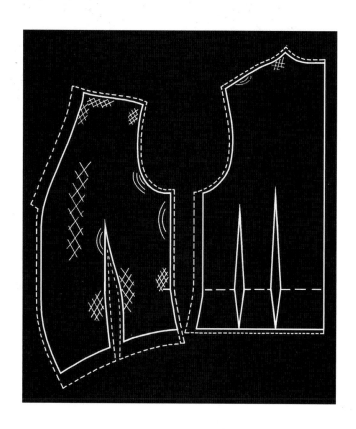

STRETCH

SHRINK

Seam allowances
The seam allowance lines are parallel to the stitching.

Iron work
The "iron work" for the waistcoat, as for the jacket, is very important for obtaining a perfect line.
The iron is used to correct the shoulder line from the point where it meets the neck to the humerus bone; where the fabric hangs loosely, it needs shrinking; the darts must be flattened and adjusted; and the right shape must be given to the side seam and armscye.

CORRECTION FOR CURVED BACK

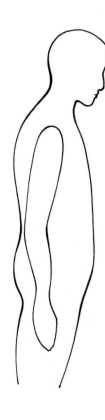

Defects
- Curvature of back 2 cm/0.79".
- Forward shift of arms 0.5 cm/0.20".

This posture is the commonest among the defects of balance, and is typical of old age.

The fulcrum of the curvature is found along the spinal column, which causes the back to hunch over and the chest to contract, with consequent forward shift of the arms, expansion of the upper back, and contraction in front.

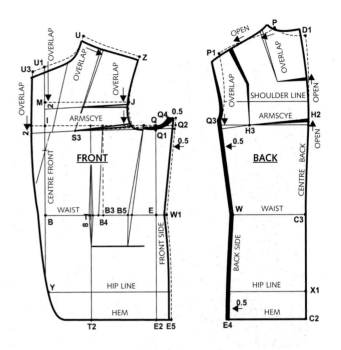

CORRECTION FOR FORWARD HIP TILT

Defects
- Tilt at waist 2 cm/079".
- Allowance for chest 0.5 cm/0.20".
- Backward shift of arms 1 cm/0.39".
- Fullest part of belly increased 2 cm/0.79".

This defect is typical of overweight people who assume this posture to support the abdominal load better, increasing the protrusion of the belly.

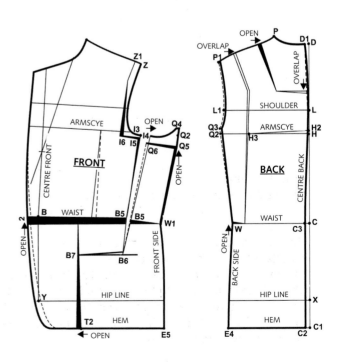

CORRECTION FOR STOUT FIGURE

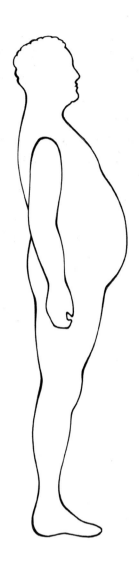

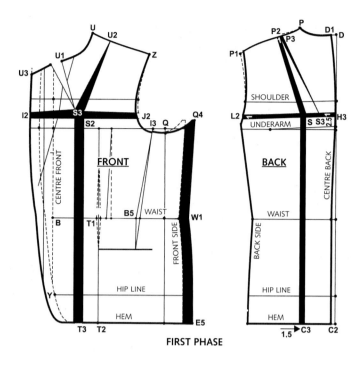

FIRST PHASE

Defects
- Torso excess 7 cm/2.76".
- Hip excess 7 cm/2.76".
- Waist excess 13 cm/5.12".
- Neck excess 1 cm/0.39".
- Arm excess 7 cm/2.76".
- Arm diameter excess 2.5 cm/0.98".

Back
- Raise by 1 cm/0.39" the upper part H3-L2-D1-P1.
- Move by 1.5 cm/0.59" the centre back S-C3-C2-H3.
- Move by 1 cm/0.39" P2-P-D1-H3-S.
- Shift point S 0.5 cm/0.20".
- Even up point P3.

First phase front
- Move the side line by 2.5 cm/0.98".
- Raise by 1.5 cm/0.59" the upper part I2-J2-Z-U-U3.
- Move by 2.5 cm/0.98" the centre front part S2-T3-I2.
- Rotate the part U2-S3-I3 and create a dart.
- Restore the vertical drape of point U3.

Second phase front
- Cut T3-S2 and open by 2 cm/0.79".
- Cut E3-I4 and open by 1 cm/0.39" at the bottom and reshape.
- Increase point B3 by 1.5 cm/0.59".
- Adjust the outlines.

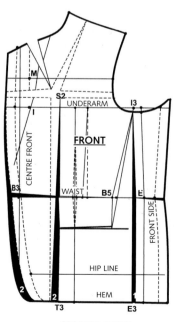

SECOND PHASE

218

CORRECTION FOR HIGH SHOULDERS

Individuals with this shape, especially when it is a question of carriage or habit, may have a thin chest.

Defects
- Shoulders raised by 1.5-2 cm/0.59" 0.79";
- Narrowness of chest 1.5 cm/0.59".

- Raise the front section Z1-S3-Q1-Q4 by 1.5-2 cm/0.59"-0.79
- Raise the back section by the same amount, as shown in figure.
- Adjust the shape of the armscye and the shoulder inclination.

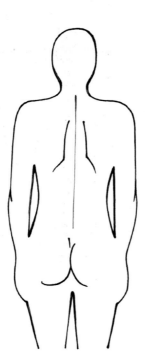

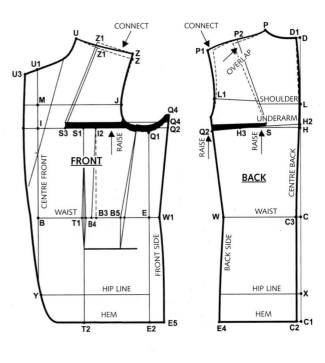

CORRECTION FOR SLOPED SHOULDERS

Individuals with this shape may have narrow chests and waists, and protruding shoulder blades.

Defects:
- Shoulders dropped by 1-1.5 cm/0.39"-0.59".
- Chest narrowness due to sloping shoulders 1.5-2 cm/0.59"-0.79".
- Allowance for protruding shoulder blades 0.5 cm/0.20".
- Waist narrowness due to sloping shoulders 1-1.5 cm/0.39"-0.59".

- Overlap point I4 and Q2 by 1-1.5 cm/0.39"-0.59".
- Open point P2 by 3 cm/1.18".
- Open point P3 by 1 cm/0.39".
- Point O overlaps as a consequence.

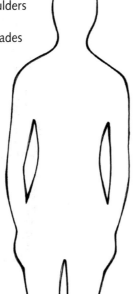

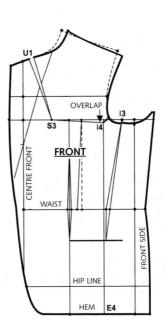

CORRECTION FOR BROAD SHOULDERS

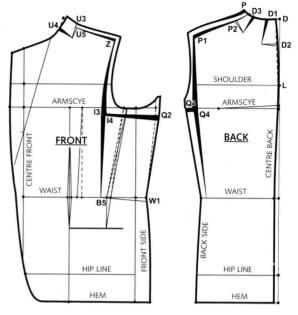

Defects:
- Shoulders raised by 1-1.5 cm/0.39"-0.59".
- Allowance for chest 2-2.5 cm/0.79"-0.98".
- Allowance for neck diameter 1.5-2 cm/0.59"-0.79".
- Allowance for shoulders 1-1.5 cm/0.39"-0.59".

- Open point D1 by 0.8 cm/0.31".
- Point D2 overlaps as a consequence.
- Open point D3 by 0.6 cm/0.24".
- Point P2 overlaps as a consequence.
- Lengthen point Q4 by 1 cm/0.39".

- Raise point Q5 by 1cm/0.39".
- Point P1 shifts as a consequence.
- Point P is 0.4/0.16" longer as a consequence.
- Open point U4 by 0.6 cm/0.24".
- Point U5 overlaps as a consequence.
- Open point I3 by 1 cm/0.39".
- Point W1 overlaps as a consequence.
- Open point Q2 by 1 cm/0.39" thus raising the armscye.
- Point Z shifts as a consequence.
- Point U5 overlaps as a consequence.

CORRECTION FOR PEAR-SHAPED FIGURE

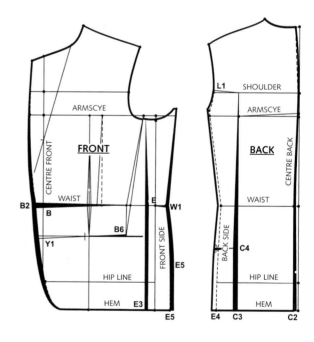

Defects:
- Allowance for waist 3 cm/1.18";
- Allowance for hips 3 cm/1.18";
- Fullest part of belly increased 1-1.5 cm/0.39"-0.59".

- Widen point C2 by 0.5 cm/0.20".
- Open points C3 and C4 by 1 cm /0.39" (1/3 hip allowance).
- Point L1 overlaps as a consequence.
- Widen point E5 by 0.75 cm/0.30" (1/4 hip allowance).

- Open point E by 0.75 cm/0.30" (1/4 waist allowance).
- Open point E3 by 0.75 cm /0.30" (1/4 hip allowance).
- Open W1 by 0.4 cm/0.16".
- Open B6 by 0.5 cm/0.20".
- Point Y1 overlaps by 0.5 cm/0.20" as a consequence.
- Open point B by 1 cm/0.39".
- Open point B2 by 0.5 cm/0.20".

Making a man's jacket

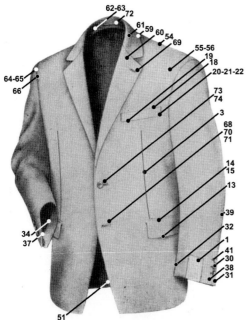

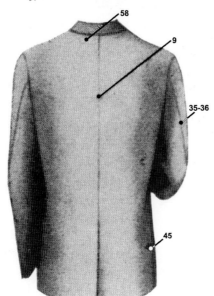

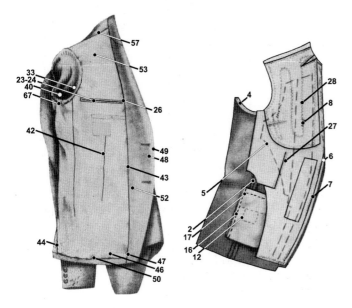

Preliminary tasks
1) Fasten the price tag.

In front
2) Sew side seams.
3) Close breast and side darts.
4) Fasten shoulder and armscye tapes.
5) Baste body canvasses.
6) Shape front, and at the same time separate basting on edges and trim canvas and fabric.
7) Baste edges.
8) Fasten pocket corners internally.

Back
9) Sew centre back seam.
10) Fasten tape to back, the armscye and the collar line.

Side pockets
11) Prepare internal pocket in the side pocket.
12) Finish internal pocket in the side pocket.
13) Make pocket flaps.
14) Pocket flap attachment seam.
15) First seam and simultaneous cut of side pockets.
16) Finish side pockets.
17) Bartacking side pocket corners.

Breast pockets
18) Sew and turn breast pocket trim inside out.
19) Fasten breast pocket.
20) Fasten breast pocket trim.
21) Fasten breast pocket trim internally.
22) Finish breast pocket.

Inner pockets
23) Make inner pocket welting.
24) First seam and simultaneous cut of inner pocket.
25) Closure inner pocket.
26) Bartacking inner pocket corners.

Interior
27) Closure of darts on canvas.
28) Stitching canvas.

Undercollar
29) Stitch and at the same time trim the undercollar.

Sleeves
30) Make buttonholes on sleeves.
31) Sew cuff pleats.
32) Sew sleeve fronts.
33) Sew front sleeve lining.
34) Sew sleeve lining hems.
35) Sew sleeve backs.
36) Sew back sleeve lining.
37) Fasten lining to sleeve hems.
38) Baste sleeve hems.
39) Fasten sleeve lining to back sleeve.
40) Baste upper sleeve lining.
41) Sew sleeve buttons

Inner lining with placket
42) Close breast dart and lining side darts.
43) Join lining to placket.
44) Close lining at sides.
45) Close sides.
46) Stitch inner lining to hem.
47) Sew and topstitch placket corners.
48) Baste placket.
49) Sew and at the same time finishing front edges.
50) Baste lining hem.
51) Baste profiling and edges.
52) Baste lining to the placket.
53) Baste upper part of inner lining.
54) Sew shoulder seams.
55) Baste padding inside shoulder.
56) Baste shoulder.
57) Close shoulder seam in lining.

Collar assembly
58) Join undercollar.
59) Join collar.
60) Baste underside of collar.
61) Baste collar.
62) Baste collar leaf and stand.
63) Sew on collar leaf and stand

Sleeve assembly
64) Sew on sleeves.
65) Sew sleeve roll.
66) Sew on shoulder padding.
67) Sew lining to the underarm part of armscye.

Finishing
68) Mark buttonholes.
69) Make lapel buttonhole.
70) Make front buttonholes.
71) Bar stitch buttonholes.
72) Sew tap for hanging jacket.
73) Sew on buttons.
74) Wrap button threads.

JACKET DETAILING

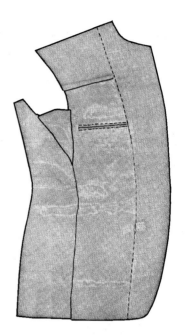

- Sew front darts.
- Apply tape to shoulder seam.
- Iron seams and darts.
- Apply iron-on reinforcement along the pocket opening and at waist height.
- Apply hip pockets and breast pocket.

- Make inner pockets with edging.
- Sew lining to the placket.

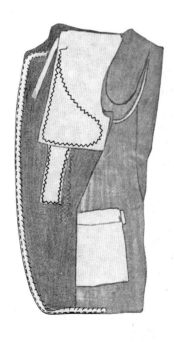

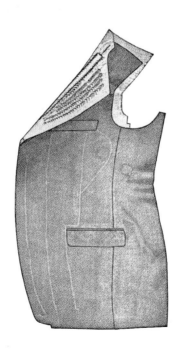

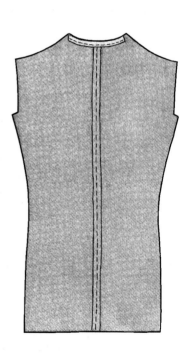

- Baste canvassing to the inside of the jacket.
- Apply tape to armscye.
- Apply tape to the front edges.

- Tailor stitching of the lapels, by hand or by a special machine with invisible stitch.

- Sew centre back seam and apply tape at collar.

JACKET COLLAR AND SLEEVES

COLLAR

1) Trim top collar and under collar.

3) Sew under collar corners by machine.

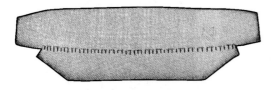

2) Apply under collar to the top collar using a hem stitch by hand or by machine.

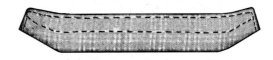

4) Turn out the collar and baste with running stitch; trim the top collar and iron well.

COLLAR ASSEMBLY

1) Baste under collar by hand or by hand basting machine.

2) Top stitch under collar by hand using machine hem stitch.

SLEEVE

- Apply facing to sleeve hem, using a running baste stitch.
- Make button holes on cuffs.

SIZE GRADING

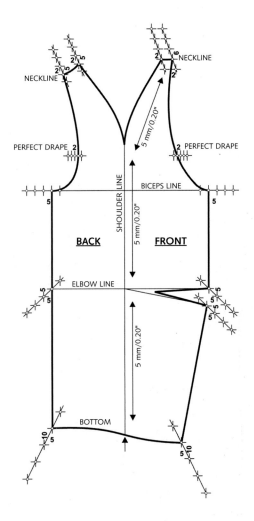

Size grading for dresses 42-50

Rates for increasing the dress size
For the size grading, the suit is divided in four sections: armscye; waistline; hips; hemline, and bust.
The increases in width per size, in order to be more precise and the better to meet the needs, must be different depending on whether they are central sizes (42–50), smaller (38–40) and over (52-56).
Anchor points
In carrying out the grading, it is necessary to have two anchor points

⊕ on the basic block, one horizontal and one vertical. These anchor points may be positioned anywhere on the pattern, selecting ones that are best for the size grading of that particular pattern.
The anchor points for regular grading are as follows: Bust line and centre back (or front); Hip line and centre back; Hem line and centre back; Bust line and bust point; Waist line and upper neckline; underarm line and side; shoulder and back dart point.

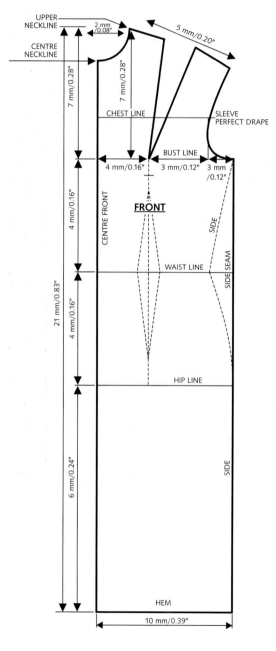
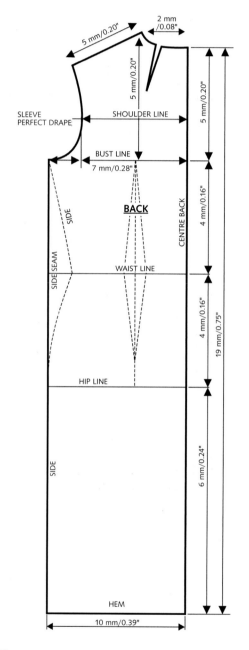

Length
The dress is lengthened a total of 19 mm/0.75" in back and 21 mm/0.83" in front.
The distribution of the values is as follows:
Back
- Armscye sector 5 mm/0.20". - Waist sector 4 mm/0.16".
- Hips sector 4 mm/0.16". - Hem sector 6 mm/0.24".
Front
- Armscye sector 7 mm/0.28". - Waist sector 6 mm/0.24".
- Hips sector 4 mm/0.16". - Hem sector 6 mm/0.24".

Width
- From centre front (or centre back) to the side taper or widen by a total of 10 mm/0.40" (overall 40 mm/1.57" as for the skirt).
Back
- Shoulder width 5 mm/0.20". - Sector 3 mm/0.12".
- Shoulder 5 mm/0.20". - Neckline 2 mm/0.08".
Front
- Centre front-Centre bust 4 mm/0.16".
- Centre bust-Sector 3 mm/0.12" - Sector 3 mm/0.12".

SIZE GRADING FOR DRESSES 38-40

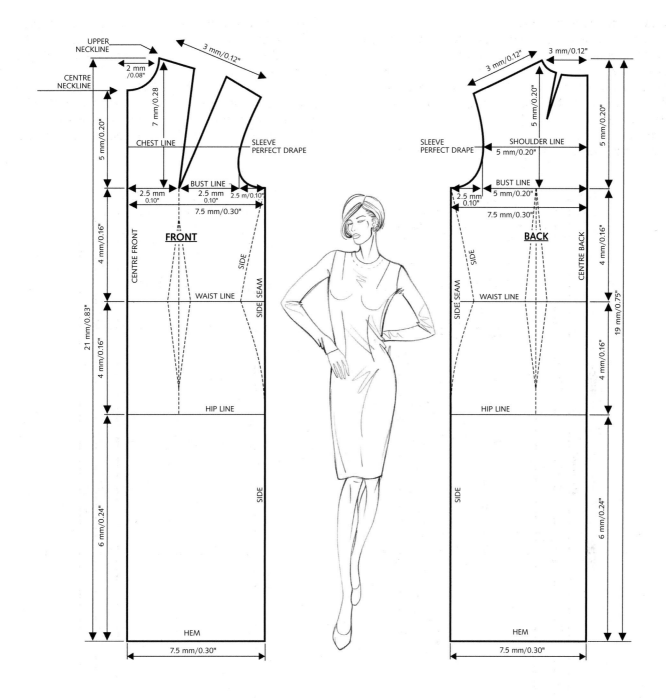

LENGTH

The dress are lengthened a total of 19 mm/0.75" for the back and 21 mm/0.83" for the front.

The distribution of the values is as for the other sizes.

WIDTH

- From centre front (or centre back) to the side taper or widen by a total of 7.5 mm/0.30 (overall 30 mm/1.18").

Back

- Shoulder width 5 mm/0.20".
- Sector 2.5 mm/0.10". - Shoulder 3 mm/0.12".
- Neckline 2 mm/0.08".

Front

- Centre front-Bust point 2.5 mm/0.10".
- Bust point-Sector 2.5 mm/0.10". - Sector 2.5 mm/0.10".

SIZE GRADING FOR DRESSES 52-54-56

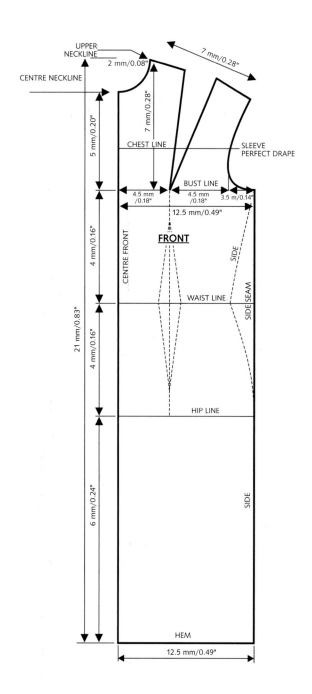

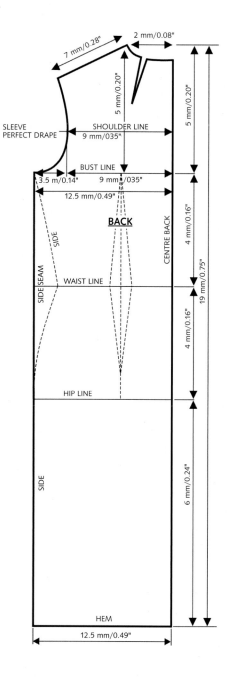

WIDTH
- From centre front (or centre back) to the side taper or widen
  by a total of 12.5 mm/0.49" (overall 50 mm/1.97").

Back
- Shoulder width 9 mm/0.35". - Sector 3.5 mm/0.14".
- Shoulder 7 mm/0.28".
- Neckline 2 mm/0.08".

Front
- Centre front-Bust point 4.5 mm/0.18".
- Bust point
- Sector 4.5 mm/0.18".
- Sector 3.5 mm/0.14".

SIZE GRADING DRESS BACK ANCHOR POINT

AND BUST LINE

The back grading, in this case, for both larger and smaller sizes, is carried out by keeping the bust line and the side line fixed.

Length measurements
The back length measurements lengthen and shorten a total of 19 mm/0.75" per size, as follows:
- Armscye sector 5 mm/0.20".
- Waist sector 4 mm/0.16".
- Hips sector 4 mm/0.16".
- Hem sector 6 mm/0.24".

Centre neckline
Squared
- Raise or drop 5 mm/0.20".
- Widen 10 mm/0.40" and reduce 7.5 mm/0.30".

Upper neckline
Squared
- Drop and raise 5 mm/0.20".
- Widen and reduce 8 mm/0.32".
Neckline dart
For grading the neckline darts drope and raise 5 mm/0.20".
- Widen 8 mm/0.32".
Perfect drape armscye
- Reduce 2.5 mm/0.10" and widen 3 mm/0.12".
Centre-back bust line
- Reduce 7.5 mm/0.30" and widen 10 mm/0.40".
Centre-back waist line
Squared
- Raise or drop 4 mm/0.16".
- Reduce 7.5 mm/0.30" and widen 10 mm/0.40".
Side waist line
- Raise and drop 4 mm/0.16".
Centre-back hip line
- Raise and drop 8 mm/0.32".
- Reduce 7.5 mm/0.30" and widen 10 mm/0.40".
Side hip line
- Raise and drop 8 mm/0.32".
Centre-back hem line
Squared
- Raise and drop 14 mm/0.56".
- Reduce 7.5 mm/0.30" and widen 10 mm/0.40".
Side hem line
- Raise and drop 8 mm/0.32".

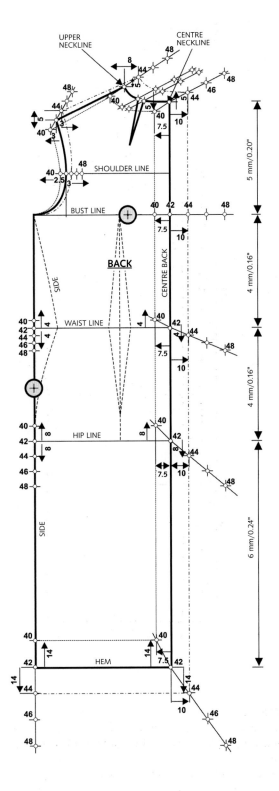

Note: *The horizontal grading values change depending on the size zone, as described above.*

Size grading dress front bust line anchor point

and bust point

The front grading, for both larger and smaller sizes, is done by keeping the bust point fixed, in order to keep the measurements more balanced, the shoulder slope, and the depth of the dart.

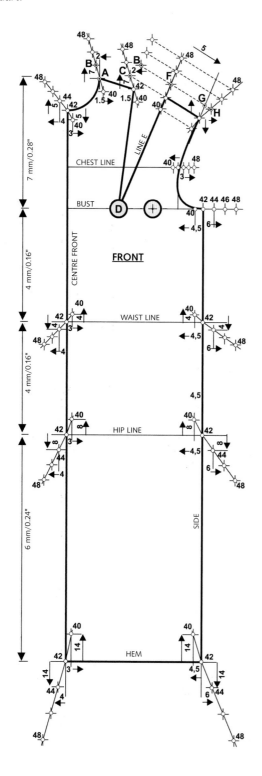

Length measurements
The length measurements of the front part are like those of the back, except in the top part, which can be made longer or shorter by 7 mm/0.28", instead of 5 mm/0.20". This is because the front with darts is almost always longer.
Centre neckline
Squared:
- Drop and raise by 5 mm/0.20".
- Widen 4 mm/0.16" and reduce 3 mm/0.12"
Upper neckline
Squared:
- Drop and raise by 7 mm/0.28".
- Widen and reduce by 2 mm/0.08".
Dart size
To carry out the grading of the bust and front shoulder darts, the procedure is as follows:
- From the intersection of the shoulder and the neckline (point A), measure 7 mm/0.28" and then, at right angles, 2 mm/0.8" (point B).
- From point B, draw a line with the same slope (so, parallel), from the shoulder and with the same length (point C); so we see that the shoulder does not narrow in this part.
- Lay a piece of tissue paper on the pattern, mark out points B and C, and, holding down point D at the tip of the dart, rotate the tissue paper until point C meets line E (suitably elongated); pass through points B and C, to reach point F.
- Extend line B–F towards the side, lay the paper pattern on this line and mark again the same width as the shoulder (point G).
- From point G, measure 5 mm/0.20" to create the new shoulder point H.
Armscye perfect drape
- Reduce 2.5 mm/0.10" and widen 3 mm/0.12".
Bust line - Side point
- Reduce 4.5 mm/0.18" and widen 6 mm/0.24".
Waist line
Squared:
- Drop and raise 4 mm/0.16".
- Reduce 4.5 mm/0.18" and widen 6 mm/0.24" on the side.
- Reduce 3 mm/0.12" and widen 4 mm/0.16" on the centre front.
Hip line
Squared:
- Drop and raise 8 mm/0.32".
- Reduce 4.5 mm/0.18" and widen 6 mm/0.24" on the side.
- Reduce 3 mm/0.12" and widen 4 mm/0.16" on the centre front.
Hem line
Squared:
- Drop and raise 14 mm/0.56".
- Reduce 4.5 mm/0.18" and widen 6 mm/0.24" on the side
- Reduce 3 mm/0.12" and widen 4 mm/0.16" on the centre front.

Note: *The horizontal grading values change depending on the size zone, as described above.*

SIZE GRADING DRESS CENTRE-BACK ANCHOR POINT

AND BUST LINE

The back grading, in this case, for both larger and smaller sizes, is carried out by keeping the bust line and the side line fixed.

Length measurements

The back length measurements lengthen and shorten a total of 19 mm/0.75" per size, as follows:
- Armscye sector 5 mm/0.20".
- Waist sector 4 mm/0.16".
- Hips sector 4 mm/0.16".
- Hem sector 6 mm/0.24".

Centre neckline
Centre neckline
Squared
- Raise or drop 5 mm/0.20".
Upper neckline
Squared
- Drop and raise 5 mm/0.20".
- Widen and reduce 2 mm/0.08".
Neckline dart
For grading the neckline darts drop and raise 5 mm/0.20".
Perfect drape armscye
- Reduce 5 mm/0.20" and widen 7 mm/0.28".
Side bust line
- Reduce 7.5 mm/0.30" and widen 10 mm/0.40".
Side waist line
Squared
- Raise or drop 4 mm/0.16".
- Reduce 7.5 mm/0.30" and widen 10 mm/0.40".
Centre-back waist line
- Raise and drop 4 mm/0.16".
Side hip line
Squared
- Raise and drop 8 mm/0.32".
- Reduce 7.5 mm/0.30" and widen 10 mm/0.40"
Centre-back hip line
- Raise and drop 8 mm/0.32".
Side hem line
Squared
- Raise and drop 14 mm/0.56".
- Reduce 7.5 mm/0.30" and widen 10 mm/0.40".
Centre-back hem line
- Raise and drop 14 mm/0.56".

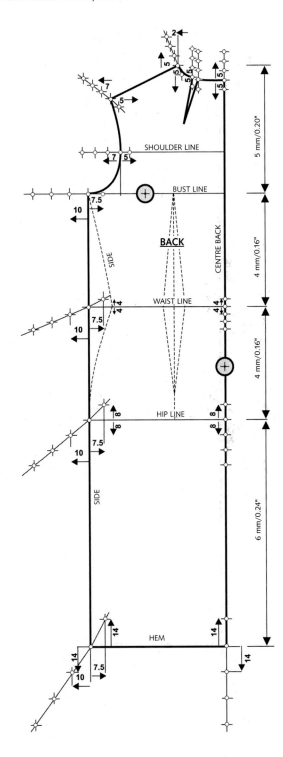

Note: *The horizontal grading values change depending on the size zone, as described above.*

Size grading dress back

Hip line and centre back anchor points

Hem line and centre back anchor points

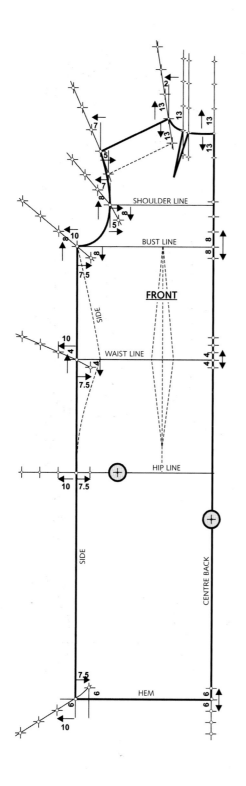

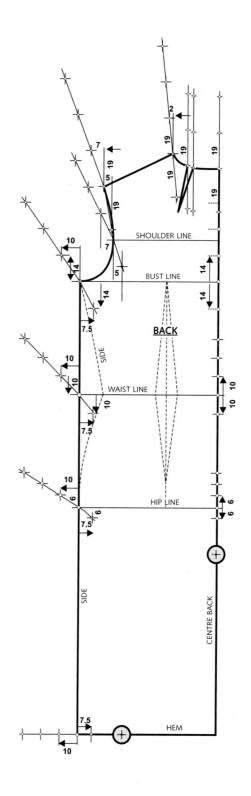

232

SIZE GRADING DRESS BACK

NECK POINT AND WAIST LINE ANCHORS

NECK AND SHOULDER POINT ANCHORS

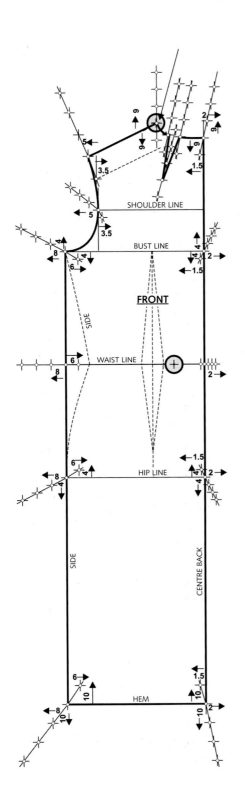

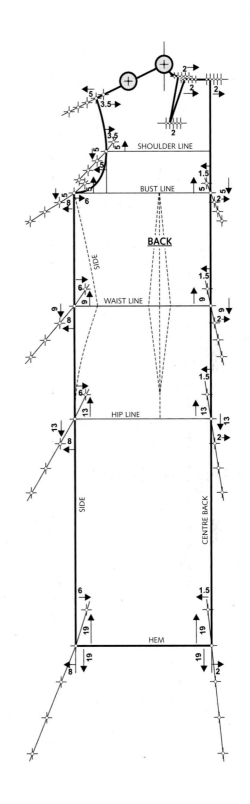

Size grading dartless dresses

The back grading, in this case, for both larger and smaller sizes, is carried out by keeping the bust line and the centre back line fixed, as for the darted dress.

Grading of the dartless front is much easier.

To increase the values, the same procedure as for the back is used. The only difference is that the top section increases and decreases by 6 mm/0.24" instead of 5 mm/0.20", with a total increase of 20 mm/0.79".

Length measurements

The length measurements of the front part are made longer or shorter by a total of 20 mm/0.79" as follows: Top sector 6 mm/0.24"; waist sector 4 mm/0.16"; hip sector 4 mm/0.16"; hem sector 6 mm/0.24".

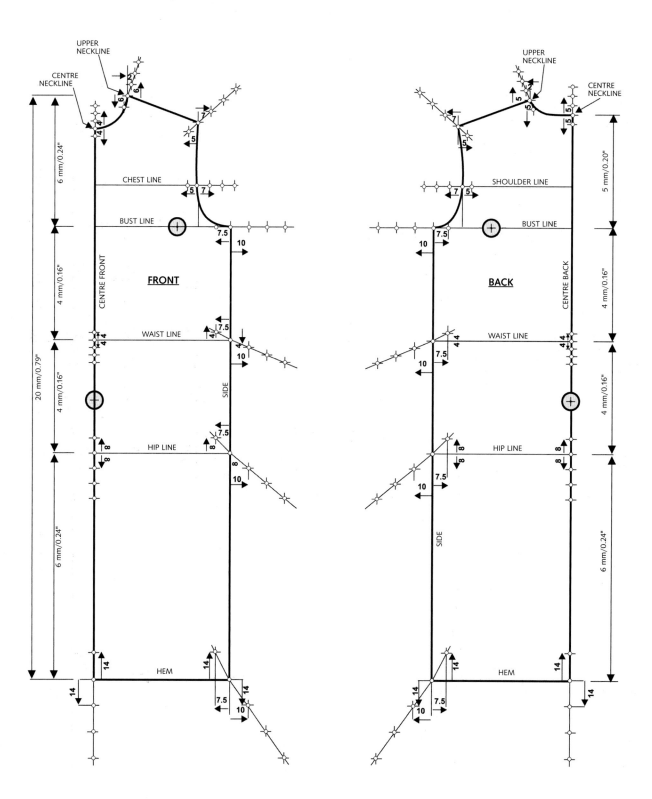

SIZE GRADING FLARED DRESS

WITH SHIFTED BUST DART

Important note
When grading a front section with bust dart open in another position (that is, it is not open on the shoulder), it is necessary to close it momentarily, re-opening it on the shoulder.

This step is necessary because the size of the dart must be increased or diminished by 2 mm/0.08" and to do this is not possible if the dart is not in the position established.

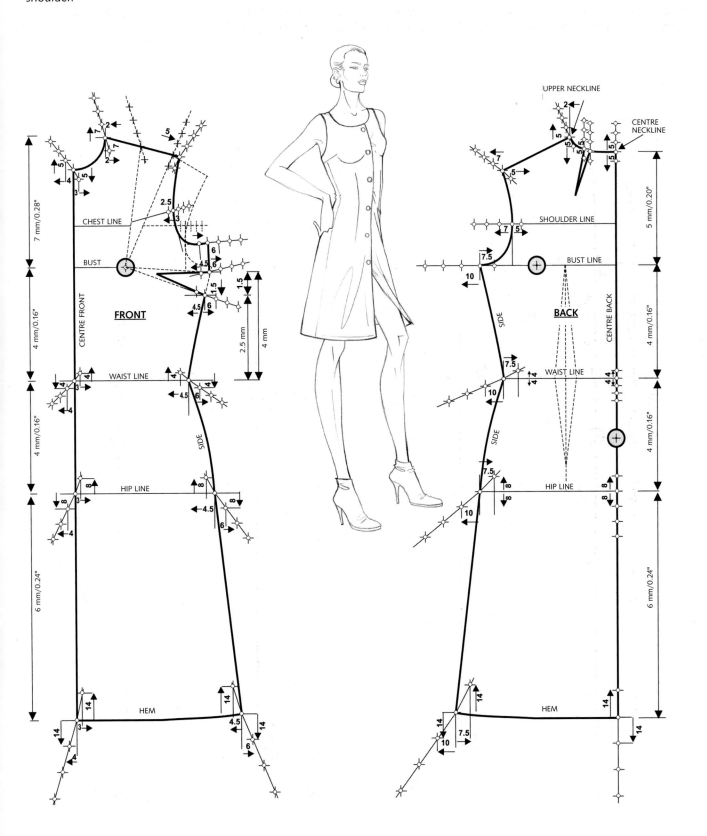

Size Grading Three-Piece Jacket

FRONT - SIDE PANEL - AND BACK

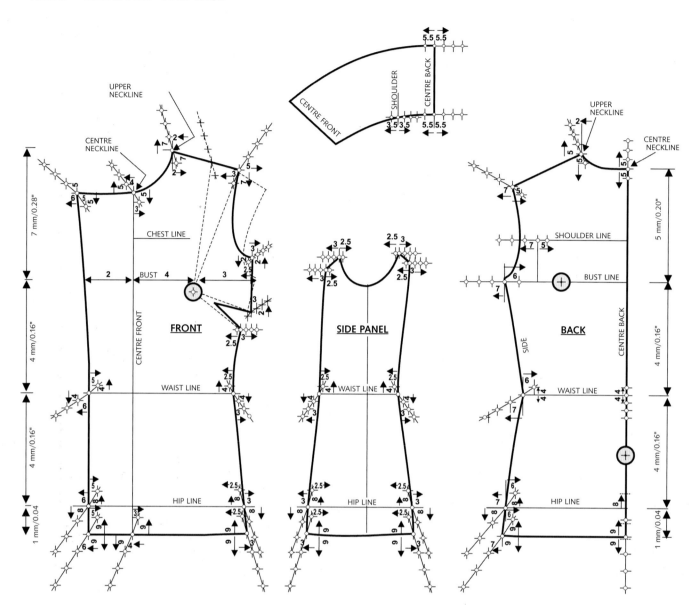

FRONT PART

Centre neckline - Squared: - Raise and drop 5 mm/0.20".
- Widen 4 mm/0.16" and reduce 3 mm/0.12".
Double breasted lapel - Squared: - Raise and drop 5 mm/0.20".
- Widen 6 mm/0.24" and reduce 5 mm/0.20".
(This fastening must be made tighter or looser in proportion to the amount taken in from the centre to the bust dart.)
Upper neckline - Squared: - Raise and drop 7 mm/0.28".
- Widen and reduce 2 mm/0.08".
Bust line - The bust dart starts from the side panel seam, so for the grading it is necessary first to open it momentarily on the shoulder, to increase or decrease its size correctly.
Shoulder point - Widen 5 mm/0.20" and reduce 3 mm/0.12".
Point where the side panel and undersleeve meet - Squared: - Raise and drop 2 mm/0.08". - Widen 3 mm/0.12" and reduce 2.5 mm/0.10".
Waist point - Squared: - Raise and drop 4 mm/0.16". - Front overlap must be widened 6 mm/0.24" and reduced 5 mm/0.20".
- Widen the side 3 mm/0.12" and reduce it 2.5 mm/0.10".
Hem point - Squared: - Raise and drop 9 mm/0.35".
- Front overlap widen 6 mm/0.24" and reduce 5 mm/0.20".

- Raise side 3 mm/0.12" and reduce 2.5 mm/0.10".
Hip point - Squared: - Raise and drop 8 mm/0.31". - Widen and reduce as hemline.

UNDERSLEEVE SIDE PANEL

Sleeve perfect drape - Widen 3 mm/0.12" and reduce 2.5 mm/0.10".
Waist point - As side front.
Hem point and hips - As side front.

BACK FACING

Centre neckline - Raise and drop 5 mm/0.20".
Upper neckline - Squared: - Raise and drop 5 mm/0.20".
- Widen and reduce 2 mm/0.08".
Waist point - Raise and drop 4 mm/0.16" on the centre back.
- Raise and drop 4 mm/0.16" on the side. - Widen 7 mm/0.28" and reduce 6 mm/0.24".
Hem point - Raise and drop 9 mm/0.35" on the centre back.
- Raise and drop 9 mm/0.35" on the side. - Widen 7 mm/0.28" and reduce 6 mm/0.24".
Hip point - Raise and drop 8 mm/0.31". - On the side widen and reduce as the bottom point.

NORMAL SPORTS COLLAR

- Widen and reduce 5 mm/0.20" on the centre back.

Size grading four-piece jacket

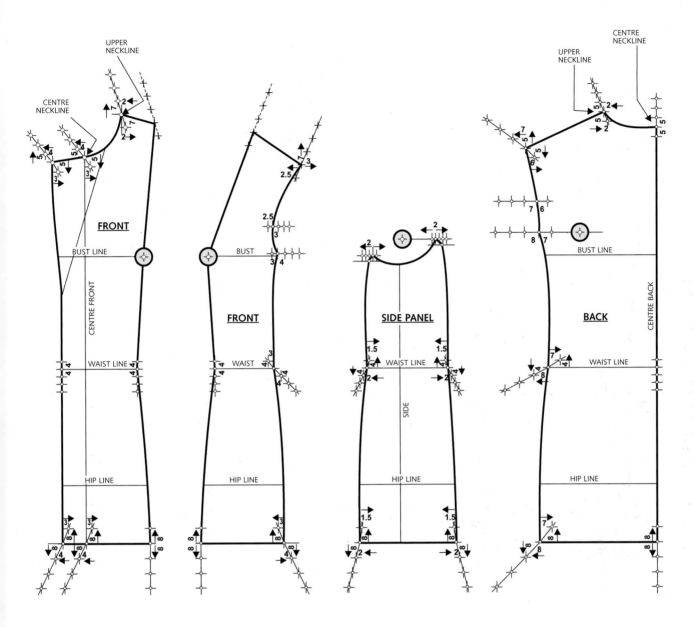

FRONT PART

Centre neckline - Squared: - Raise and drop 5 mm/0.20"
- Widen 4 mm/0.16" and reduce 3 mm/0.12".

Single-breasted lapel - Squared: - Raise and drop 5 mm/0.20".
- Widen 4 mm/0.16" and reduce 3 mm/0.12".

Upper neckline - Squared: - Raise and drop 7 mm/0.28".
- Widen and reduce 2 mm/0.08".

Bust point - The bust dart is part of the seam.
- The procedure is similar to the one described above.

Waist point - Raise and drop 4 mm/0.16".

Hem point - Squared: - Raise and drop 8 mm/0.31".
- Front overlap must be widened 4 mm/0.16" and reduced 3 mm/0.12". - Side must not be widened.

FRONT SIDE PANEL

Shoulder point - Widen 3 mm/0.12" and reduce 2.5 mm.
Point where the side panel and undersleeve meet. - Widen 4 mm /0.16" and reduce it 3 mm/0.12".

Waist point - Squared: - Raise and drop 4 mm/0.16". - Widen the side 4 mm/0.16" and reduce it 3 mm/0.12".

Hem point - Squared: - Raise and drop 8 mm/0.31". - Front overlap must be widened 4 mm/0.16" and reduced 3 mm/0.12".

BACK FACING

Centre neckline - Raise and drop 5 mm/0.20".

Upper neckline - Squared: - Raise and drop 5 mm/0.20".
 - Widen and reduce 2 mm/0.08".

Waist point - Raise and drop 4 mm/0.16" on the centre back.
- Raise and drop 4 mm/0.16" on the side. - Widen 8 mm/0.31" and reduce 7 mm/0.28".

Hem point - Raise and drop 8 mm/0.31" on the centre back.
- Raise and drop 8 mm/0.31" on the side, widen 8 mm /0.31" and reduce 7 mm/0.28".

UNDERSLEEVE SIDE PANEL

Sleeve perfect drape - Widen 2 mm/0.08" and reduce 1.5 mm/0.06".

Waist point - Squared: - Raise and drop 4 mm/0.16".
- Widen 2 mm/0.08" and reduce 1.5 mm/0.06".

Hem point and hips - Squared: - Raise and drop 8 mm/0.31".
- Widen 2 mm/0.08" and reduce 1.5 mm/0.06".

Size grading fitted sleeve

Before starting to size grade a fitted sleeve, you need to measure by how much the armscye of the front and back bodice has increased. To find this value, you start at the perfect drape point (point L) on the paper pattern for the back, and, moving in the direction of the new shoulder (point M), you measure the difference (in this case we found 3.5 mm /0.14" for the back and 4 mm/0.16" for the front).

Then, keeping the pattern on the perfect drape point L, move in the direction of the graded side (point N), and measure the difference (in this case, we found 3 mm/0.12", from point L to point N, both front and back).

These values are marked on the sleeve pattern.

Now draw the sleeve and set the line R-S square with respect to the straight grain.

On the paper pattern, from the perfect drape point on the front, point A, measure 4 mm/0.16" towards the shoulder (this is how much the sleeve is to be increased or decreased on the front) and lay this new point on the front perfect drape point; mark the new armhole on the straight grain up to the shoulder on the paper pattern.

Keeping to the paper pattern, from the shoulder moving towards the perfect drape point on the back, measure 3.5 mm/0.14", and lay this point on the new shoulder marked S at the end of the armhole (ever respecting the straight grain) and draw the curve of the sleeve head, including the perfect drape point and the end of the armhole (point T).

From point T measure 3 mm/0.12" and from point R on the front 3 mm/0.12".

Finish by lengthening the sleeve by 10 mm/0.39" from points R and S, down to the cuff on the straight grain.

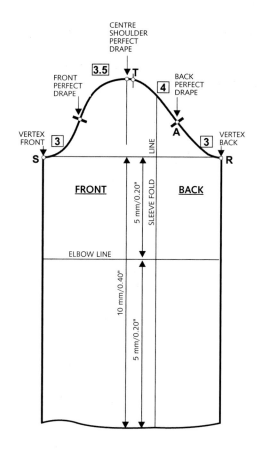

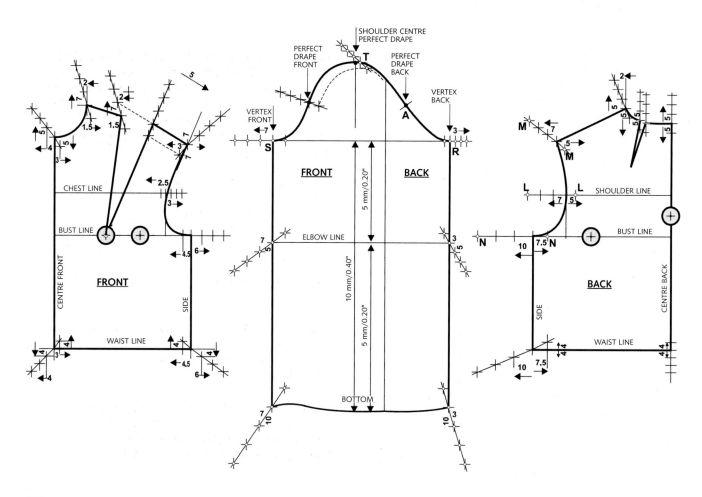

Size Grading Two-Piece Fitted Sleeve

For size grading the two-piece sleeve with centre shoulder seam, proceed as for the whole sleeve.
Just copy the values written on the front and back shoulder-cuff seamlines.

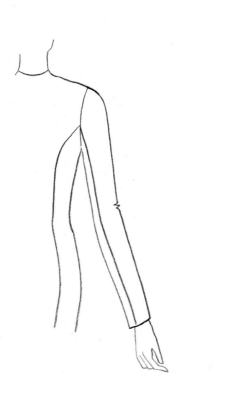

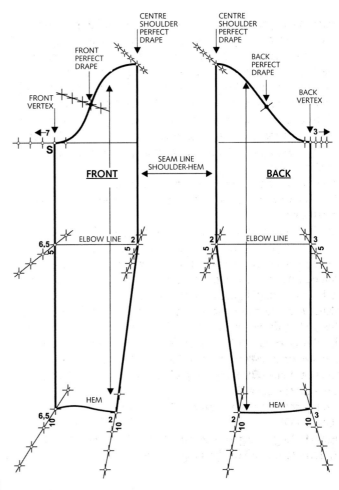

Size Grading Sleeve with Undersleeve

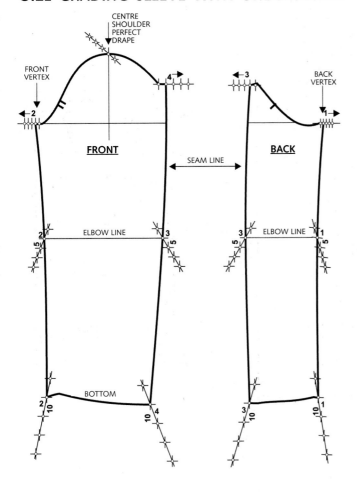

Oversleeve
- Lay the basic bodice block over the new front perfect drape point and measure the difference between the basic block shoulder and that of the upper and lower pattern.
- Drop or raise by 3 mm/0.12" the sleeve pattern on the shoulder drape and, keeping it perpendicular to the centre shoulder line, draw the outlines as far as the front and back perfect drape.

Front vertex
- Widen and reduce 2 mm/0.08".

Seam vertex
- Widen and reduce 4 mm/0.16".

Elbow line
- Widen and reduce 2 mm/0.08", raise and drop 5 mm/0.20" on the front.
- Widen and reduce 4 mm/0.16", raise and drop 5 mm/0.20" on the seam line.

Hem point
- Widen and reduce 2 mm/0.08", raise and drop 10 mm/0.39" on the front.
- Widen and reduce 4 mm/0.16", raise and drop 10 mm/0.39" on the seam line.

Undersleeve
- Reduce and widen di 3 mm/0.12" on the seam line.
- Reduce and widen 1 mm/0.02" on the back.
- Raise and drop 5 mm/0.20" on the elbow line.
- Extend and shorten 10 mm/0.39" on the hem.

SIZE GRADING A RAGLAN BODICE BLOCK

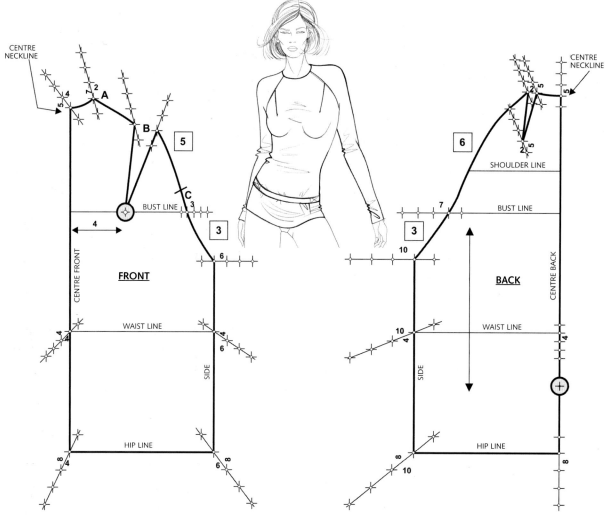

Front
Centre neckline
Squared:
- Drop and raise 7 mm/0.28".
- Widen 5 mm/0.20" and reduce 4 mm/0.16".

Upper neckline
Squared:
- Drop and raise 7 mm/0.28".
- Widen and reduce 2 mm/0.08".
- Mark off the first part of the shoulder that runs from the neckline point to the dart (which remains unchanged), holding the paper pattern in alignment, join it to the bust point which is raised 3 mm/0.12". Measure the length thus obtained and copy it to the other leg of the dart, proceeding with the system used for the fitted sleeve block.

Bust hem-side point
- Reduce 3 mm/0.12" and widen 4 mm/0.16".

Sleeve bottom-side point
- Reduce 4.5 mm/0.18" and widen 6 mm/0.24".

Waist line
Squared:
- Drop and raise 4 mm/0.16".
- Reduce 4.5 mm/0.18" and widen 6 mm/0.24" on the side.
- Reduce 3 mm/0.12" and widen 4 mm/0.16" on the centre front.

Hemline
Squared:
- Drop and raise 8 mm/0.31".
- Reduce 4.5 mm/0.18" and widen 6 mm/0.24" on the side 0.

- Reduce 3 mm/0.12" and widen 4 mm/0.16" on the centre front.

BACK
Centre neckline
Squared:
- Drop and raise 5 mm/0.20".
- Widen and reduce 2 mm/0.08".

Upper neckline
Squared:
- Drop and raise 5 mm/0.20".

Neckline dart
- For making the neckline dart, drop and raise 5 mm/0.20".
- Widen and reduce 2 mm/0.08".

Bust line-sleeve seam
- Reduce 5 mm/0.20" and widen 7 mm/0.28".

Sleeve hem-side point
- Reduce 7,5 mm/0.30" and widen 10 mm/0.39".

Waist line-side point
Squared:
- Drop and raise 4 mm/0.16".
- Reduce 7.5 mm/0.30" and widen 10 mm/0.39".

Waist line-centre back
- Raise and lower 4 mm/0.16".

Hem line-side
Squared:
- Drop and raise 8 mm/0.31".
- Reduce 7.5 mm/0.30" and widen 10 mm/0.39".

Hem line-centre back
- Raise and drop 8 mm/0.31".

Size grading a two-piece raglan sleeve

Front

- Measure against the basic block how much longer the upper line is and how much shorter the lower line is at points C – B – A of the bodice.
- Copy the same measurements on the sleeve by the points C1 – A1.
- Squaring up, raise or drop by the value found (5 mm/0.20").
- Draw the outline of the sleeve pattern block up to the shoulder perfect drape point (point D).
- Widen and reduce 2 mm/0.08" from point D and draw the line down to the hem.

Hem point
Squared:
- Raise and drop 10 mm/0.39". - Widen and reduce 2 mm/0.08" on the seam above. - Widen and reduce 3 mm/0.12" on the seam below.

Elbow point
Squared:
- Raise and drop 5 mm/0.20". - Widen and reduce as hem.

Armscye point
- Widen and reduce 3 mm/0.12". - Biceps line: widen and reduce 2 mm/0.08".

Back

Follow the same procedure as for the front. Only the neckline value changes: it is raised or dropped by 6 mm/0.24".

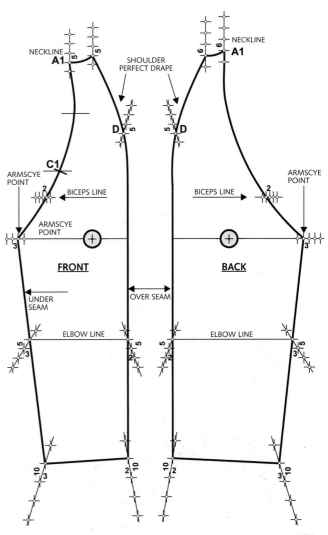

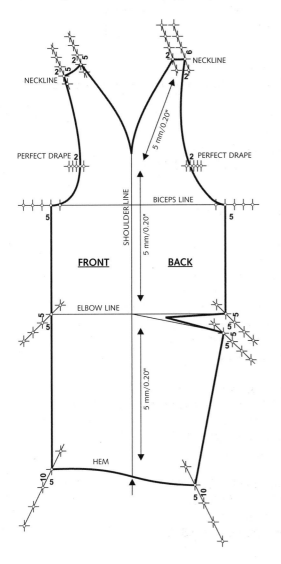

Size grading a one-piece raglan sleeve

Front

Drop and raise the two neckline points of the sleeve by the amount found measuring the basic bodice block against the smaller or larger size (5 mm/0.20").

Perfect drape
- Widen and reduce 2 mm/0.08".

Biceps line
- Widen and reduce 5 mm/0.20".

Elbow point
Squared:
- Raise and drop 5 mm/0.20".
- Widen and reduce 5 mm/0.20".

Bottom point
Squared:
- Raise and drop 10 mm/0.39".
- Widen and reduce 5 mm/0.20".

Back

Follow the same procedure as for the front. Only the neckline value changes: it is raised or dropped by 6 mm/0.24".

Size grading a kimono

The best way to size grade the kimono is to keep the front and back sides fixed.

Front
Centre neckline
- Drop and raise 5 mm/0.20".
- Widen and reduce 10 mm/0.39".
Upper neckline
- Drop and raise 7 mm/0.28".
- Widen and reduce 8 mm/0.31".
- Keeping the basic block squared up, mark the new perfect drape point, widening and reducing by 5 mm/0.20".
Bust point
- From the bust point widen and reduce by 6 mm/0.24".
- Draw the first part of the shoulder (which remains unchanged).
- Draw the new dart line and carry the same measurement over to the second leg of the dart, which is the starting point for the rest of the shoulder, joined with the sleeve, drawn using the basic block.
Centre back hem
- Drop and raise 4 mm/0.16".
- Widen and reduce 10 mm/0.39".
Side hem line
- Raise and drop 4 mm/0.16".
Sleeve hem
- Lengthen and shorten 10 mm/0.39".

Back
Centre neckline
- Drop and raise 5 mm/0.20".
- Widen and reduce 10 mm/0.39".
Upper neckline
- Drop and raise 5 mm/0.20".
- Widen and reduce 8 mm/0.31".
- Keeping the basic block squared up, mark the new perfect drape point, widening and reducing by 5 mm/0.20".
Centre back hem
- Drop and raise 4 mm/0.16".
- Widen and reduce 10 mm/0.39".
Side hem line
- Raise and drop 4 mm/0.16".
Sleeve hem
- Lengthen and shorten 10 mm/0.39".

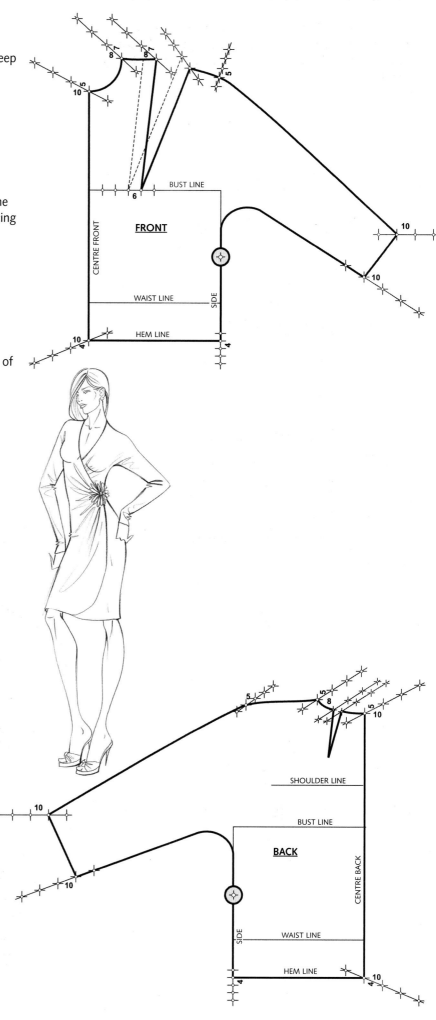

242

Size grading a kimono with gusset

For the size grading of a kimono with gusset, follow the same procedure as the classic kimono without gusset. Change only the part regarding the front and back undersleeve, which widens or tightens by 2 mm/0.08".

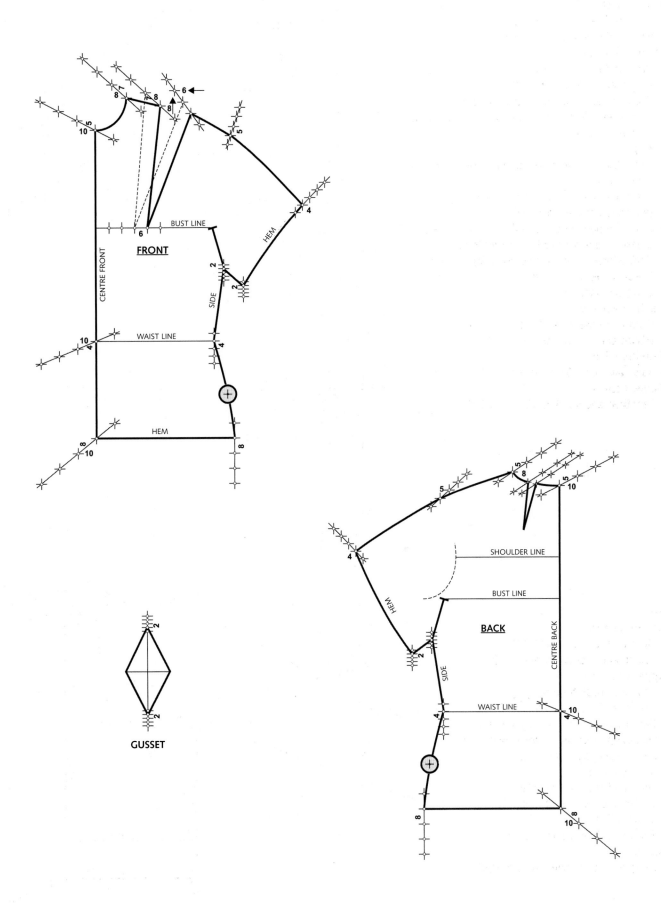

SIZE GRADING A JUMP SUIT

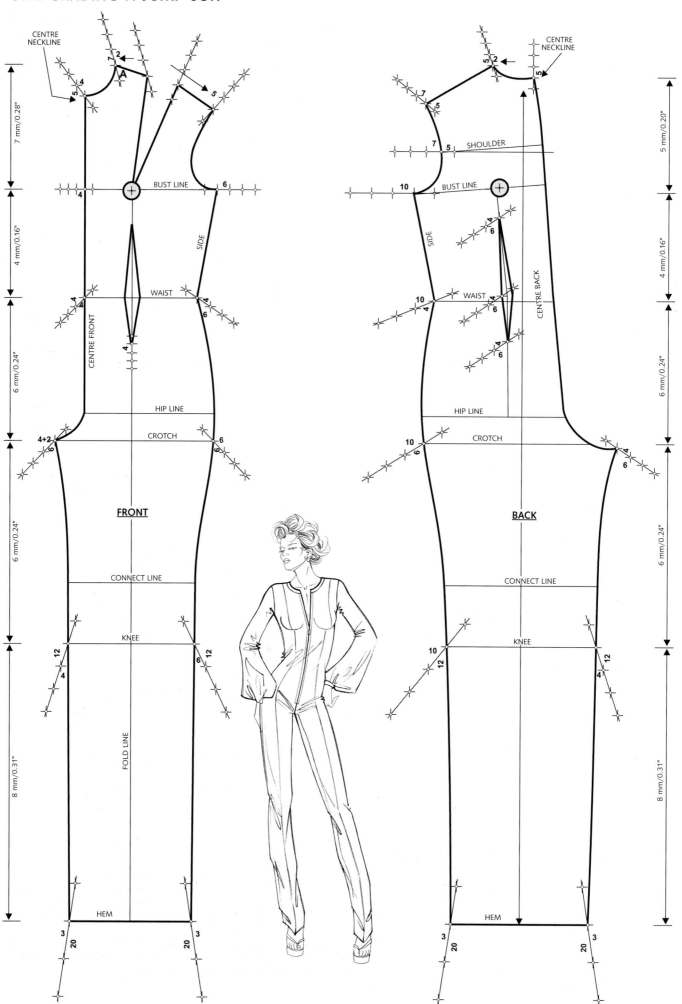

FRONT

BACK

SIZE GRADING COLLARS

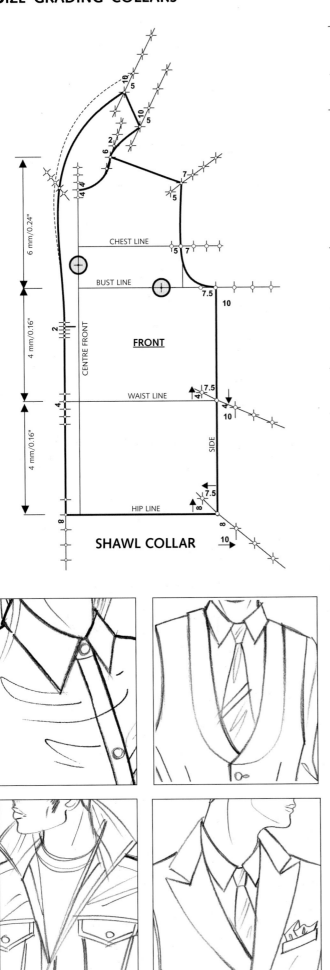

CHEST LINE

BUST LINE

FRONT

CENTRE FRONT

WAIST LINE

SIDE

HIP LINE

6 mm/0.24"

4 mm/0.16"

4 mm/0.16"

SHAWL COLLAR

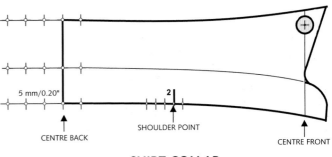

5 mm/0.20"

CENTRE BACK   SHOULDER POINT   CENTRE FRONT

SHIRT COLLAR

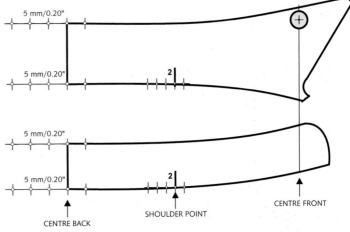

5 mm/0.20"

5 mm/0.20"

5 mm/0.20"

5 mm/0.20"

CENTRE BACK   SHOULDER POINT   CENTRE FRONT

SHIRT COLLAR WITH DETACHED BAND

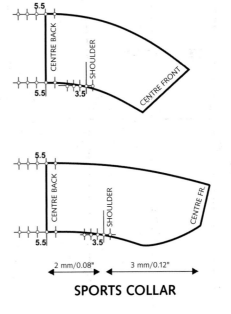

5.5
CENTRE BACK
SHOULDER
5.5   3.5
CENTRE FRONT

5.5
CENTRE BACK
SHOULDER
5.5   3.5
CENTRE FR.

2 mm/0.08"   3 mm/0.12"

SPORTS COLLAR

Note: *Knitwear size differential – With men's knitwear, the size differential is usually an increase of 4 cm/1.57" for sizes over L and 3 cm/1.18" less for all the smaller sizes, while in women's knitwear, we have an increase of 3 cm/1.18" for all sizes over M and we have 2 cm/0.79" less for all the smaller sizes.*
As far as shorts, briefs, tangas, bras and tops are concerned, we have an increase of 2 cm/0.79" for all sizes over the standard sizes (L and M) and 1 cm/0.39" less for all the smaller sizes.

THE PATTERN LAYOUT

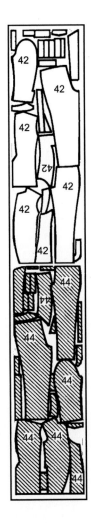

The pattern layout graphic is the cutting path obtained with the arrangement of the pattern parts, in their various sizes made in cardboard, placing them one next to the others, spread across the width of the fabric in the best way possible, with logical schemes that ensure that fabric use is reduced to a minimum. When the layout is done using a material that allows the production of several copies, it is called a marker.

For a clothes manufacturer, the optimization of fabric use is fundamental for determining the cost of the finished garment, especially nowadays, when raw materials are so expensive.

CRITERIA FOR MAKING THE GRAPHIC

Before making the layout, it is necessary to analyze some technical factors inherent to the fabric and to the type of pattern, as well as to the garment itself. These are:

1) The height of the fabric; 2) The business classification of the fabric; 3) The symmetry of the pattern (symmetrical or asymmetrical pattern); 4) The number of sizes to lay out (one-size-fits-all or various sizes); 5) The layout technique to use; 6) The professional skill of the operator.

The height of the fabric

The fabric height can be: simple, if 100 cm/39.37" (80 cm/31.50" o 100/39.37") or less; or double, if over 100 cm/39.37" (usually 140-150 cm/55.12"-59.16").

Summer fabrics are usually simple, while men's fabrics and woolens are double.

Nowadays, however, for industrial manufacturing requirements, fabrics are almost all double in height, independently of the seasons or the fibre makeup.

There are fabrics that reach a height of 200 cm/78.74" or even 300 cm/118.11", produced using ordinary or circular looms.

Fabrics used in industrial manufacturing are already prepared wound on small-diameter cylinders, at full height and with the right side in.

Instead, fabrics used by tailors are folded in half and wound on a rectangular core with the right side on the inner part of the fold.

The business classification of the fabric

The characteristics and the types of fabrics are numerous, so companies often draw up a classification and a codification for internal use, for the purpose of indicating the qualities; these serve above all in the pattern layout.

This fabric codification, using abbreviations and code names, essentially involves the following factors and characteristics:

- Fabrics without a right side and a wrong side and without a nap (*Class A* – e.g. Nonwoven facings).
- Fabrics with a right side and a wrong side, without a nap (*Class B* – e.g. Fabrics for linings or laminated fabrics).
- Fabrics with semi-obligatory cutting direction (*Class C* – e.g. fabrics with slight nap).
- Fabrics with obligatory cutting direction (*Class D* – e.g. Velvet, loden, prints, etc.)
- Special fabrics to be decided individually (*Class E* – e.g. plaids, checks, etc.)

Class A fabrics, without a right side and wrong side and without a nap offer the best return in terms of consumption, while as requirements and conditions grow, consumption for the same garment increases.

The fabric's structure and its pattern are elements that determine the direction in which the pattern pieces have to be laid.

Other important factors to bear in mind are:

- *The straight grain of the fabric*, which is any segment that runs parallel to the warp or the selvedge of the fabric.
- *The straight grain of the pattern*, which must be clearly indicated on every pattern piece, with a line with arrows and the inscription Straight grain.

When the straight grain of the pattern coincides with the straight grain of the fabric, the garment is said to be "standing".

When the pattern is positioned with the straight grain parallel to the weft, the garment is said to be "crosswise".

When the straight grain of the pattern is positioned on the diagonal of the fabric, that part is described as "on the bias".

The straight grain line drawn on the pattern should in any case always be positioned in the direction of the warp, so the position that the pattern is given on the layout graphic is practically automatic.

THE GRAIN OF THE FABRIC

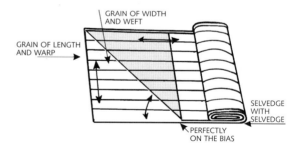

GRAIN OF WIDTH AND WEFT
GRAIN OF LENGTH AND WARP
SELVEDGE WITH SELVEDGE
PERFECTLY ON THE BIAS

CHARACTERISTICS OF THE FABRIC TO BE CUT

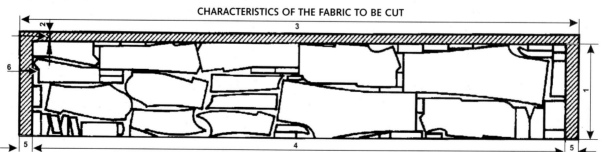

1) Usable height – width of the fabric minus the width of the selvedges.
2) Selvedge waste – Cutting waste on the width of the cloth.
3) Default length – Length of the graphic + head and foot.
4) Length of the layout graphic.
5) Cutting head and foot – Cloth remnants at the top and the bottom of the fabric.
6) Cutting waste – fabric scraps from within the pattern layout.

PATTERN ARRANGEMENT

The pattern arrangement
The pattern arrangement can be "matched", or "dove-tailed", when two perfectly identical pieces (e.g., the front) become a right and a left only because they are laid out facing one another on the fabric.

Or it can be "not matched", or "in a row", but in this case the two perfectly identical pieces (e.g., the front) can be worn only on one side of the person (e.g., left), and furthermore, this arrangement is usually used for fabrics without a right side and without nap (Class A).

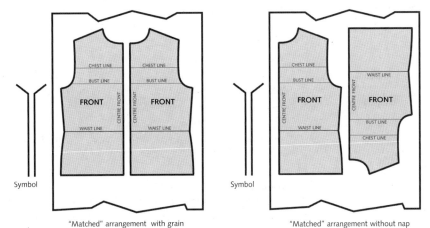

"Matched" arrangement with grain

"Matched" arrangement without nap

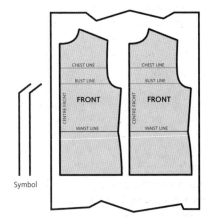

"Not matched" arrangement

Combination of sizes and grain of the pieces
Clothing manufacturers rarely make as many layouts as there are sizes sold: this would create a lot of scrap and greater consumption of fabric.
The most widely used solution is to keep track of sale and establish whether it is worthwhile to combine two or more sizes (or several articles of the same size) in a single layout.

Size symbols
To make the layout decided on perfectly clear, here, too, companies use a symbol code to indicate the types of pieces to lay out and the type of arrangement to use.

Examples of size symbols

Sizes laid out in the same direction

One size laid out in one direction and the other in the opposite direction

Free layout of sizes

SUMMARY OF SYMBOLS

FABRIC				SIZES / LAYOUT	
	A	Fabric without a right side or wrong side, and without nap			Sizes laid out on the same grain
	B	Fabric with a right side and a wrong side, but without nap			One size laid out on one nap and the other in the opposite direction.
	C	Fabric with semi-obligatory cutting direction (slight nap, small pattern)			Free layout of sizes
	D	Fabric with obligatory cutting direction (velvet, prints, etc.)			1 - ZIG-ZAG layout with right side in and opposite nap
	E	Fabric with special characteristics (Checks, plaids, etc.)			2 - Layout on a slant with right side in and opposite nap
PATTERN		Matched pattern pieces			3 - Layout on a slant with right side in and the same nap
		Not-matched pattern pieces			4 - Layout on a slant with right side out and the same nap
		Pattern pieces laid out on the same nap			5 - Layout on a slant with right side in and opposite nap
		Pattern pieces laid out on opposite naps			6 - Special layout with specific instructions

LAYOUT NAPS

Nap of patterns of the same size
The various pattern pieces of the same size, such as, for example, the front, the back, the sleeves, etc., are laid out in different ways, depending on the nap of the fabric.
To indicate the nap of the fabric, companies use symbols, as for the layout and the sizes.

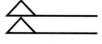

Pattern pieces laid out on the same nap

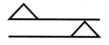

Pattern pieces laid out on opposite naps

Layouts without a nap
For Class A and B fabrics, which do not have a grain, the pattern pieces are laid out any which way, as in the following example, where a back, a front, and a sleeve are laid out in one direction, while a front and another sleeve are positioned in the opposite direction.

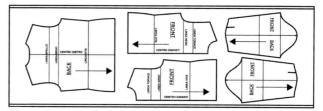

Layout of pattern pieces of the same size without nap

Layout with a nap
For Class C and D fabrics, which have a nap, the pattern pieces are laid out with attention to the nap, as in the following example, where the back, the front, and the sleeves are positioned all in the same direction.

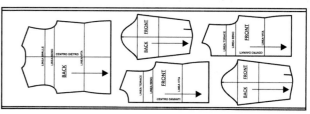

Layout of pattern pieces of the same size with nap

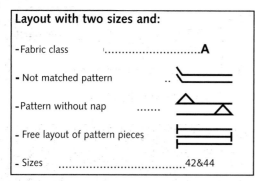

Layout with two sizes and:

- Fabric class ....A
- Not matched pattern ..
- Pattern without nap ....
- Free layout of pattern pieces
- Sizes ....42&44

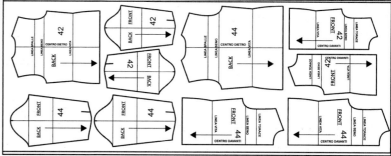

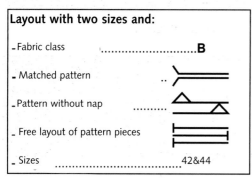

Layout with two sizes and:

- Fabric class ....B
- Matched pattern ..
- Pattern without nap ....
- Free layout of pattern pieces
- Sizes ....42&44

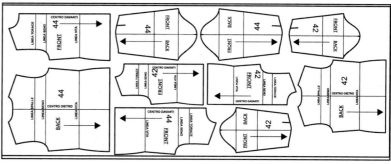

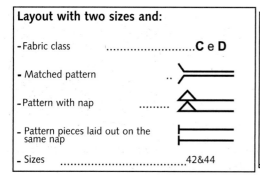

Layout with two sizes and:

- Fabric class ....C e D
- Matched pattern ..
- Pattern with nap ....
- Pattern pieces laid out on the same nap
- Sizes ....42&44

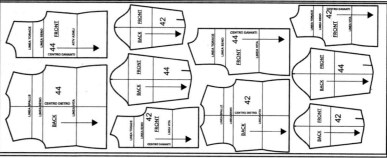

LAYOUT STRATEGIES

Layout with all the pieces
The complete layout is carried out with all the pattern pieces: right- and left-hands, plackets and facings, collars, cuffs, etc.
This graphic is used by the industries, with fabrics laid out at full height.

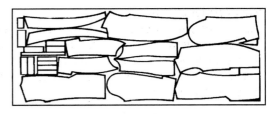

Layout with all the pieces

Single-size layout
This is the graphic rendition of the layout using only one size pattern pieces.
This layout is quite simple and has advantages for order planning, but, compared to several-size layouts, it has the disadvantage of greater fabric consumption.

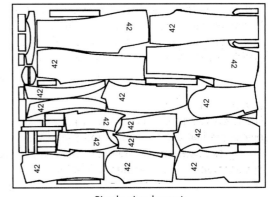

Single-size layout

Layout with half the pieces
The layout using only half the pattern pieces (for example, with the right or the left half) is done with a double layer of fabric (face to face) or tubular fabrics.

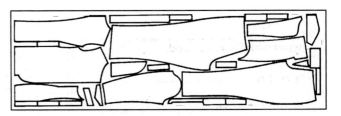

Layout with half the pieces

Sectional layout
This layout is done with one or more sizes, positioned in sequence, one after the other, with the pieces arranged in a rectangular "section".

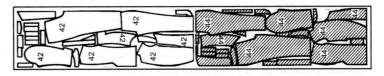

Sectional layout

Interlocking sectional layout
This layout is done with two adjacent sizes, dovetailed together.

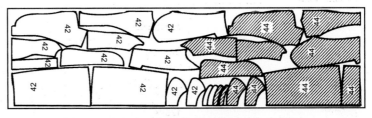

Interlocking sectional layout

Mixed multi-size layout
This layout gets the most out the fabric as it uses pattern pieces of various dimensions, in all the available space.

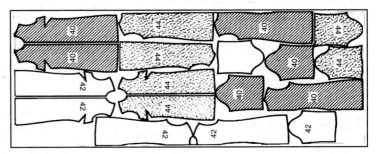

Mixed multi-size layout

LAYOUT TECHNIQUES

The best-known layout techniques at the present time are as follows: *1. Direct manual layout; 2. Reduced scale layout; 3. Computer-assisted layout.*

Direct manual layout

This is the simplest method and it consists in arranging the cardboard pattern pieces manually on the fabric, one next to the other, done directly by the technician, who is entrusted with maximizing the use of the fabric.

The "Direct manual" layout can be performed in the following ways:

a) - Directly on the fabric, drawing the outlines with chalk or a coloured pencil.

b) - Directly on the fabric, drawing the outlines using dabbers or with a chalk spray pistol.

c) - Drawing the pattern outlines in pencil on cardboard; going over them with the perforator and then dabbing the "marker" (the diagram of the layout) with the special powders.

d) - Laying out the pattern on the "marker", drawing the numbered piece outlines and laying the marker on top of the layers of fabric to be cut.

e) - Laying out the pattern on the "marker", drawing the numbered piece outlines on carbon paper and then tracing the outlines in pencil.

f) - Laying out the pattern, drawing the numbered piece outlines in pencil. The layout thus obtained is called a "marker" and is used to make successive copies.

Layout with reduced silhouettes

The original patterns are reduced to scale 1:30 or 1:5 using pantographic spirals and then cut. The reduced scale pattern pieces are placed on a table in the same small scale for the study of the best layout.

This method allows you to have a better overall view and therefore a better result in the least time.

The marker obtained is photographed or photocopied for archiving.

To make the cut you have to enlarge the marker again, drawing it in 1:1 scale.

Layout with the use of computers

The last way to study the optimization of the cutting layout consists in the use of computerized systems. This is carried out by an independent work unit dedicated to the study, execution and storage of layouts for the cutting room, using tables and rules and with checks and modification of the parts stored and preparation of the work sequence, style, order placement, review and restructuring files.

The layout function is made on a video graphic using 256 and more colours, from which it is also possible to access the program of control and manipulation of the digitalized pieces.

When the layout order is requested, the screen will show the area of the fabric with the height requested and a menu of the pieces required for the specific layout.

Direct manual layout.

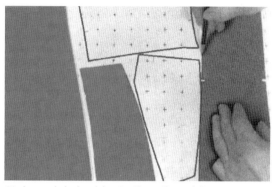

Marker made by hand-drawing the outlines of the pattern pieces.

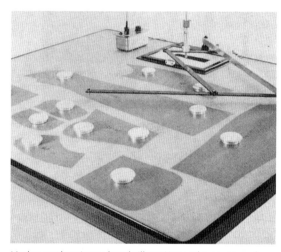

Marker made using reduced silhouettes and a pantograph.

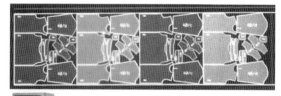

Marker made using the computer.

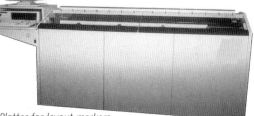

Plotter for layout markers.

Pattern data sheet

The pattern data sheet, usually drawn up by the designer along with the patternmaker, is an indispensable tool for defining and completing the description of all the details that make it up.

The data sheet should include the technical sketch of the pattern, rendered as clearly as possible and which, if necessary, should highlight all the details needed to understand every part of it.

Furthermore, there should be a detailed description of any instructions concerning the layout and any accessories, the dimensions of any appliqués, the type of fabric to use, the most important measurements, and the features of the pattern.

This card must be a reliable guide for the accurate realization of the garment conceived.

NOTES OF THEIR GARMENT FEATURES	PATTERN	
	SIZE	
	CLASS	
	SKETCH PATTERN	

INTERIOR AND ADHESIVES

INSTRUCTIONS FOR MAKING

DO NOT SEW THE GARMENT BEFORE GETTING APPROVAL

BUTTONS

ELASTIC

EPAULETTES

ZIPPER

HOOKS

OTHER ACCESSORIES

SPECIAL

SPECIAL

MEASURES										FABRIC		HEIGHT	TYPE

DESIGNER/PATTERNMAKER | DATE

COST ANALYSIS SHEET

The cost analysis sheet, usually put out by the production planning department, flanked by the designer and the head of purchasing, should contain all the information necessary for making the pattern for the garment; the type of fabric and its cost; the accessories that go along with the garment, and their costs; and the time needed for individual processing and the relative costs. This sheet is very useful for the production of the garment, especially to define the costs and, if these prove to be too high with respect to the target market's expectations, it provides the opportunity to intervene on the factors that determine it.

GENERAL INFORMATIONS			FABRIC INFORMATIONS		GARMENT INFORMATION	
TYPE	RISE	SIZE	RESOURCES		DEPARTMENT	
			PATTERN		NAME OR N.	
			WIDTH		PRICE	
			PRICE		SEASON	
			CONTENTS		REFERENCE N.	
			COLOURS		DATE	
			AGENT		ARTICLE	
			TEL.		SIZE	
			BLEND		COLOURS	
					COMPOSIT.	

1 - MATERIAL	ESTIMATED WASTE	EFFECTIVE WASTE	PRICE PER METER	TOTAL PRICE	DESIGN
LINING					
INTERIOR					

TOTAL COST OF ALL OTHER MATERIAL USED _____

2 - ACCESSORIES	ESTIMATED QUANTITY	EFFECTIVE QUANTITY	PRICE EACH	TOTAL PRICE
BUTTONS				
ZIPPER				
WAISTBAND				
PLEATS				

TOTAL COST OF ACCESSORIES _____

3 - WORKS	ESTIMATED TIME	EFFECTIVE TIME	TOTAL COST
CUTTING			
MANUFACTURING			

TOTAL COST OF WORK _____

TOTAL COST		
MARKUP	%	
WHOLESALE PRICE		
VAT		
TOTAL		

NOTES

SPECIAL

CHIEF TECHNICAL OFFICE   DATE

OTHER BOOKS

FASHION PATTERNMAKING TECHNIQUES [Vol. 3]
How to make jackets, coats and cloaks Women / Men

Antonio Donnanno
Illustrations by Elisabetta Kuky Drudi

ISBN 978-84-16504-18-3

This third volume of this collection completes the exploration of patterns for women and men. It focuses on the shaping of men's and women's outwear. The wide range of patterns examined includes basic forms of jackets, coats and cloaks. The book also offers detailed descriptions of drafting techniques.

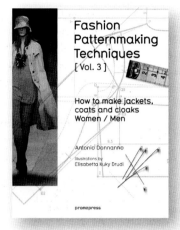

Release July 2016

FASHION PATTERNMAKING TECHNIQUES [Vol. 1]
How to make skirts, trousers and shirts Women / Men

Antonio Donnanno
Illustrations by Elisabetta Kuky Drudi

ISBN: 978-84-15967-09-5

This volume, divided into eight chapters, offers a wealth of in-depth knowledge relating to pattern design, beginning with a detailed study of people's measurements and builds, textile technology and tailoring terminology. It contains a comprehensive study of all types of skirts and trousers, from the most basic to the most elaborate. It also explores making patterns for men and examines making alterations for different sizes.

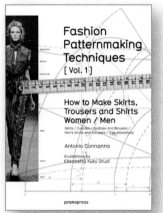

PATTERNMAKING IN PRACTICE
A step by step guide

Lucia Mors de Castro

ISBN: 978-84-92810-07-9

Using four basic garments (skirts, dresses, jackets and coats), this volume explores contemporary patternmaking in detail and explains how to draw, cut and mount patterns. This book helps the reader to understand the more complex processes and teaches how to customize and adapt basic models and recreate patterns from pictures. This book describes the traditional methods used and today's advanced body-shaping techniques.

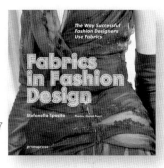
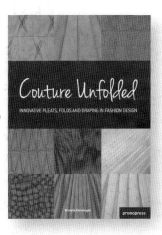